ALEXANDER I

PROFILES IN POWER

General Editor: Keith Robbins

ALEXANDER I

Janet M. Hartley

LONGMAN
London and New York

Longman Group UK Limited,
Longman House, Burnt Mill,
Harlow, Essex CM20 2JE, England
and Associated Companies throughout the world.

Published in the United States of America
by Longman Publishing, New York

© Longman Group UK Limited 1994

First published 1994

ISBN 0 582 05271 8 CSD
ISBN 0 582 05259 9 PPR

British Library Cataloguing-in-Publication Data

A catalogue record for this book is
available from the British Library

Library of Congress Cataloging in Publication Data

Hartley, Janet M
Alexander I / Janet M. Hartley.
p.   cm. – (Profiles in power)
Includes bibliographical references and index.
ISBN 0-582-05271-8 (cased). – ISBN 0-582-05259-9 (pbk.)
1. Alexander I, Emperor of Russia, 1777-1825. 2. Russia–Kings and
rulers–Biography. 3. Russia–History–Alexander I, 1801-1825.
I. Title. II. Series: Profiles in power (London, England)
DK191.H37   1994
947'.072'092–dc20
[B]
93-11656
CIP

Set by 7P in 10½/12pt Baskerville
Produced by Longman Singapore Publishers (Pte) Ltd.
Printed in Singapore

CONTENTS

CONTENTS

NOTE AND ACKNOWLEDGEMENTS

While most of the rest of Europe adopted the Gregorian or New Style calendar Russia retained the Julian or Old Style calendar until February 1918 (although Peter I moved the beginning of the year from March to 1 January). In the eighteenth century Old Style dates lagged eleven days behind New Style dates; in the nineteenth century the difference was twelve days. For the sake of simplicity and compatibility with the rest of Christian Europe all dates in this text are in New Style. Transliteration of Russian is by the Library of Congress system, but -sky has been used instead of -skii in surnames (in the text but not in bibliographical references) and the names of the Russian rulers have been anglicized. Emphasis in quotations is not my own but has been reproduced from the source indicated in the footnote.

I should like to thank the kind friends who read my manuscript and gave me much useful advice and constructive criticism: Dr John Klier, Professor Isabel de Madariaga, Dr Mia Rodriguez-Salgado, Dr Hamish Scott. I am also grateful to my husband, Dr Will Ryan, for reading the final draft and, with just sufficient tact, pointing out yet more weaknesses which had to be overcome. Finally, I should mention my two-year-old son, Benedict, who makes my work worthwhile, and the staff of the Nursery of the London School of Economics and Political Science, who make it possible.

TO MY PARENTS

Chapter 1

INTRODUCTION: ALEXANDER AND POWER

The distinguished Russian writer and historian Nikolai Mikhailovich Karamzin addressed Alexander on his accession in 1801 with the words:

> Let there be under your sceptre a Russia [that is] the epitome of goodness and happiness . . . . You are the father of the fatherland, the second creator for your subjects. God and virtue are with you.[1]

Alexander's own statements on power, however, suggest that Karamzin's assertion that the tsar had an almost divine authority over his subjects would have held little appeal for him. Before he came to the throne Alexander confided to his closest friends that he felt unworthy to rule and desired only to escape from the real world. He told his former tutor, La Harpe, that he wished to live on a farm near him in Switzerland, and confided to his friend Prince Viktor Pavlovich Kochubei in 1796 that 'My plan is to settle with my wife on the banks of the Rhine, where I shall live peacefully as a private person finding happiness in the company of friends and in the study of nature'.[2] Even at his moment of greatest triumph in late 1812, when Napoleon's army had just been expelled from Russia, he confessed to Madame de Choiseul-Gouffier, Countess Tiesenhausen, that 'No, the throne is not my *vocation*, and if I could honourably change my condition I would do it gladly'.[3] As late as 1819 he spoke with members of his family about his wish to 'rid myself of my duties and to retire from the world' leaving the European stage to

1

younger rulers. There is even a legend that Alexander faked his own death and started a new life as a holy man in Siberia.

Yet Alexander's seeming modesty about his lack of ability to rule and his professed aversion to exercising power seem at odds with the record of his reign. Despite his declared unwillingness to rule, he in fact came to the throne in 1801 through a violent *coup* in which his own father, Paul I, was murdered. He claimed to favour constitutions and representative institutions and in 1813 even asserted to John Capodistria (later his foreign minister) 'You love republics and so do I'.[4] Yet he never implemented the constitutional projects which were put before him or made changes to the governmental structure which would have resulted in any diminution of his power. Indeed, he responded with anger when his subjects dared to assert what they assumed to be their rights. When in 1803 a group of senators tried to exercise the right of representation, which they believed the Senate had acquired when it was reformed in 1802, Alexander chose to regard this as 'evil intent' on their part. In 1811 the central administration was restructured and Ministries were set up headed by ministers who were given considerable powers. But, according to an anecdote recorded by the writer Nikolai Ivanovich Turgenev, when Admiral Nikolai Semenovich Mordvinov tried to establish the extent of ministerial responsibility, by asking Alexander whether a decree would still be binding if a minister refused to sign it, he received the blunt reply 'Certainly, a decree must in all circumstances be implemented.'[5]

Nor did Alexander take kindly to his subjects misusing, in his view, the privileges which he had graciously bestowed upon them. In 1815, he introduced a constitution into the newly-formed Congress Kingdom of Poland, which was formally linked to the Russian Empire by virtue of the fact that the tsar was also the king of Poland. The constitution established the composition and function of the representative body, the *Sejm*. Alexander's relations with the first Polish *Sejm* were quite amicable but when deputies in the second *Sejm* in 1820 dared to challenge some governmental actions as 'unconstitutional' they were told that the tsar could take away the constitution just as easily as he had granted it. He also responded with hostility to any attempt by his subjects to take the initiative on reforms, even when they expressed sentiments which he claimed to share. When, late in his reign, some noble landowners took it upon themselves to present the tsar with a proposal for the emancipation of the serfs, the tsar is supposed to have responded 'leave me to promulgate the laws which I consider the most useful to my subjects'.[6] This was despite the fact that Alexander had himself expressed his abhorrence of serfdom and during his reign had commissioned several studies of the feasibility of freeing the serfs.

Alexander's record abroad also fails to support the image of a ruler trying to escape from the unpleasant duty of exercising power. In fact, he consistently wanted to have his views heard and respected by other continental statesmen and rulers, even in the early years of his reign when Russia was in no position to control events. He asserted his right to interfere throughout all Europe in all diplomatic decision-making, from territorial settlements to the determination of the internal form of the governments of states, irrespective of whether these arrangements had any strategic significance for Russia. He consistently displayed, for example, an interest during the Napoleonic Wars in the territorial and constitutional arrangements of the small German states, expressed concern for the fate of the King of Sardinia and maintained a particular interest in the constitutions of Switzerland. After the defeat of Napoleon, Alexander assumed that Russia would play a dominant role in resolving future European problems. When revolts broke out in the Iberian and Italian peninsulas in the 1820s, the tsar volunteered to send Russian troops across Europe to assist in the restoration of legitimate authority; an offer which the other great powers, not surprisingly, greeted with suspicion.

Furthermore, Alexander projected bold visions about the future organization of Europe and the conduct of her affairs. In 1804 he presented a proposal to William Pitt for the reorganization of Europe into a league of liberal and constitutional states founded on 'the sacred rights of humanity' under the paternalistic care of Britain and Russia. At the same time he suggested that codes of law and of the rights of man should be introduced for the whole of Europe. In 1804 Alexander was too weak to enforce his views but after the defeat of Napoleon, in which Russian troops had played such a vital part, the tsar was in a position to assert his ideas about European organization more powerfully. His Holy Alliance of 1815 (see below pp. 133–6) was dismissed contemptuously by statesman at the time but, nevertheless, within Europe only the Prince Regent in England and the Pope were able to avoid adherence to it (the Turkish sultan was not invited).

Alexander confidently assumed that his principles would receive general support as they were intended to benefit all European peoples. He always asserted that his policies were not narrowly national, but were aimed at resolving the problems of the whole continent; indeed at one point he claimed that his policy was 'in the interest of the entire universe'.[7] For himself, he expected that others would recognize his 'known principles of moderation and disinterestedness'. Yet such moderation and disinterestedness had not prevented Alexander from extending his control over large and strategically important territories during his reign – Finland in 1809 (from the Swedes), Bessarabia in 1812 (from the Ottoman Empire) and, above all, the Congress Kingdom of Poland in 1815 (mainly from the lands acquired by Prussia in the three Partitions of Poland in the late eighteenth century). The tsar had extended the borders of his Empire more than either of his two illustrious predecessors in the eighteenth century – Peter I and Catherine II – and had brought Russian power into the heart of Europe.

. . . .

The contrast between Alexander's private statements on his wish to retreat from the world and the vigorous way in which in practice he asserted his authority at home and abroad is just one example of the seeming contradictions between his words and his actions throughout his reign. He declared that he 'loved constitutional institutions' and 'loved liberty' but rejected the draft constitutions for Russia which were submitted to him; he frequently expressed his abhorrence of serfdom but did not in fact weaken it; he talked about the 'rights of man' but forced thousands of soldiers and peasants into military colonies against their will. This has led to portrayals of him as blatantly hypocritical ('playing at liberalism' in Lenin's words) or inconsistent and weak, governed by more ruthless and stronger-willed advisers. Historians have given him labels such as 'the sphinx' (*Le Sphinx du nord* is the title of Henri Troyat's biography of Alexander) or the 'enigmatic tsar' (the title of Maurice Paléologue's biography) in an attempt to convey his complex personality. Napoleon concluded that there was 'something wanting' in him and Castlereagh simply considered that he was mentally unbalanced. Alexander's subjects were sharply divided about their ruler. Some saw him as a saintly figure (which partly accounts for the success of the legend about him becoming a holy man); yet police apparently found a portrait of the tsar in the possession of the Preobrazhensk Old Believer community in Moscow in which he was depicted as Antichrist, with a horn and tails.

Alexander certainly possessed the ability to say what he knew his listeners wanted to hear – he was able to convince, at least for most of the time, such diverse individuals as his grandmother Catherine II, his tutor La Harpe, his Polish friend Prince Adam Czartoryski, his foreign minister John Capodistria, his sister Catherine, his minister for religious and educational affairs Prince Aleksandr Nikolaevich Golitsyn, the quaker William Allen and the mystic Madame Julie de Krüdener that he genuinely shared their aspirations and sentiments. He aired his views on matters such as despotism and republicanism in correspondence with, amongst others, Jeremy Bentham, Thomas Jefferson and Tadeusz Kosciuszko, in a manner which sometimes suggested either naivety or hypocrisy. But the evidence does not suggest that Alexander was essentially a weak person, despite his moments of self-doubt. He showed resoluteness in the face of the greatest challenge to his throne by refusing to compromise with Napoleon when he invaded Russia and entered Moscow. He not only successfully resisted any attempt by his advisers to force changes in the governmental structure on him against his will but was prepared to follow policies which he knew were unpopular, such as concluding the

Treaty of Tilsit with Napoleon in 1807, supporting his minister Mikhail Mikhailovich Speransky's introduction of examinations for officials (see below p. 84), and giving a constitution to Poland in 1815. Nor was he at the mercy of his advisers. He was quite prepared to act against their wishes; neither Czartoryski nor Capodistria when nominally in charge of foreign affairs was in practice able to direct Alexander to favour their chosen policies for Poland or Greece. He was also able to dismiss seemingly important advisers – of whom the most notable was Count Petr von Pahlen who had been one of the conspirators who had brought Alexander to the throne – or simply to use people who were not likely to question his initiatives, like Count Aleksei Alekseevich Arakcheev to implement his scheme for military colonies and Count Karl Nesselrode as foreign minister in the later part of his reign.

Some historians and contemporaries considered that Alexander's statements on his dislike of absolute rule were simply the product of youthful idealism, in part discarded on his accession and then totally rejected in the 1820s and replaced by 'the dark forces' of mysticism, militarism and reaction. More recent studies have stressed the essential continuity of Alexander's thought and policies. Alexander is portrayed by the historian Marc Raeff as a conservative reformer who believed that the reform process should be entirely in the hands of the ruler. In this respect his declared liking for 'constitutions' should not be seen as an indication of his hypocrisy or naivety; rather, this reflected the limited sense in which he understood the meaning of the word 'constitution'; that is as an orderly form of rule according to the law, essentially a *Rechtsstaat*. In Raeff's interpretation Alexander remained consistent in his principles and aims throughout his reign. The most recent scholarly biography of Alexander in English, by Allen McConnell, argues with a rather different emphasis that Alexander only seriously considered introducing legislation to limit his power in the first few months of his reign, when he felt himself to be at the mercy of the leaders of the conspiracy who had brought him to power. Once he had dismissed Pahlen, one of the chief conspirators, he 'never again assented to any restraints on his autocratic power within Russia'[8], although he was prepared to introduce them elsewhere and to carry out educational and administrative reforms at home as a 'Paternalistic Reformer' once his initial insecurity had been overcome.

Unfortunately, the nature of Alexander's education (see chapter 2) and the limitations of his intellect meant that he was unable to express the principles which he followed with either clarity or consistency. He had a poor understanding of concepts and frequently expressed himself in a naive or superficial manner. Prince Clement von Metternich commented in 1822 that '. . . of all children the Emperor Alexander is the most childish'.[9] His views were often ill-formed or only partially developed and it was only when his thoughts were harnessed by more able advisers that they acquired some intellectual cohesion. This was the case in 1804 when Alexander's rather ingenuous and vague statements on European organization, and on the role of Russia within this new organization, were brought together in a fully developed plan which was presented to William Pitt. Unlike his grandmother, Catherine II, he never took on the role of writer or critic himself. While Catherine synthesized and adapted the writings of Montesquieu, Beccaria, Bielfeld and others in her *Great Instruction* of 1767, Alexander relied upon others to produce draft constitutions or projects for the emancipation of the serfs. His own rare compositions, such as the Holy Alliance of 1815 or his speech to the Polish *Sejm* of 1818 (see below pp. 166–7), displayed his carelessness in the use of potentially ambiguous or dangerous statements and his lack of appreciation of the potential consequences of his words.

Nevertheless, the lines of Alexander's thinking remained constant throughout his reign. Despite informing Czartoryski that he considered 'that hereditary monarchy was an unjust and absurd institution'[10] he in fact retained a clear view of his role and prerogatives as ruler, and his understanding of such concepts as 'constitution', rule by law and the rights and privileges of his subjects remained consistent. He also had a genuine dislike of serfdom, a distrust of the nobility as a class and a sincere wish to improve the lot of his people through the extension of education and the encouragement of philanthropic endeavours. Abroad, he consistently expressed his desire for peace, not just for Russia but for the whole continent, and throughout his reign asserted the right of Russia as a major European power to play a part in all aspects of European diplomacy. After Alexander's spiritual experience during the French invasion of Russia in 1812 the language in which he expressed his concerns, both at home and abroad, changed but his assumptions and aspirations remained essentially the same.

This characterization of Alexander as holding consistent, albeit often hazily expressed, views rather than being simply hypocritical, weak or confused, does not mean that there were no variations in policy or approach in his reign. Circumstances at home and abroad affected Alexander's freedom of action and his ability to put his ideas into practice. The structure of this book reflects the view that his reign fell into several distinct stages, broadly defined as 1801 to 1807, 1807 to 1815, 1815 to 1820, and 1820 to 1825.

The period between 1801 and 1807 was one of hesitancy at home and frustration abroad. The two fundamental issues which dominated Alexander's reign – the introduction of a constitution and the emancipation of the serfs – were discussed. The new tsar invited, and received, suggestions for fundamental reform of the governmental structure and of serfdom but in practice did little beyond some reorganization of central government institutions (see chapter 3). He seemed not so much insecure as uncertain how to proceed. The lack of a well thought out and coherent approach which hindered reform at home was equally evident in Alexander's early foreign policy (see chapter 4). At this time Russia lacked the military power to challenge Napoleon effectively or, indeed, to dominate the alliance against him. Alexander had grandiose plans for the maintenance of European peace and for the establishment of new forms of European organization, but had neither the military strength nor the diplomatic authority to enforce his views on either his enemy or his allies. His first experience of Napoleonic warfare was a disaster. The Russian army, with Alexander at its head, was humiliated at the battle of Austerlitz in 1805; a further defeat followed at Friedland in 1807. Alexander then had to acknowledge French superiority in the Treaty of Tilsit.

In the years between 1807 and 1815 Napoleon and

Alexander vied for dominance within Europe (see chapters 5 and 6). In theory, the Tilsit peace divided Europe into two spheres of influence – French in the West and centre and Russian in the East – and gave Alexander the opportunity to pursue an expansionist foreign policy in the north against Sweden and in the south against the Ottoman Empire and to turn his attention again to reform at home. In practice, the alliance between France and Russia was always likely to collapse; Russia could never accept the rebirth of part of Poland under French protection (the Duchy of Warsaw) and her economic interests were harmed by the Continental System, while the ambitions of both countries in the Balkans were irreconcilable. War had become inevitable by 1811; by this time the far-reaching constitutional plans of Speransky had also been shelved. The French invasion of 1812 proved to be the turning point of the Napoleonic Wars. Napoleon's Grande Armée was destroyed by a combination of battle casualties, partisan and peasant attrition, disease and cold. Alexander, who had undergone a religious experience during the invasion, now led the coalition against Napoleon and entered Paris in triumph at the head of his troops in December 1814. Russia was now the strongest military power on the continent and her international position had been transformed.

In many ways the period 1815 to 1820 is particularly important for understanding Alexander's principles and aims. The tsar was now at the peak of his power and was at last in a position to put some of his ideas into practice. Outside Russia, Alexander did not hesitate to use his new authority to the full (see chapter 7). At the Congress of Vienna he played a dominant role in the territorial and constitutional settlement of Europe. His Holy Alliance of 1815 repeated many of his earlier thoughts about European organization, although they were now couched in more spiritually uplifting phrases reflecting his own religious experience. In 1815 the other great powers were no longer able to ignore or deflect these ideas. The culmination of Alexander's influence arguably came not in 1815 but in 1818, at the Congress of Aix-la-Chapelle, when the other powers had to accept, at least in part, his policy towards France, and when the final protocol of the Congress formally incorporated some of his sentiments about Christian principles and the shared obligations of the great powers. At home, there were expectations that Alexander would now turn to domestic reform and in particular that he would extend to Russia the type of constitution which he had introduced into the Congress Kingdom of Poland. Indeed, in these years the tsar commissioned both a constitution for Russia from Nikolai Nikolaevich Novosil'tsev and several projects on emancipation of the serfs. This period also saw the introduction of military colonies and an expansion of the work of charitable and philanthropic institutions (see chapter 8).

Events in the early 1820s, however, halted any further move towards fundamental change to the Russian governmental or social structure and changed Alexander's perception of the international situation. The revolts which broke out in the Iberian and Italian peninsulas and the so-called 'mutiny' of the prestigious Semenovsky guards regiment (see p. 216) shook Alexander's belief in the stability of the new Europe which he had helped to create. The conviction that Europe was yet again faced with a revolutionary threat made him wary of antagonizing the Russian nobility and risking social disorder by pursuing the question of emancipation. It also made him lose faith in the value of constitutions, at home and abroad, as a means of ensuring the stability of regimes and the well-being of subjects. The last few years of his reign were also marked by a disillusionment with the ability of the great powers to act collectively to maintain peace and stability – at the time of his death in 1825 it looked as if Russia was about to embark on another war with the Ottoman Empire.

Alexander had on several occasions expressed his unfitness and unwillingness to exercise power and yet left a legacy that was intimately associated with power; Russian power in Europe and the power of tsarist absolutism in Russia. By 1825, Russia was more powerful in Europe than at any previous time in her history. Essentially this domination was military; Russia had triumphed over the Napoleonic armies and her military might was feared by all. It was not until the Crimean War exposed Russian weaknesses that this fear subsided. At home, Alexander had failed to make any fundamental changes to the structure of

Russian absolutism. Far from fulfilling his declared ambition to escape from the responsibilities of office to some pastoral idyll, Alexander had instead resolved to retain all his power when presented with the opportunity of sharing some of it with his subjects. The conclusion inevitably drawn by many educated Russians from this (see chapter 9) was that tsardom could not, or would not, reform itself.

. . .

NOTES AND REFERENCES

1. Stephen Lessing Baehr, *The Paradise Myth in Eighteenth-Century Russia: Utopian Patterns in Early Secular Russian Literature and Culture*, Stanford, 1991, p. 44.
2. Alan Palmer, *Alexander I: Tsar of War and Peace*, London, 1974, p. 24.
3. Madame la Comtesse de Choiseul-Gouffier, *Historical Memoirs of the Emperor Alexander I and the Court of Russia*, translated by Mary Berenice Patterson, London, 1904, p. 137.
4. C.M. Woodhouse, *Capodistria: The Founder of Greek Independence*, London, 1973, p. 80.
5. N. Tourgueneff [Turgenev], *La Russie et les Russes*, 3 vols, Paris, 1847, II, p. 291.
6. S.V. Mironenko, *Samoderzhavie i reformy. Politicheskaia bor'ba v Rossii v nachale XIX v*, Moscow, 1989, p. 81.
7. W.P. Cresson, *The Holy Alliance: The European Background of the Monroe Doctrine*, New York, 1922, p. 70.
8. Allen McConnell, *Tsar Alexander I: Paternalistic Reformer*, New York, 1970, p. 29.
9. C.W.N.L. von Metternich, *Mémoires, documents et écrits divers laissés par le Prince de Metternich chancelier de cour et d'état*, 8 vols, Paris, 1881, III, p. 531.
10. *Memoirs of Prince Adam Czartoryski and his Correspondence with Alexander I*, edited by Adam Gielgud, 2 vols, London, 1888, I, p. 117.

Chapter 2

THE RELUCTANT RULER

. . .

CATHERINE II AND ALEXANDER

Alexander was born on 24 December 1777, the first child of Paul (son of Catherine II) and the Grand Duchess Maria Fedorovna. As Paul himself had been removed from his mother at birth by the Empress Elizabeth, so Alexander was not entrusted to his parents by Catherine, who took responsibility for his upbringing, and that of his younger brother Constantine, born in 1779. Catherine regarded herself as something of an expert on educational matters. She read the latest educational theorists and had followed the fortunes of the foundling homes established in Moscow and St Petersburg by Ivan Betskoi, which attempted to put some of Rousseau's educational theories into practice. She had also set up a commission on education whose work culminated in the Statute on National Education of 1786, which laid the foundations for state primary and secondary schools in Russia. She took a personal interest in the educational methods and the curricula of these new schools. Corporal punishment, for example, was specifically forbidden and Catherine personally commissioned the publication of 'The Duties of Man and Citizen' based on a book by the Augustinian Abbot Felbiger who had worked for the Prussian king Frederick II in Silesia, which instructed pupils on their duties towards society and government. Her grandsons now gave her the opportunity to put into practice some of the new theories. The boys slept on leather mattresses filled with hay in the wing of the palace facing the Admiralty Dockyard to accustom them to the sound of cannon fire; Alexander subsequently developed deafness in one ear. Catherine even designed a one-piece suit for the baby Alexander of which she was extremely proud: in 1781 she gave the details, including a sketch, in a letter to her correspondent in Paris, Melchior von Grimm, and informed him that 'the King of Sweden and the Prince of Prussia have asked for and obtained the pattern of the outfit of M. Alexander'.[1]

More significant for the development of Alexander's character was the choice by Catherine of Frédéric César de La Harpe, a Swiss republican and noted scholar, as one of his tutors in 1784. (His other tutors were the French writer Frédéric Masson and three Russians, M.N. Murav'ev, A.Ia. Protasov and A.A. Samborsky.) At this time Catherine, who had devoured the writings of the leading figures of the Enlightenment, saw no harm in entrusting a future tsar to the influence of a committed republican. Indeed, she read the first French constitution of 1791 (which, of course, was a monarchical constitution albeit with legal restrictions on the monarch's power) to the boys herself, and encouraged them to learn it by heart. Alexander's instruction at the hands of La Harpe and his other tutors was of a very high intellectual quality and led, amongst other things, to some knowledge of five languages. (Alexander's musical instruction, in contrast, was a late addition to his education. Catherine herself was unmusical and professed an aversion to her grandson's instruction in the violin because it reminded her of her former husband, Peter III – dethroned by her in 1762 – who had played the instrument.)

La Harpe's method and the content of his instruction undoubtedly had a pronounced effect on Alexander's mental development. He proved to be particularly susceptible to La Harpe's influence; Constantine who was subjected to the same regime, seems to have been quite unaffected. For example, La Harpe's insistence that the boys should dwell on their failings played on Alexander's natural tendency to self-doubt and introspection. La Harpe's so-called 'archives of shame of the Grand Duke Alexander' obliged his pupil to be publicly reminded of his shortcomings. One such passage which he had to write out and display read:

The Grand Duke Alexander having forgotten himself so far as to say uncivil things, has been sent away, and to remind him that incivility is inexcusable, this paper is hung up in his study as a fit ornament for it.

Another piece, written by Alexander when he was thirteen, read:

Instead of redoubling my efforts to profit by the years of study which remain to me, I become every day more careless, inattentive, and incapable. The older I grow, the more I approach zero. What shall I become? Nothing, according to all appearances.[2]

On several occasions, both before he became tsar and during his reign, Alexander asserted in conversation and on paper that he lacked the ability to rule. His letter to his friend Viktor Kochubei in May 1796, in which he also expressed his longing to escape his responsibilities and settle by the Rhine (see above p. 1), was similar in tone to his lines for La Harpe written six years earlier:

There is incredible confusion in our affairs. In such circumstances, is it possible for one man to rule the State, still less correct abuses within it? This is beyond the strength not only of someone endowed with ordinary abilities like myself, but even of a genius; and I have always held to the rule that it is better not to attempt something than to do it badly.[3]

Alexander frequently displayed self-denigration, mixed with stubbornness, in his relationships, be it with members of his family, with his advisers or with Napoleon; it was a combination which most found difficult, if not impossible, to comprehend and to overcome.

Furthermore, Alexander was impressionable and enthusiastically absorbed the writings recommended to him by La Harpe which endorsed his own views on the evils of despotism and the necessity for rule under the law. The content of Alexander's reading was far too ambitious for his age and ability; he was reading philosophical writings on the necessity of the rule of law and for restraints on despotism at the age ten or twelve and was taught languages through translations of writers such as Rousseau,

Montesquieu and Gibbon. Although Alexander was intelligent he lacked the time and maturity to study these ideas fully and had the habit, then and later on, of voicing views without fully reflecting on their true meaning or on the consequences of their practical implementation. As his friend the Polish Prince Adam Czartoryski (who had been brought to the Russian court by Catherine) noted, 'While he was Grand-Duke, Alexander did not read to the end a single serious book', and his mind 'was filled with vague phrases, and M. de la Harpe did not sufficiently make him reflect on the immense difficulty of realizing these ideas'.[4]

Alexander's education was incomplete. It was hampered by his early marriage to Princess Louise of Baden (who took the name Elizabeth Alekseevna when she was received into the Orthodox Church) in 1793 when he was only fifteen years old and his bride only fourteen. Catherine delighted in the role of matchmaker and in the accompanying court celebrations. She enthused to Melchior von Grimm when Alexander and Elizabeth first met, and then again at their betrothal, that 'never was a couple more suited to each other – as lovely as the day, full of grace and spirit . . . . Everyone said they were two angels pledging themselves to each other'.[5] Furthermore, Catherine hoped that if Alexander were to provide an heir this could ease the way to debarring his father from the throne (see below pp. 18–19). Elizabeth soon fell in love with Alexander; Alexander was unable to respond in kind. His studies were neglected in the year that it took for the marriage arrangements to be completed and then by the necessity for the young couple to set up a separate household in the Winter Palace.

His programme of education was finally cut short by the dismissal of La Harpe two years later when Catherine's horror at the developments taking place in revolutionary France (and in particular the execution of Louis XVI in 1793) led to suspicion falling on her chosen tutor. By this time, however, it was too late. Czartoryski recorded that in conversations with Alexander in 1796:

His opinions were those of one brought up in the ideas of 1789, who wishes to see republics everywhere, and looks upon that form of government as the only one in conformity with

the wishes and the rights of humanity . . . . I had constantly
to moderate the extreme opinions expressed by Alexander. He
held, among other things, that hereditary monarchy was an
unjust and absurd institution, and that the supreme authority
should be granted not through the accident of birth but by
the votes of the nation, which would best know who is most
capable of governing it.[6]

The adolescent Alexander was flattered to share the
company of the older and more sophisticated Czartoryski
and wanted to display his own knowledge and maturity; he
confided his ideas to Czartoryski because, in his own rather
priggish words, 'he could not mention them to any
Russian, as none were yet capable even of understanding
them'.[7] At this time, of course, Alexander was discussing
principles rather than contemplating the practical
problems which he would face if ever he became ruler of
Russia; nevertheless, later in his reign both Napoleon and
the writer N. Karamzin, when in conversation with the tsar,
found themselves in the rather strange situation of having
to oppose his negative views on monarchical rule.

Alexander's youthful views, had they been made public,
would have had the rare effect of uniting in outrage both
his father and his grandmother, who normally found it
difficult to agree on anything. Alexander and Constantine
had been isolated from Paul who had a separate
establishment at Gatchina, but Alexander saw more of his
father during Catherine's later years (ironically it was La
Harpe, whose views were detested by Paul, who encouraged
father and son to have more contact). He and Constantine
became frequent visitors to Gatchina and had to witness
and learn the arts of the precise military manoeuvres and
ceremonial parades of Paul's private army. It has often
been said that it was through this necessity to please
simultaneously his grandmother (by being the perfect
courtier at St Petersburg) and his father (on the parade
ground) that Alexander learnt the arts of dissimulation
which remained with him throughout his adulthood. While
there is some truth in this, and Alexander certainly had to
learn to keep his opinions to himself in both places, this
does not mean that he disliked the visits to Gatchina. The
mass of trifling procedures which had to be applied in
military manoeuvres did not come easily to Alexander, and

he had to seek the help of Colonel Aleksei Arakcheev, later a close adviser, to overcome some of his awkwardness and protect him from Paul's anger. He wrote to Arakcheev in 1799 concerning the formation of a military square:

> I ask you in all friendship to explain to me in detail what is wrong. Tomorrow is the day for manoeuvres. God knows how it will go; I doubt that all will be well . . . .[8]

He admitted to Czartoryski, however, that he enjoyed military ceremonial, and, indeed, all his life he retained a liking for parades (150,000 Russian soldiers are said to have taken part in the Russian victory parade staged outside Paris in 1815 after the Russian troops had triumphantly entered the city in 1814). Alexander recorded nothing of his attitude towards his father at this time but there is no evidence that he disapproved of his life style at Gatchina, let alone any suggestion that he considered him to be unsuitable to rule.

In fact, dissimulation was probably required less of Alexander at Gatchina than at Catherine's court where he developed an abhorrence for its luxury and decadence. He also grew to despise both Catherine's behaviour and some of her policies, a fact of which she remained happily oblivious. Catherine enthused to her correspondents about Alexander's good looks, delightful manners and intelligence. Her grandson in the meantime was freely criticizing her government to his friends and in particular her partitions of Poland and repression of the Polish uprising of 1794, (this was also condemned by Paul, suggesting that father and son shared more than just an interest in military parades.) Czartoryski, who of course encouraged Alexander in his pro-Polish sentiments, recorded that he

> . . . did not in any way share the ideas and doctrines of the Cabinet and the Court; and that he was far from approving the policy and conduct of his grandmother, whose principles he condemned. He had wished for the success of Poland in her glorious struggle and had deplored her fall. Kosciuszko, he said, was in his eyes a man who was great by his virtues and the cause which he had defended, which was the cause of humanity and of justice.[9]

Alexander liked to please and must have known that he was expressing views which his Polish friend would welcome, but there is no doubt that he took a poor view of Catherine's government. 'What is happening is incomprehensible: everyone steals, one hardly meets an honest man, it is monstrous' he wrote to La Harpe in February 1796.[10] Alexander, of course, saw Catherine in the last years of her rule. He witnessed the crushing of the Polish revolt and final Partitions of Poland in 1793 and 1795, and also the repressive measures taken by Catherine in the wake of the French Revolution against Russian writers. These included Aleksandr Radishchev, whose book *A Journey from St Petersburg to Moscow* (published in 1790) had sharply criticized Russian landowners and government and had provoked Catherine to say that it was infected by 'French poison'. (Alexander gave Radishchev a post when he came to the throne.) He also witnessed the somewhat degrading spectacle of the elderly Catherine becoming involved with young and rather frivolous lovers, and in particular he resented the circle which grew around her favourite Prince Platon Aleksandrovich Zubov.

Catherine remained unaware of her grandson's true feelings, and in the last few years of her reign rumours circulated that she intended to name him as her successor. According to the succession law of Peter the Great, tsars could name their own successor and there was therefore no automatic hereditary succession; Catherine would therefore have been theoretically within her rights to do this. There would be dangers, however, in disregarding so openly the obvious heir, her son Paul. Catherine's grounds for his disqualification were: doubts about his mental stability, his expressed dislike for her policies and his understandable resentment of the *coup* which had brought her to power and resulted in the death of Peter III (whom Paul assumed to be his father, although this is uncertain). Catherine raised the issue of the succession in an audience with La Harpe in 1793 but he refused to be drawn into a discussion of this with Alexander. In the summer of 1796 Catherine apparently put a proposal to Maria Fedorovna, Paul's wife and Alexander's mother, that her son should reign instead of her husband, which she refused to sign. In September 1796 Catherine held an audience with Alexander during which some important papers were entrusted to him. The content of their conversation was not recorded, but it is probable that the question of the succession was raised. Alexander politely, but ambiguously, wrote to Catherine afterwards thanking her for her trust in him and agreeing with the contents of the documents without further committing himself or being more explicit. While Catherine was dying in 1796, Paul destroyed some of her documents which may have included these 'important papers'. Alexander, however, was not in the process of making plans for his succession at this time. Instead he was telling Kochubei that he longed to retire to the banks of the Rhine and La Harpe that he would happily give up his station for a farm near his tutor. He was indulging in high-minded conversations with Czartoryski on the evils of despotism rather than contemplating disinheriting his father and facing the awkward task of putting these ideas into practice.

Catherine suffered a stroke on 16 November 1796. Paul, quickly summoned by Nikolai Zubov (brother of Catherine's favourite, Platon Zubov), arrived at the palace and took his place in the room next to his mother's bedchamber. While Catherine lingered rumours persisted about Alexander's succession, but he had immediately sent his own messenger to Gatchina when his grandmother was taken ill and showed no signs of disloyalty to his father or involvement in intrigue. When Paul arrived at the Winter Palace he was met by his two sons, already dressed in 'Gatchina style' army uniforms. The last rites were administered to Catherine on 17 November and she died late that evening. Oaths were immediately taken to Paul as the new tsar. Some days later, Alexander joined his family in a gruesome procession following the disinterred coffin of Peter III as it was transported from the St Alexander Nevsky monastery to the Winter Palace where it was to lie in state next to Catherine's coffin.

. . .

PAUL I AND ALEXANDER

Paul had waited a long time to assume the throne and was not hesitant in using his new authority. Estimates by historians of the precise number of new laws passed by Paul vary (from 2,179 laws and decrees for the whole reign to 48,000 orders, rules, and laws for the year 1797 alone) but historians do not disagree about his enthusiasm for making changes. But many of his decrees seemed trivial and capricious to his subjects. His hatred of the French Revolution led to the banning of French dress, hairstyles, words, and sheet music; and he insisted on serving native kvass and vodka instead of wine in the palace. Everyone, including pregnant women, had to dismount from their carriages and kneel down in the muddy street to greet the tsar if he passed by. Such behaviour led some contemporaries and later commentators to regard Paul as insane. Charles Whitworth, the British ambassador in Russia, wrote that 'the Emperor is literally not in his senses',[11] but this was written in respect of his shift in foreign policy against Britain and in the knowledge that he was going to be recalled. (Castlereagh made a similar remark about Alexander in 1815, so perhaps not too much should be made of the opinion of British diplomats regarding the tsars' sanity.) Certainly Paul had an uncontrollable temper and could order harsh punishments for the most trivial military imperfection on parade. But these characteristics suggest emotional instability rather than actual madness. What was important was that his methods and policies threatened the most powerful groups in the state, namely the court and provincial nobility, the officer corps and, ultimately, Alexander himself.

Paul's domestic policies were far-reaching: he made significant modifications to the structure of local government established by Catherine in 1775, reorganized the workload and composition of the Senate (created by Peter I in 1711) and tried to improve Russia's parlous financial situation by, among other things, establishing a Bank of Assistance for the Nobility. He also advised the restriction of the *barshchina*, or labour days, performed by serfs for their masters to a maximum of three days a week. All these actions were regarded with suspicion by the nobility. Paul's pronouncement on serf labour did not fundamentally challenge the institution of serfdom (the manifesto, issued at the coronation, simple *suggested* that landowners should restrict labour services) and was ignored in practice. Nevertheless it raised fears amongst the nobility that this was only the first step towards emancipation of the serfs which in turn could mean the end of their privileged position in the state and result in social upheaval. (Count Semen Romanovich Vorontsov feared Paul's policies would 'plunge Russia into popular revolt, producing millions of Stenka Razins and Pugachevs'; that is, Cossack leaders of popular revolts in the seventeenth and eighteenth centuries.)[12] The fact that Paul had deemed it appropriate for the state to pronounce on the regulations governing the relationship between nobles and their serfs was seen as unwarranted and unprecedented interference.

Many nobles who held elective offices in the provinces following Catherine's reform of local government resented Paul's reform of central and local government because they saw that the purpose was to reduce their employment opportunities (Paul removed the middle tier of provincial courts which provided several elective posts as judges or assessors for members of the nobility) and to give greater powers to a professional bureaucracy at their expense. The fears of the nobility about losing their social and political positions seemed justified when Paul rescinded the rights granted in Catherine's Charter to the Nobility of 1785 by imposing travel restrictions on nobles and disregarding their immunity from corporal punishment. The nobles also distrusted the new Bank of Assistance for the Nobility which was intended to provide credit facilities for them but which they feared, not without some justification, would lead to a greater number of sequestrations of estates if they were unable to meet the stringent conditions for the repayment of loans. It was never assumed that loans would be voluntary; the bank was empowered to make forced loans against identified plots of land which were overvalued, and the intention was clearly to force the nobility to handle their income more responsibly. Paul was convinced of the decadence of most of the nobility and wanted to discipline them into giving up life styles which they could not afford. This also applied to the wealthy and cosmopolitan nobility in St Petersburg and Moscow who were particularly hit by Paul's restrictions on foreign dress and, in the last months, from his ban on the import of luxury goods from Britain.

In the army, harsh punishments were inflicted not only on ordinary soldiers who made the slightest error on parade but also on officers. The patriotic sentiments of the officers of the élite guards regiments were particularly offended by Paul's insistence on uncomfortable Prussian-style uniforms and wigs and the imposition of Prussian drill. They also resented the favours shown to the Gatchina regiments in which many Ukrainians served, and feared, with some justification, that Paul intended to eliminate their influence and status. Three-and-a-half thousand officers, about one-quarter of the entire officer corps, showed their disapproval by resigning during Paul's reign. Officers, and other members of the nobility, also felt humiliated by Paul's seemingly capricious foreign policy.

Paul's first acts had been to reverse Catherine's foreign policies; he cancelled her plans to send Russian troops to join the First Coalition against France and formed an alliance with the Ottoman Empire. At first, it looked as if Paul was determined upon peace in order to concentrate on reforms at home, but within a year he was playing a leading part in the formation of the Second Coalition of Britain, Austria and the Ottoman Empire against Napoleon, largely as a result of his commitment to the defence of the Island of Malta. The Knights of St John of Malta (originally a crusading order) had appealed to Paul's chivalrous instincts after the French Directory had confiscated their property in France, and he formally became their Protector in late 1797. When Napoleon captured Malta in June 1798 on his way to Egypt, Paul was therefore committed to come to the assistance of an island (and extensive properties elsewhere) which, realistically, Russia could not hope to defend by herself. Far from trying to evade his new and awkward responsibilities, Paul became grand master of the Order in November 1798 and promptly demanded the withdrawal of French forces. This led contemporaries, and some historians, to portray Paul as a rash romantic in foreign affairs, governed by idealism rather than by Russia's real interests. There were, however, practical reasons for opposing further French advancement. France seriously threatened Russia's interests in the Balkans and vis-à-vis the Ottoman Empire by her control of the Mediterranean. In addition to her occupation of Malta, France had seized the Ionian islands (Corfu being the most important) in 1797 and her conquests in Italy upset the balance of power in the whole Mediterranean area. Paul also feared the threat posed to the social and political order by the French Revolution, although he was soon to be disillusioned in his belief that Napoleon would restore traditional values in France. In his mind, championing the cause of the Knights of Malta was linked with the crusade against the revolutionary ideas of the Revolution.

During the war of the Second Coalition, Russian troops, under the leadership of General Aleksandr Vasil'evich Suvorov, successfully campaigned in Italy and Switzerland, and joined with British troops in an abortive landing in Holland. Paul, however, soon felt disillusioned with the conduct of his allies; he saw that the Austrians preferred to concentrate their efforts on making gains in Italy rather than supporting the Russian army in Switzerland, and that the British were not prepared to allow Russian troops to assist in the garrisoning of Malta, which they had captured in September 1798. After the defeat of the Russian army at Zurich in September 1799 (made less serious by Suvorov's daring escape with at least part of the army through the Alps), Paul withdrew from the coalition, although without formally making peace with France. He then proceeded to infuriate Britain by seizing British ships and crews in Russian ports, imposing an embargo on British trade and in December 1800 reviving Catherine II's League of Armed Neutrality of 1780. The League had been designed by the empress to assert the right of neutral vessels to continue trading with belligerent countries and to challenge Britain's power to condemn cargoes and ships in her admiralty courts. Paul's new anti-British stance also prevented the export to Britain from the Baltic of vital supplies for her navy, such as masts, tar, hemp and pitch. He also planned a Cossack expedition to march though central Asia and conquer India, a foolhardy and reckless plan which had no chance of success but which, nevertheless, increased British suspicion of Russia. These rash actions were met with disapproval and concern by army officers and by the court nobility: Nikita Petrovich Panin, the vice-chancellor, wrote in November 1799 that

'In several months Russia will be the laughing-stock of all Europe'.[13]

Paul's suspicions of plots against him had led to a large increase in the number of arrests and members of the social élite were disproportionately at risk. Although the total number of people arrested in his reign has not been calculated (12,000 were amnestied by Alexander when he came to the throne) it is known that they included seven fieldmarshals, 333 generals, and 2,261 officers. Many of these people were tried by the Secret Expedition of the Senate. Peter III had abolished the Secret Chancellery during his brief reign and its function as the main security agent of the state (investigating crimes such as *lèse-majesté*, treason and sedition) then passed to the Secret Expedition. In Catherine's reign this body had investigated individuals such as the Cossack rebel Pugachev, who claimed to be Peter III, and the satirical writer N.I. Novikov, who was suspected of treasonous activities. But under Paul its use was far more widespread and heightened the atmosphere of fear because of its secrecy and the commonly-held belief that torture was used in its interrogations. By 1799 there was a dangerous atmosphere of uncertainty and fear amongst the élite, especially in St Petersburg and Alexander's friend Viktor Kochubei wrote:

> The type of fear in which we now live in St Petersburg cannot be described . . . . True or false, denunciations are always listened to. The fortresses are full of victims. A black melancholia has taken possession of everyone . . . . To mourn a parent is a crime. To visit an unfortunate friend is to become the *bête noire* of the authorities. The torments one suffers are incredible.[14]

By the end of 1800 rumours circulated about plots against Paul; rumours of 'mass arrests' in March 1801 further heightened the tension. General Sablukov (who remained loyal to Paul throughout his reign although he disapproved of his policies) recalled, albeit with a somewhat rosy view of the recent past that 'The pressure of despotism falling on the most trifling and trivial circumstances, became more goading because it followed a period of perfect personal liberty'.[15]

Paul trod dangerously by offending the officer corps and

the nobility but it required a serious group of conspirators, and a willing successor, to put his throne at risk. The leaders of the conspiracy were Panin, Count Petr von Pahlen (governor-general of St Petersburg, head of the College of Foreign Affairs and director of the post), the Zubov brothers (who had been favourites in the last years of Catherine II), and General Levin Bennigsen. Panin, who in particular opposed the shift in foreign policy against Britain, may have been in receipt of funds from Charles Whitworth, the British ambassador in St Petersburg, although the evidence for this is not conclusive. The conspiracy was not, however, narrowly focused on the court but involved a wider circle of officers, two-thirds of whom were in the élite guards regiments, and members of the aristocracy (including sons of the leading families like the Dolgorukovs, Viazemskys and Golitsyns), showing that dissension was rife amongst the most important social groups in the state. (Paul was generally held to be popular amongst ordinary soldiers and serfs, who falsely believed that he intended to emancipate them, but this support was of little political importance.)

In order to succeed, Pahlen and Panin needed to persuade Alexander to support the conspiracy. During Paul's reign Alexander's position as heir had been assured by the new law of succession which formally established the rule of primogeniture, and he was also given an important role in government as member of the Supreme Council and the Senate, president of the War College, honorary colonel of the Semenovsky regiment and military governor of St Petersburg, although he had no influence over his father's policies. Alexander's pleasure in drilling the troops must have been tempered by Paul's comments, on finding a sentry badly positioned, that his son was 'an imbecile' and 'an animal'. His post as military governor of St Peterburg also proved onerous, as Sablukov recorded:

> The Grand Duke Alexander was still young and of a timid disposition: moreover, shortsighted and a little deaf; one can therefore imagine that the office he held was no sinecure, and he passed many a sleepness night in consequence.[16]

Alexander was deeply affected by the seeming

arbitrariness of Paul's rule, which was so contrary to the precepts of rule under the law which had been the foundation of La Harpe's teaching. His letter to his tutor in late 1797 (taken out of Russia by one of Alexander's new friends, Nikolai Novosil'tsev) shows a mixture of idealism and naivety coupled with a shrewd understanding of the shortcomings of Paul's rule and a realization that he might after all have a duty to come to the throne in order to save his country and give it a representative body before he could make his longed-for retreat from the world:

> My father, on succeeding to the throne, wished to reform everything. The beginning, it is true, was sparkling enough but what followed did not fulfil expectations. Everything has been turned upside down at once; something which has served only to increase the already too great confusion which reigned in our affairs. The military take up almost all his time, and that in parades. For the rest, he has no plan to follow; he orders today what a month later he countermands: he never permits any representation except when the harm has already been done. Finally, to speak plainly, the well-being of the State counts for nothing in the regulation of affairs . . . . You have always been acquainted with my ideas of leaving the country. At the moment I see no means to execute them; moreover, the unfortunate situation of my country has made me fashion my ideas differently. I have thought that if ever the time should come for me to rule, instead of leaving my country *I would do better to work to make my country free* and to preserve it from serving in the future as the plaything of a madman . . . . Our [Alexander and his friends, Czartoryski, Pavel Stroganov and Novosil'tsev] idea is that during the present reign we should translate into Russian as many useful books as possible. . . . Once, on the other hand, my turn comes, then it will be necessary to work, little by little, to create a representation of the nation which, directed, will create a free constitution, after which my authority will cease absolutely; and, if Providence supports our work, I will retire to some spot where I will live contentedly and happily, observing and taking pleasure in the well-being of my country. This is my idea my dear friend.[17]

In early 1801 there were rumours that, despite the new succession law, Alexander himself was in danger of being replaced as heir by the Empress's nephew, Prince Eugene of Württemberg, and that his own life could be in danger.

While Alexander might have liked to have spent his time translating 'useful books' with his friends, circumstances now demanded that more active measures were taken. For some six months, Pahlen tried to persuade him to support the conspiracy, using arguments skilfully calculated to appeal to his sensitivities, such as Paul's despotism, his disregard for the rights of his subjects and his cruelty. He finally succeeded, although Alexander insisted that Paul's life should be spared. This proviso has sometimes been regarded as an illustration of Alexander's hypocrisy, or at least gross naivety, as the chances of Paul willingly accepting abdication were slight. Pahlen was more realistic; when asked by an officer what would happen if Paul resisted he replied: 'You all know messieurs that to make an omelette you need to break eggs'.[18] But Alexander's horror on hearing that his father had in fact been murdered and the remorse which stayed with him throughout his life, are testimony to his genuine belief that Paul would survive. This is an example of his habitual failure to reflect more than superficially on the consequences of his actions, as well as a certain reluctance to face reality, rather than one of calculating cynicism. And in the event he showed more astuteness than naivety in apparently getting Pahlen to agree that the attempted *coup* should be postponed for two days until the Semenovsky regiment, of which he was the honorary colonel, was on duty, and in his insistence that nothing should be said to his brother Constantine about the plot.

By the middle of March 1801 Paul had become aware that a conspiracy had formed and was deeply suspicious of Pahlen (Panin had been dismissed at the end of 1800 and exiled to his estates). Although seemingly not aware of any direct involvement of his son, Paul heightened the tension in his own way. When he found that Alexander had left his copy of Voltaire's *Brutus* open at a page describing Caesar's assassination, he instructed that his son should be brought a copy of the history of Peter the Great, opened at the page which described the death of the tsarevich Aleksei for treason. On 21 March Paul sent a messenger to recall Arakcheev, whom he had dismissed from service and banished from St Petersburg, but the messenger was intercepted by Pahlen who had the audacity to present

Paul with his own note to Arakcheev, claiming that it was a forgery although it was obviously genuine. Paul was too terrified to deny this and had to insist that the note should be delivered. Clearly, however, Pahlen had to act quickly before Paul could rally support, and the conspirators resolved on 22 March to act the following evening when the Semenovsky guard would be on duty. Alexander was again reassured that no harm would come to his father. The events of the night of 23 March showed Alexander to be irresolute in the face of his first crisis. A group of officers, led by Bennigsen, entered Paul's bedroom. In the scuffle that followed Paul was struck down by Nikolai Zubov and finally strangled by one of the officers. When Alexander was informed of Paul's brutal murder by a group led by the Zubov brothers and Bennigsen, he was almost helpless with despair and remorse: 'I cannot go on with it, I have no strength to reign. Let someone else take over from me' was his first response.[19] Maria Fedorovna, Paul's wife and Alexander's mother, at first refused to speak to her son, and even attempted to claim the throne herself. It was only the resoluteness of Alexander's wife, Elizabeth and the firmness of Count Pahlen ('That is enough of playing the child; come and rule!') which persuaded him to receive the oath of loyalty from the not entirely enthusiastic guards regiments.

The memory of the unhappy means by which he came to the throne haunted Alexander during his reign, and was possibly made even more poignant by the death from natural causes of all his own children. (Elizabeth bore him two daughters, Maria born in 1799 and Elise born in 1806, both of whom died in convulsions at fourteen and eighteen months respectively; his main mistress Maria Naryshkina bore him three daughters, all of whom died, two in childhood and the youngest, Sophia, at the age of eighteen from consumption.) 'I am the unhappiest man on the earth' confessed Alexander to Count Karl Stedingk, the Swedish ambassador, on the first day of his reign.[20]

· · ·

NOTES AND REFERENCES

1. *Sbornik Imperatorskago russkago istoricheskago obshchestva* (hereafter *SIRIO*), XXIII, p. 205.

2. C. Joyneville, *Life and Times of Alexander I. Emperor of all the Russias*, 3 vols, London, 1875, I, pp. 38-9.
3. Alan Palmer, *Alexander I: Tsar of War and Peace*, London, 1974, p. 24.
4. *Memoirs of Prince Adam Czartoryski and his Correspondence with Alexander I*, edited by Adam Gielgud, 2 vols, London, 1888, I pp. 128, 130.
5. *SIRIO*, op. cit. pp. 580, 583.
6. *Memoirs of Prince Adam Czartoryski*, p. 117.
7. Ibid., p. 111.
8. Kenneth R. Whiting, *Aleksei Andreevich Arakcheev*, unpublished Ph.D. thesis, Harvard, 1951, p. 65.
9. *Memoirs of Prince Adam Czartoryski*, pp. 110–11.
10. *Correspondance de Frédéric-César de la Harpe et Alexandre Ier*, 3 vols Neuchâtel, I (1785-1802), 1978, p. 157.
11. James J. Kenney, Jr, 'Lord Whitworth and the Conspiracy against Tsar Paul I: The New Evidence of the Kent Archive', *Slavic Review*, vol 36, 1977, p. 213.
12. James J. Kenney, Jr., 'The Politics of Assassination' in Hugh Ragsdale, ed., *Paul I: A Reassessment of his Life and Reign*, Pittsburgh, 1979, p. 137.
13. Constantin de Grunwald, *L'Assassinat de Paul Ier tsar de Russie*, Paris, 1960, p. 173.
14. Ibid., p. 169.
15. N.A. Sablukov, 'Reminiscences of the Court and Times of the Emperor, Paul I, up to the Period of his Death', *Fraser's Magazine for Town and Country*, London, 1865, p. 230.
16. Ibid., p. 234.
17. *Correspondance de Frédéric-César de la Harpe*, II, pp. 215–16.
18. Grunwald, op. cit., p. 18.
19. Palmer, op. cit., p. 45.
20. N. Ia. Eidel'man, *Gran' vekov. Politicheskaia bor'ba v Rossii konets XVIII – nachalo XIX stoletiia*, Moscow, 1982, p. 259.

Chapter 3

THE HESITANT REFORMER: 1801–1807

. . .

THE CONSTITUTIONAL QUESTION

Alexander's accession was greeted with great enthusiasm by the population of St Petersburg. The French historian J.H. Schnitzler wrote '. . . the accession of Alexander was hailed with sincere and universal delight'. His physical appearance and manner charmed everyone: 'The prince was of majestic figure and striking beauty: his words and manners were clothed with a seductive grace'.[1] Even in later years Alexander was able to make an impact, particularly on women. Madame de Choiseul-Gouffier, Countess Tiesenhausen, from one of the aristocratic families of Vil'na, gave this description of Alexander, then aged thirty-five:

Notwithstanding the regularity and delicacy of his features, the brightness and freshness of his complexion, his beauty was less striking, at first sight, than that air of benevolence and kindness which captivated all hearts and instantly inspired confidence. His tall, noble and majestic form, which often stooped a little with grace, like the pose of an antique statue, already threatened to become stout, but he was perfectly formed. His eyes were blue, bright and expressive; he was a little short-sighted. His nose was straight and well shaped, his mouth small and agreeable. The rounded contour of his face, as well as his profile, resembled that of his august mother. His forehead was somewhat bald, but this gave to his whole countenance an open and serene expression, and his hair, of a golden blond, carefully arrranged as in the heads on antique cameos or medallions, seemed made to receive the triple crown of laurel, myrtle, and olive. He had an infinity of shades of tone and manner. When he addressed men of distinguished rank, it was with dignity and affability at the same time; to persons of his retinue, with an air of kindness almost familiar; to women of a certain age, with deference; and to young people, with an infinite grace, a refined and attractive manner, and a countenance full of expression.[2]

Alexander never failed to charm the ladies in his company, and his gallantry never flagged even under the stress of his campaigns against Napoleon.

Alexander started his reign in a manner which suggested a rejection of Paul's policies and methods and a return to the ways of Catherine II. In his accession manifesto he promised to rule 'according to the spirit and laws' of his grandmother, a formula which was sufficiently vague to sound reassuring. That Alexander, during the later years of his grandmother's court, had been so openly disapproving of its 'spirit' and conduct was set aside. His first series of decrees confirmed Catherine's laws and reversed some of the actions of his father's reign which had most offended the Russian élite. Alexander reaffirmed Catherine's Charter to the Nobility of 1785. This had restated the rights of the nobility to the exclusive ownership of serfs, had decreed that they were not to be deprived of their titles, rank or property without the due legal process; and had confirmed their rights of freedom from compulsory service, exemption from the poll tax and from providing quarters for troops, immunity from corporal punishment and freedom to travel abroad. (These last two rights had in practice been ignored by Paul.) Alexander also reaffirmed Catherine's Charter to the Towns (promulgated in 1785) which had established a structure of municipal representative bodies to deal with urban affairs, although he did not reverse Paul's simplification of Catherine's local government structure. He restored the Russian names and old uniforms to regiments, so appeasing the officer corps, and cancelled the restrictions on exports and imports which had affected both the export of grain from noble estates and the life styles of the wealthy nobles in St Petersburg and Moscow who relied on the import of foreign luxuries. Furthermore, he took measures to demonstrate that the arbitrariness and cruelty associated with Paul's reign was now at an end. The hated Secret Expedition (see above p. 24) was abolished and the police and lower courts were instructed to observe the prohibition of torture. He released an estimated 12,000 prisoners held under arrest and amnestied fugitives hiding abroad for crimes other than murder. In June 1801 he appointed a commission to draw up a new law code, and included the radical Aleksandr Radishchev (who had been released from internal exile by Paul) as a member.

The first few years of Alexander's reign were dominated by the question of internal reform. The issues at the heart of this remained the same throughout the reign of reform – the merits of a 'constitution' and the abolition of serfdom. In the first few years of his reign both issues were debated at length and proposals which would have resulted in a diminution of tsarist power and challenged some aspects of the institution of serfdom were proposed but then put aside. On the one hand, proposals were put forward by the conspirators against Paul (Pahlen and Zubov) and by senior officials who had served under Catherine which would have given central government institutions more authority within the state. On the other hand, the Unofficial Committee (*Neglasnyi komitet*) of Alexander's 'young friends' (Adam Czartoryski, Nikolai Novosil'tsev, Count Pavel Aleksandrovich Stroganov and Viktor Kochubei) discussed the stages by which a 'constitution' could be introduced into Russia. But no fundamental change took place in the relationship between central government institutions and the tsar, or between serfs and masters, and a constitution was not introduced. This does not mean, however, that these years are without interest. On the contrary, the period between 1801 and 1803 is crucial in highlighting the different strands of the reform movement within Russia and in understanding Alexander's own attitude towards reform and the principles which he felt should apply in government.

Alexander has often been portrayed as vague and insincere in his attitude to reform. It is true that he could make vague and sweeping generalizations about rights and freedoms. In August 1805 he wrote to Thomas Jefferson, expressing his admiration for the United States and its '. . . free and wise constitution which assures the happiness of each and every one'.[3] On 18 April 1806 Jefferson wrote to Lovett Harris, United States consul at St Petersburg:

> . . . the Emperor entertained a wish to know something of our Constitution. I have therefore selected the two best works we have on the subject, for which I pray you to ask a place in his library.[4]

Alexander liked to project an image of himself which he knew would please his audience, but although he could be seemingly careless about his vocabulary, he was neither weak nor hypocritical when it came to fundamental questions of government. There are many testimonies to his stubbornness in discussion and to his insistence that the initiative and responsibility for reform was his alone. He always, for example, ended the discussions in the Unofficial Committee (see below pp. 39–42). Nor could he be pressurized into any change which he did not approve. The discussions in the Unofficial Committee resulted in several disagreements between Alexander and his 'young friends'. For example, he 'energetically' opposed the suggestion of Kochubei that a chancellery of ministers should replace all the colleges (the previous organs of central administration) and wanted instead to retain some of the colleges for a time. Despite the opinions of Novosil'tsev and Stroganov that this would prove impossible because the collegiate form of administration would hinder the ministers, Alexander refused to be moved and took a final decision on the matter without further discussion.

Alexander consistently viewed with hostility any attempt by individuals or institutions to assert their rights or to take independent initiatives but this does not mean that he did not understand concepts of reform or that he was essentially reactionary. In the early years of his reign he frequently stated the view that the ruler was not above the law and expressed abhorrence of arbitrary and despotic rule, which had been, in his view, practised by Paul. The Secret Expedition was abolished on 14 April 1801 because, according to Alexander's decree, 'in a well-ordered state all offences must be comprehended, judged and punished by the force of the law'. The Commission for the Codification of the Laws was set up, in the same year, because 'in fortunate circumstances all other measures could be taken in a state, but only the law could establish them forever'. Nor was Alexander entirely insensitive to the vocabulary of reform. When D.P. Troshchinsky (state secretary under Catherine, Paul and Alexander) opened his proposed manifesto on the prerogatives of the Senate with the words 'Decree to Our Senate' (that is, the tsar's Senate) Alexander objected that 'the Senate is not ours – it is the Senate of the Empire'. He also insisted that subjects should be referred to in decrees as 'Russian' and not 'our' subjects.[5]

Nor can it be said that Alexander was vague or hypocritical in his understanding of the word 'constitution'. Essentially he understood 'constitution' in a modified *ancien régime* sense, meaning an orderly system of government based on law. He did not in principle rule out representative institutions but any restructuring would be introduced on the initiative of the ruler and would not therefore be an expression of popular sovereignty. He was opposed to the establishment of enshrined, inalienable rights and principles. The well-being of the state would always come first and in Alexander's view the ruler was best equipped to determine what the country needed. Given this line of thinking, it would be sensible to give constitutions only to countries which had reached an appropriate level of development and so were able to use a constitution wisely. Thus it was not entirely inconsistent for Alexander to encourage the introduction of constitutions elsewhere in Europe, and even in the non-Russian parts of his own Empire, while not introducing one into Russia itself. At various points in his reign Alexander considered the possibility of introducing a constitution into Russia, but he never quite had the confidence that she had reached this necessary level of development. It was only towards the end of his reign that he finally put aside constitutional plans.

The overthrow and murder of Paul meant that the leaders of the conspiracy were dominant in the early months of Alexander's reign. According to the memoirs of Vigel', Pahlen 'reigned in Russia' in the first three months after Paul's assassination.[6] Pahlen, and to a lesser extent the Zubov brothers, seemed to have plans to use their position to limit Alexander's powers. Indeed, the Bavarian chargé-d'affaires, Olry, wrote that '. . . Pahlen and Zubov as leaders of the conspiracy put to Alexander as a *conditio sine qua non* the limitation of the supreme power, and they rather freely pronounced the word 'constitution'.[7] There were rumours that Platon Zubov had a piece of paper with him at the time of Paul's assassination which contained the text of an agreement between tsar and the people.[8] A. von Kotzebue, director of the German theatre in St Petersburg, wrote in his memoirs that 'Pahlen without doubt had the good intention of introducing a moderate constitution; Count Zubov had the same intention' and recorded that Alexander had told his sister Catherine, on the first day of his reign, that he had asked the conspirators to do just this, with the words 'do the rest, define the rights and duties of the sovereign; without that the throne will not have great attraction for me'.[9] Even if this account can be believed, it points more to panic and depression felt by Alexander in the aftermath of his father's death than to a serious proposal to introduce a constitution. Czartoryski's memoirs also testified to the influence of Pahlen and the other conspirators but, in his view, this was due more to Alexander's state of mind and psychological inability to act against the murderers of his father than to their real hold over him:

> For a few months he believed himself to be at their mercy, but it was chiefly his conscience and a feeling of natural equity which prevented him from giving up to justice the most guilty of the conspirators . . . . The proclamations issued at that time were all signed by him [Pahlen]; nothing could be done except through him and with his consent; he affected to protect the young Emperor, and scolded him when he did not do what he wished, or rather ordered. Alexander, overcome with sadness and despair, seemed to be in the power of the conspirators; he thought it necessary to treat them with consideration and bend his will to theirs.[10]

It was not clear exactly what Pahlen had in mind, if indeed he possessed a plan at all, but by the word 'constitution', he is unlikely to have been referring to a French Revolutionary or American-style document. Rather, as representatives of the bureaucracy and the nobility, the conspirators sought to increase the power of central government institutions *vis-à-vis* the tsar, institutions in which of course they served and could therefore bring influence to bear. Pahlen and the Zubov brothers were members of the so-called Permanent Council (*Nepremenyi sovet*) which was established by Alexander on 11 April 1801 'to examine and comply with state affairs and decrees'. This Council was the most important central institution in the first few years of the reign and took part in discussion of measures such as the reaffirmation of the Charter to the Nobility, the abolition of the Secret Expedition and the question of foreign relations with Britain. It prepared an instruction (*nakaz*) for Alexander to promulgate on the establishment of a new Council, which would replace the Permanent Council and become the head of the central administration. There are several drafts of this instruction which differed in defining the Council's areas of competence and its authority *vis-à-vis* the tsar; one draft stated that the Council had only a consultative function and another gave it the right to initiatate legislation. As, however, the dates of the different drafts cannot be conclusively established it is impossible to know whether these differences reflect a shifting balance of power between Alexander and the conspirators. In any event, a new Council was not created until 1810, and then under different circumstances and as a result of different influences (see below pp. 89–90).

Nevertheless, the Permanent Council showed that it could take an independent line on policy and was prepared to disagree with the tsar. This became clear when, in April, Alexander put the question before the Council of whether Georgia should be annexed. Georgia had entered a military alliance with Russia, and Paul had promulgated a decree to annex the country on 30 January 1801. The unanimous decision of the Council was that annexation should go ahead. A recent publication by the Russian historian Safonov (see footnote 8), based on the records of the Council, shows that Alexander did not share this view but that the Council refused to change its opinion. The tsar made known to the Council his 'extreme loathing' of the annexation proposal and instructed it to look again at the matter, but it refused to alter its opinion. In August, a report on the current situation by the commander-in-chief in Georgia, General B.F. Knorring, with comments by

Count Aleksandr Romanovich Vorontsov and Kochubei opposing annexation, were submitted to the Council for further deliberation but still it supported annexation. Platon Zubov prepared a further memorandum for Alexander on the wisdom of annexation, but both Novosil'tsev and Stroganov rejected his arguments. Despite this, Alexander ('reluctantly', according to Safonov) accepted the view of the Council on this matter and issued a manifesto annexing Georgia on 24 September 1801.

The relationship between Alexander and the Council in the first half of 1801 shows that the latter was not prepared tamely to endorse his views. It is unlikely, however, that Alexander saw the issue of Georgia as a real test of his authority, or that he felt seriously threatened by the Council. Zubov was forceful in his views on Georgia, but by the time Alexander issued the manifesto on annexation Pahlen, the most powerful of the conspirators, had already been removed from office. Stroganov recorded at a meeting of the Unofficial Committee on 25 August 1801 that Alexander was undecided over the future of Georgia, so perhaps his action simply signified that he had changed his mind. By the end of June 1801, Alexander had felt confident enough of his position, and the loyalty of the troops, to challenge Pahlen directly and dismiss him. Pahlen's departure was followed by the exile of Panin and then the dismissal of the Zubov brothers. General Beningsen was also dismissed but, unlike the other conspirators, was recalled, in 1806.

The American historian McConnell (see footnote 7) has seen the dismissal of Pahlen as a turning point in Alexander's reign. According to his interpretation, many of Alexander's early liberal decrees and promises were forced on him. After Pahlen's fall the flow of liberal decrees slowed down and early steps towards institutional and legal reform halted. Furthermore, McConnell argues, the experience of being under Pahlen's control led Alexander to be wary of any restrictions on his autocratic power later in his reign. Although it is true that Pahlen was influential, Alexander's own understanding of constitutional change, and the views held by his other advisers, made the whole process of reform a complex one in which the role of Pahlen was only one of many factors. The dismissal of

Pahlen 'made much noise at St Petersburg'[11] but did not lead to any direct opposition to Alexander or rallying to the fallen minister. In fact the process of tentative reform did not stop abruptly; the 'Charter to the Russian People' (discussed below), for example, was only submitted to the Unofficial Committee in August and to the Permanent Council in September, that is, *after* Pahlen's fall.

Whatever the intentions of Pahlen and his fellow conspirators, their chance of forcing fundamental constitutional change on Alexander against his will were slight. Pahlen and the Zubov brothers were not fully representative of the court bureaucracy. Indeed, they were not popular and the influential brothers, Counts Aleksandr and Semen Romanovich Vorontsov, disliked the seemingly all-powerful Pahlen and had urged Alexander not to accept any diminution of his own power. The lack of unity between the leaders of the conspiracy and the court bureaucracy meant that little real pressure could be put on the tsar. Members of the court bureaucracy who had served under Catherine II felt that the Senate should take on a more positive and legally-defined role in the government apparatus and also sought legal confirmation of the rights of the nobility as a class, after their experience under Paul. This loose grouping of individuals, referred to by historians as the senatorial party although there was never any formal organization, was led by the Vorontsov brothers. It is thought that Count Aleksandr Vorontsov was the main author of the 'Charter to the Russian People', written with the intention that it should be read out at Alexander's coronation. Influenced by the practice of government in England and by the French 'Declaration of the Rights of Man and of the Citizen', the Charter aimed to establish the security of property and person, the right of free speech and freedom from arbitrary arrest (the introduction of the English principle of *habeas corpus*) and confirmed the privileges given to the nobility in 1785. Vorontsov envisaged that the Russian nobility would no longer be 'beneath the tsar' but 'alongside him'. Although the Charter did not challenge the tsar's power directly, it would have confirmed the rights of the nobility as an estate. It would also have raised the status of the Senate in that it stated that all new laws had to be submitted to the Senate for ratification. The first draft of the Charter was prepared in June 1801; Alexander gave it to the Unofficial Committee for discussion in August; and the final amended version was submitted to the tsar on 25 August and was accepted by him subject to some minor modifications. It was submitted to the Permanent Council on 21 September (that is, six days before the coronation) and approved, but Alexander did not promulgate it and it was quietly put aside.

It was on Alexander's initiative that proposals for reform of the Senate were requested from senators, to be collated by P.B. Zavadovsky (Catherine II's ex-lover). It has been suggested that this was done reluctantly by Alexander and was an indication of his initial insecurity on the throne, but there was no reason for him in principle to oppose the Senate since he regarded it as a necessary safeguard against arbitrary government. The various proposals asserted, amongst other things, the Senate's right to: propose taxes, present candidates for the posts of governors-general and presidencies of certain colleges; submit 'the nation's needs' to the tsar; and the right of representation if a law or decree proved 'contrary to those previously published or harmful or unclear'. Representations to Alexander from the Vorontsov brothers, Troshchinsky, Zavadovsky and the Zubov brothers tried to convince Alexander to 'restore' the Senate to its position of supremacy over all other institutional bodies. Count Aleksandr Vorontsov even rather naively hoped that Alexander would not object to the Senate having the right of veto: 'I dare to hope for the granting of the right of veto to the Senate as the occurrence of this would be rare and the ruler would not be burdened by this'.[12] In September 1802 a decree confirmed the prerogatives of the Senate more or less on the lines of the senators' proposals. Its right to maintain the law and to supervise the operation of executive bodies in the state was confirmed, and it also formally acquired the right to return a law to the tsar if a majority of senators considered it to be 'unsuitable'.

The potential influence of the conspirators and the court bureaucracy was diminished by the existence of a rival body of reformers – the Unofficial Committee, or 'Committee of Public Safety' as Alexander jokingly called it – comprising Alexander's 'young friends': Czartoryski, Novosil'tsev, Stroganov and Kochubei. Czartoryski,

Novosil'tsev and Kochubei had had to leave Russia during Paul's reign, but were now summoned back by Alexander. These young men were more familiar with events and conditions abroad than was Alexander; Novosil'tsev had lived in England, Stroganov had been a visitor at the Jacobin club in Paris during the French Revolution. In the words of the senator and poet G.R. Derzhavin they were both 'filled with French and Polish constitutional spirit'.[13] There was much enthusiastic talk in the Committee about the 'rights of man' and the intro- duction of a constitution into Russia (much of it, admittedly, from Alexander himself) but little in the way of practical results. As Czartoryski put it, the Committee was 'like a masonic lodge from which one entered the practical world'.[14]

In fact, despite the enthusiasm expressed by the 'young friends' for a constitution ('Arrivez mon ami . . . . Nous allons avoir une constitution', wrote Stroganov to Novosil'tsev in London after Paul's death)[15], they were quite cautious in their proposals to bring this about and on what it entailed. Stroganov maintained that a proper administrative framework had to be established before the introduction of a full constitution. Indeed, Stroganov's definition of what he meant by a constitution is significant:

> One can divide the constitution into three parts: the establishment of rights, the means to employ them and their guarantee. In our case, the first two parts exist at least in part [through the Charters to the Nobility and the Towns and the Senate], but the absence of the third nullifies the other two completely . . . . The constitution is the law which regulates the method which has to be observed in the drawing up of administrative laws, which having necessarily to approve modifications, explanations etc., must submit these changes in a manner which is known, fixed, invariable, which closes the door on all *arbitrariness* and, in consequence, reduces the harm which can arise from the difference in the capacities of those who are at the head of the State. This is what I mean by a constitution.[16]

This is not an assertion of the rights of man and popular sovereignty; it is more the traditional view of the orderly governed state regulated by the law; a *Rechtsstaat*. This was something which the arbitrariness of Paul's reign had shown Russia did not yet possess; it was also, of course, very much in line with the thinking of Alexander himself.

Furthermore, the 'young friends' resisted the proposals made by the senatorial party. Novosil'tsev suggested to Alexander that the adoption of the principle of *habeas corpus*, proposed by Count Aleksandr Vorontsov, would be dangerous, arguing that it would be better not to adopt something which might in the future have to be revoked. Such a view was shared by the tsar: 'His Majesty said that that was the very observation he had already made to Count Vorontsov'.[17] Alexander had been willing to set up a commission to prepare a law code but he was not prepared in practice to establish a recognized legal procedure in case it should restrict his prerogatives. The 'young friends' were particularly suspicious of any attempt to increase the authority of the Senate, pointing out to the tsar that this would limit his own power. Novosil'tsev warned that increasing the authority of the Senate in the way proposed by Zavadovsky and others would 'bind your hands and would make it impossible to do all that had been planned for the general good and would mean coming up against the ignorance of these people'.[18] He expressed the wish that the tsar's decrees should be issued in such a way that all the Senate would have to do was publish them. His negative view of the Senate was shared by Czartoryski, who scathingly wrote that ' . . . it was nothing but a name; it was composed of men who were for the most part incapable and without energy, selected for their insignificance . . . a receptacle for the indolent and the superannuated'.[19] The 'young friends' believed that the best hope for reform was to entrust it to the tsar. There was some historical justification for this; Peter the Great had forced reform and modernization on a reluctant country, and Catherine had given charters to the nobles and townspeople. They distrusted the court bureaucracy who, they believed, thought only of their own self-interest. Alexander's former tutor La Harpe, who had been invited back to Russia, was also opposed to the Senate increasing its powers. Alexander submitted all the proposals for reform by the senators to the Unofficial Committee for scrutiny and comments. The result was that any possible diminution of the tsar's power was pointed out to

Alexander at this stage and the divisions and antagonisms between the two sets of reformers were exposed.

Alexander's handling of the reform proposals at the beginning of his reign illustrates both his methods of dealing with potentially threatening advisers and his attitude towards institutional change. He was obviously under some pressure from Pahlen and the Zubov brothers in the first few months, but the evidence suggests that his power was never seriously threatened, even before Pahlen's dismissal. There was never a united reform movement. Personal differences, such as the Vorontsovs' dislike for Pahlen and, in turn, the 'young friends' ' dislike of the Vorontsovs and Zubov, prevented any concerted action. The opposition by the members of the Unofficial Committee to the Senate strengthened Alexander's hand. Alexander has sometimes been portrayed as deliberately playing off the two sides against each other but there was really no need for him to be so devious. In the final analysis, reform could not be imposed upon him against his will. He accepted the 'Charter to the Russian People' but never implemented it and could not be forced to do so. He was not compelled to adopt the proposals of the Senate; the proposals were made on his initiative and the decree on the Senate of 20 September 1802 was not a concession wrung out of him.

Indeed, Alexander showed how conscious he was of his own authority in his dealings with the Senate in the early years of his reign. On the same day that the prerogatives of the Senate were recognized, another decree established eight Ministries for all branches of government administration, domestic and military: internal affairs, finance, justice, foreign affairs, war, navy, education and commerce. From the beginning there were contradictions in the relationship between the Ministries and the Senate, and overlapping functions which weakened the latter's authority. The heads of the Ministries were appointed by the tsar and personally responsible to him; in other words, they did not come under the Senate's control despite the confirmation of its supervisory powers over executive organs of the state. Ministers had direct access to the tsar and could submit to him projects for new laws or amendments to existing ones which, if approved, would then be announced to the Senate. But ministers also had to submit an annual report to the First Department of the Senate about their activities, and could be asked to provide 'explanations', and the Senate in turn reported to the tsar on the performance of the minister. The situation was further complicated by the fact that ministers were also members of the First Department of the Senate. In 1809, for example, of the nineteen members of the First Department six were ministers, three were former ministers, one was a deputy minister and four had quasi-ministerial posts, so that ministers were in effect justifying their performance in a body in which they could have a majority. Ministers also became *ex-officio* members of the Permanent Council. This has led the American historian LeDonne to talk about 'ministerial despotism'.[20] Yet the Ministries had no real independence or power either, and certainly were no more able than the Senate to control the tsar. Alexander confidently wrote to La Harpe in late 1802 that business was being conducted through the Ministries with 'a great deal more clarity and method',[21] but in practice central government had been made neither more efficient nor more independent.

Alexander's understanding of his relationship with the Senate was more clearly defined in an incident which took place a year after the decree on the Senate. In 1803 the senator Count Severin Osipovich Potocki attempted to exercise the Senate's right of representation on 'unsuitable laws', which it was generally believed to have acquired in 1802, on a law concerning the retirement of noble army officers. This, he thought, contradicted earlier decrees on the subject. A group of senators, including Potocki, wished to return the decree to Alexander for reconsideration. Derzhavin, who chaired the Senate, recommended Alexander to forbid further discussion of the issue in the Senate. The tsar, however, resolved that the Senate should debate it. This was duly done and a majority of the senators voted that the decree should indeed be returned to the tsar for reconsideration. As Derzhavin refused to do this (mainly because he was in favour of the decree, rather than on any constitutional grounds), a delegation led by Potocki presented a petition themselves. Alexander was furious at the impertinence of the Senate, met their delegation coolly and, being 'of the opinion that there was evil intent on the part of the Senate', proceeded to pass an edict which effectively made this right meaningless by restricting their right of comment to laws passed only after 1802, without reference to earlier laws. The matter was put before the Unofficial Committee; this body's clarification of the Senate's prerogatives accorded with Alexander's views, although it was expressed in more measured tones as a misunderstanding by the Senate of the meaning of the original decree. The 'young friends' had, of course, shown themselves to be hostile towards any attempt of the Senate to increase its powers at the expense of the tsar, so it is perhaps not surprising that they took this view.

Czartoryski was scathing about this illustration of Alexander's limited understanding of the meaning of liberty (writing, however, after the tsar had disappointed his hopes for a restored Poland):

> The Emperor liked forms of liberty as he liked the theatre; it gave him pleasure and flattered his vanity to see the appearances of free government in his Empire; but all he wanted in this respect was forms and appearances; he did not expect them to become realities. In a word, he would willingly have agreed that every man should be free, on the condition that he should voluntarily do only what the Emperor wished.[22]

The Senate's new authority had proved to be illusory but neither Alexander nor the senators seemed to be aware that anything significant had taken place or that the Senate's powers had been irrevocably weakened. The historian Yaney aptly summed up the situation thus: 'Perhaps the clearest indication of the general inability of Russia's statesmen in the late eighteenth and early ninteenth centuries to comprehend the nature of a legal institution is that this mortal blow to government by legal institutions was unintentional and that it went virtually unnoticed . . . the Senate did not lose its institutional position in 1803, because it never had one'.[23]

. . .

THE SERF QUESTION

The first few years of Alexander's reign also demonstrated that he did not have any great respect for the Russian nobility in particular or for the established structure of Russian society in general. Although he confirmed Catherine's Charter to the Nobility, which included the confirmation of freedom from compulsory service originally granted by Peter III in 1762, he expressed the opinion that a distinction should be drawn between those who served and those who did not. Indeed, at a meeting of the Unofficial Committee on 27 July 1801 he claimed that 'it was against his will that he had revived the Charter to the Nobility because of its exclusive rights which had always been repugnant to him'.[24] He supported the right of non-nobles to buy serfs on the dubious grounds that they would treat serfs better and would not make slaves of them. He was also prepared to go some way to attack the institution of serfdom itself, in which any change would, of course, affect the privileged position of the nobility *vis-à-vis* other social estates.

Alexander had expressed his abhorrence of serfdom from an early age. At some time between 1798 and the end of 1800 he wrote in his exercise book that:

> Nothing could be more degrading and inhuman than the sale of people and a decree is needed which will forbid this forever. To the shame of Russia slavery still exists.

He then outlined the decrees which would ensure this, concluding that 'All this will have two advantages; firstly freemen will be made from slaves; and secondly, by degrees conditions will be equalized and classes will be abolished'.[25] The sentiments expressed here were partly the product of La Harpe's teaching, but Alexander consistently deplored the existence of serfdom, and there is no reason to think that his sentiments were not genuine. The problem was not, of course, recognizing the injustice of serfdom, but finding a means to end it without endangering the throne either by arousing too much hostility from the nobility or by encouraging social upheaval in the countryside. In the early years of his reign Alexander approached the issue tentatively by supporting proposals for piecemeal steps which aimed to alleviate the condition of the serfs and to make some challenge to the exclusive rights of the nobility to own land and serfs.

Understandably, any move in this direction would be opposed by many members of the nobility. In practice, even members of the Unofficial Committee who had expressed their abhorrence of serfdom and contempt for the nobility (Stroganov said of the nobles during a discussion about serfdom in the committee: 'It is the most ignorant, the most debauched, class'),[26] found reasons in practice to be wary of the piecemeal and minor changes in the relationships between serfs and landowners put before it. In the summer of 1801, Platon Zubov prepared a project which proposed, amongst other things: allowing nobles to free their house serfs in towns with financial compensation from the state (the ex-serfs would register in the towns as *meshchane* – that is, artisans – and enter the town guilds); forbidding the change in status of agricultural serfs to house serfs; forbidding the sale of land without serfs; and setting out regulations for serfs wishing independently to buy their freedom. It has been estimated that 8.1 per cent of the urban population were house serfs, and that, in all, this group totalled approximately 190,000 people, so Zubov was addressing an important point. His proposals were then put before the Unofficial Committee in August, and its members opposed them, partly because of personal dislike of Zubov as Catherine's favourite, and partly on the financial grounds that it would cost the treasury too much to purchase the freedom of house serfs. This latter objection ignored the fact that Zubov recommended the purchase by the state not of all house serfs, but only of those whom the landowners wished to part with. Alexander continued to support the project despite the disapproval of the 'young friends' but did not act on it.

In late 1801 a further memorandum on serfdom by Admiral Mordvinov proposed extending the right of non-noble classes to buy populated and unpopulated land. The Unofficial Committee was asked to look at this proposal in November and to give further thought to Zubov's proposals. The 'young friends', although they were not in principle opposed to ending the nobles' monopoly to own serfs, in practice found the right to purchase both land and serfs by non-nobles 'too great an innovation' and one which could have unfortunate economic consequences such as an increase in the price of land. Zubov's proposals could result in 'dangerous excess' on the part of the serfs and 'too great dissatisfaction' on the part of the landowners. Novosil'tsev warned that disorder could arise if the serfs thought that the tsar were planning to emancipate them fully. The tsar demonstrated his independence, and heated debates took place between himself and his 'young friends' on the two proposals in general and the issue of the sale of serfs without land in particular. For example, while Alexander accepted the main points of Mordvinov's proposal he also accepted the opinion of the 'young friends' that the project should be promulgated as a decree and not as a manifesto (as Mordvinov had wished), on the grounds that this would be less provocative. At the same time he opposed putting the proposal before the Permanent Council, as his 'young friends' wished, on the grounds that the Council 'could not approve such an concept, that it was necessary to do this by the force of absolute [that is, tsarist] authority'. He insisted, against the advice of his 'young friends', that the Permanent Council should only be allowed to accept or reject the proposal. He was eventually persuaded to put the project before the Council, possibly when he was assured that there would be no major objections to it. In the event, it restricted its opposition to a suggestion that there should be a special tax on land acquired by this means. The right of merchants, artisans, state peasants and free cultivators to buy unpopulated land was granted in a decree on 24 December 1801, Alexander's birthday. The noble monopoly of landownership had been broken, but neither the right of other estates to own 'populated' land (that is, land on which there were serfs) nor the Zubov proposals had been accepted.

In November 1802, Sergei Petrovich Rumiantsev submitted a further proposal to Alexander which would have allowed landowners to free individual serfs or whole villages if they wished to do so for a sum determined by the landowner. Despite the moderation of this proposal it excited hostility from many nobles who feared that it would lead to unrest as the serfs would believe that the decree was the prelude to complete emancipation. Despite doubts expressed in the Permanent Council that the freed peasants could find themselves subject to onerous terms imposed by their former landowners, the proposals were accepted by Alexander and became the basis for the Free Cultivator's Law passed in March 1803. This allowed landowners to petition the tsar for permission to free whole villages of serfs, with the land which they worked, and thereby created a new class of Free Grain Cultivators. But in practice few landowners took the opportunity voluntarily to free their serfs, and by the end of his reign it has been estimated that only 47,153 male serfs had been freed by this method (13,371 as a result of the action of one nobleman, Prince Aleksandr Nikolaevich Golitsyn). The law was passed, incidentally, without being offered for discussion in the Senate which, following Derzhavin's lead, would probably have raised objections to it.

In early November 1803 the Unofficial Committee looked at the disorders which had occurred in the Ukraine (Malorossiia) following the introduction of new regulations on peasants relating to their rights as Cossacks. Alexander was reluctant to cancel the regulations (the Committee was split on this issue) because 'this would be completely against what he had started, which was the emancipation of the peasants'. But later in the month when the question of the rights of merchants to purchase serfs was discussed again in the Committee, both the tsar and his 'young friends' acknowledged the core of the problem. Stroganov reported that:

. . . The Emperor repeated what he had always said, that he had to satisfy the bulk of the population; that if they should ever make an outcry and become aware of their power this would be dangerous. We replied by making him see the consequence of attacking the nobility too much, who also made up a considerable section of the population which could very easily acquire influence; that popular opinion counted for very little and that one should not diverge from the great principle of not wronging anyone.

Little practical progress was made during this discussion: 'As he [Alexander] spoke as ever of his favourite ideas of finding a standard for duties owed by the peasant to his lord, we opposed him with all that one could say on such an occasion'.[27] After all the discussions only minor changes had been made in the regulations concerning serfdom.

Advertisements for serfs for sale in the St Petersburg and Moscow gazettes, which had offended the sensibilities of Alexander, were now forbidden but this had little bearing on the institution of serfdom.

OTHER REFORMS

The early years of Alexander's reign were not entirely barren in terms of domestic reform. Attention was paid to the administration of the Empire's non-Russian subjects, to the administration of the army and to education and welfare.

Alexander consistently showed a degree of flexibility in his approach to the non-Russian lands in his empire. To some extent, he used these areas as a testing ground for reforms in Russia. The only major change concerning the relationship between serfs and landowners took place in the Baltic provinces of Estonia, Livonia and Courland (which had become part of the Empire in the early eighteenth century during the reign of Peter I). Here, unlike in Russia, at least some of the nobles, most of whom were ethnically German or Swedish, had shown some interest in ending serfdom and there had been a debate on the issue since the 1760s. Alexander took a personal interest in these discussions, hoping that Russian landowners might be inspired in turn to propose some form of emancipation. He expressed the hope in the Unofficial Committee in February 1802 that 'the province will provide an example to the rest of the Empire'.[28] Partly in response to pressure from Alexander the diets of Estonia and Livonia acted between 1802 and 1804 to pass statutes which regulated the obligations of serfs to their landowners and gave leaseholders hereditary rights to their lands.

In 1775, Catherine II had established a new structure of provincial administration for Russia, including courts and fiscal bodies. This institutional framework was introduced in the Baltic provinces and replaced their traditional institutions, although they were permitted to continue to use their own law codes within the new structure of courts. Paul restored their traditional institutions and special rights and privileges. Alexander did nothing to reverse this but his recognition of the rights and privileges of the Baltic provinces in September 1801 was tempered by the phrase 'in so far as they are in agreement with the general decrees and laws of our state'. In practice, this simply meant that the provinces retained a separate administrative infrastructure but that this could be modified or overridden if necessary. In 1801, for example, the Russian military governor of Riga was put in charge of the administration of all three Baltic provinces. Later, in 1810, Estonia was separated from Courland and the province (*guberniia*) of Lithuania (the latter having been created after the acquisition of territory by Russia as a result of the partitions of Poland). All three provinces were reunited in 1819, and then in 1823 Pskov province was added. Unlike Catherine, however, Alexander showed little inclination to interfere in local Baltic affairs or to impose Russian institutions. He made no attempt to exploit the conflict which broke out in the town of Riga over the merits of retaining traditional guilds as opposed to readopting Catherine's urban institutions (set up in her Charter to the Towns of 1785) or to take advantage of the conflict within the Livonian diet in 1803 about the merits of restoring Catherine's 1775 local government institutions.

Georgia, in the Caucasus, had been annexed in 1801, but Alexander allowed the province to retain its own 'constitution'. By 'constitution' he meant that Georgia retained its own laws and social organization and was governed by its own administrative structure. This was similar, therefore, to his attitude towards government of the Baltic provinces. Neither territory was given a new constitution of the kind that was later given to the Congress Kingdom of Poland (see below p. 132). The Georgian monarchy was allowed to remain and the status of the Georgian Orthodox church was left unchanged. Georgian nobles, however, were integrated into the Russian Table of Ranks and given Russian titles, but there was little opposition to this by the local nobility as they benefited by being allowed to participate in local government. Unlike in Russia, social groups other than the nobility had been allowed to own serfs (including the clergy, merchants and even serfs themselves). Alexander made no attempt to alter this and the practice continued during his reign, finally being abolished in 1832 during the reign of Nicholas I. In

1821, however, Alexander did abolish the practice of free peasants being allowed to 'volunteer' for bondage in Georgia.

Alexander also gave some attention to the Jewish population, subjects of the Russian Empire as the result of the three Partitions of Poland in Catherine's reign. Historians have disagreed about the number of Jews in the Empire. Their estimates have ranged from 32,000 to 200,000, although latest research suggests that the lower estimates are more likely to be accurate. The Jews posed an administrative anomaly in the former Polish provinces, as their *kahal* structure gave them a separate administrative, judicial and educational organization. They also created (or were thought to create) an economic problem, being popularly blamed for the economic hardship suffered by the peasantry. Catherine had tried to address the problem of poverty in the countryside by obliging the Jews to register in the urban estates. She also imposed late in her reign a double poll tax (which was naturally resented) and recruiting tax (in lieu of actual recruits), which set the precedent of treating the Jews as a separate social estate, with different obligations from the others. The precise rights and obligations of the Jews in the towns remained unclear and Alexander set up a special commission to examine the question in November 1802. Members of this Committee for the Organization of Jewish Life included Derzhavin (later replaced by P.V. Lopukhin), Valerian Zubov, Speransky, Kochubei, Czartoryski and Potocki. Their work resulted in the Jewish Statute of 1804 which had two aims; first, to reform and assimilate Jewish society by encouraging Jews to attend state schools and institutions of higher education; and secondly, to protect the peasantry from economic exploitation by the Jews by excluding the latter from participation in the liquor trade and by seeking to resettle them from the countryside. The statute did not abolish the *kahal* structure (which, amongst other things, retained the right to apportion taxation within the community) and failed to clarify the status of Jews and their rights of representation in the elected municipal institutions (which remained as set out in the local government reform of 1775). Jews were allowed to register as farmers, and encouraged to resettle in certain areas to compensate them for their loss of revenue in the liquor trade, but in the short term their economic position only worsened. There was, however, a gradual erosion of the double taxation, which had disappeared by 1807.

Alexander's experience of Gatchina life had left him with a genuine love of the minutiae of military life. In the first years of his reign, following the peace with Britain and France (see below pp. 61–2), he turned his attention to the reorganization and modernization of the armed forces. Arakcheev, who had befriended and helped Alexander in the Gatchina days, was recalled in 1803 and given a free hand to reorganize and modernize the artillery. He approached the task with some vigour, separating the artillery from the infantry, establishing schools of artillery for officers, and starting a publication, *The Artillery Journal,* which attempted to improve the status and *esprit de corps* of the artillery. Lieutenant Zhirevich, his adjutant in the Guards' Artillery Battalion, wrote in his memoirs concerning the artillery that 'everyone in Russia knows that its present condition is the work of Arakcheev, and if it has since been perfected, it was he who laid the firm foundation'.[29] Considerable changes were made to the structure of the army. In 1808 Arakcheev was made head of the new Ministry of Land Forces and greatly expanded its role. A committee was also set up in 1802 to reform the navy and a Ministry of Naval Forces established (renamed the Marine Ministry in 1815). Little improvement, however, was made in the conditions of ordinary soldiers and nothing was done to mitigate the brutality of military justice. Early in Alexander's reign 'merciless' and 'cruel' punishments were outlawed but such adjectives were not thought to apply to the cruellest military punishment, that of running the gauntlet, during which most victims died from the blows.

In 1786, Catherine had established state schools at the district (*uezd*) and provincial (*guberniia*) levels, although in practice there were not sufficient teachers, financial backing, textbooks or pupils to ensure that the system worked everywhere as she had envisaged. In 1803, Alexander created a comprehensive educational structure, including village schools and universities. The country was divided into six educational regions, each headed by a university which had responsibility for overseeing schools in its area. A ladder of schools was established: parochial schools in every village with one year of instruction; district schools in every district town with two further years of instruction; provincial schools (*gimnaziia*) in every provincial town with four years of further instruction; and universities in six large cities.

The main influences on the new educational system were Polish and French. Czartoryski wrote a memorandum on education in 1802, and the statute of 1803 which dealt with the structure of schools and the curriculum in the Vil'na educational district (which included Lithuania and Belorussia, where there were many Polish-speaking nobles, but also part of the Ukraine and the Russian provinces of Minsk, Mogilev and Volhynia) was a modification of the Polish Statute on Schools of 1783. A major influence was the Marquis de Condorcet's report which was presented to the French National Assembly in 1792. The curricula of the new schools were based on Condorcet's belief in the utility of education and established a clear gradation from lower to higher schools. Thus the teaching of the following subjects showed an emphasis on technological subjects: parochial schools taught reading, writing and arithmetic, religion and morals, elements of natural science, agriculture and hygiene; district schools taught religion, law, Russian, history, geography, mathematics, physics, natural science, technology, local industry, drawing and, in addition, Latin and German for those pupils who were entering the provincial schools; provincial schools taught mathematics, physics, technology, natural science, psychology, logic, ethics, aesthetics, law, political economy, history, geography, statistics, Latin, German, French and drawing. The syllabus was highly ambitious and, inevitably, was going to be very difficult to implement in full. In 1811, S.S. Uvarov, the supervisor of schools in the St Petersburg educational district, proposed that the curriculum should be simplified and made less 'encyclopedic' and that the course of study should be increased from four to seven years in order to make the system more workable.

In principle, as in Condorcet's project, schools were open to both sexes and all classes, and free tuition and books were to be provided for children from poor families.

We know that at least some girls were educated in state schools: in 1808 there were twenty girls in the *gimnaziia* of Vitebsk, thirteen in Mogilev, three in Novgorod and seven in Pskov. It was only in the reign of Nicholas I that formal restrictions were placed on the participation of girls in the state education system, when they were forbidden to enter any but parochial schools. Serfs in principle could also attend these schools, although in practice probably very few did. Fees were introduced in the schools in the St Petersburg region in 1819, but orphans and children of poor parents were exempted. However, as the need for qualifications rose (especially after examinations were introduced for the civil service, see below p. 84) the higher schools became more the province of the gentry. The schools were given insufficient funding and it proved impossible to establish them except in towns; nevertheless, by the end of Alexander's reign there were three élite *lycées* (see below pp. 83–4), 57 *gimnazii*, 370 district schools, 600 private schools and three major schools (schools in major provincial towns; the name comes from Catherine's statute of 1786). This meant a total of 1,411 schools and 69,629 pupils, compared with only 317 schools and 19,915 pupils in 1801.

The new structure required the establishment of three new universities at St Petersburg, Kazan' and Khar'kov in addition to the existing universities of Moscow, Vil'na (which was largely Polish) and Dorpat (largely German). Education reform was less controversial, of course, than alterations to the structure of government or to the institution of serfdom. Even so, the provisions of these reforms illustrate some of Alexander's persistent concerns. We have seen that he had little respect for the nobility; the universities, like the schools, were made open to all classes of society, despite opposition from the provincial nobility. Alexander also had a poor opinion of the calibre of the bureaucracy in Russia. During a discussion in the Unofficial Committee on 22 February 1802 the 'young friends' stressed the necessity of appointing good governors-general; Alexander's response was 'It is true, but find me such people'.[30] The new universities were to remedy these defects by providing useful state servants. The statute for Moscow University in 1804 (the statutes for the universities of Kazan' and Khar'kov were almost identical) defined the university as:

> . . . the highest learned organization, founded for the dissemination of learning. In it youth prepare for entrance into the various branches of state service . . . . Among the sciences taught at the university are those necessary for all who wish to be useful to themselves and to the Fatherland, no matter what role in life or which service they choose.[31]

Students who completed the three-year course were awarded the twelfth rank in the Table of Ranks; that is, officer status. The same emphasis on utilitarian education and technological and scientific subjects which had been apparent in the curricula of secondary schools was present in the university syllabuses. A new faculty of Physical and Mathematical Sciences was established at Moscow University in 1804 and by 1820 similar faculties had been opened in the other universities. A new statute was given to the Russian Academy of Sciences in 1803 which emphasized its role in furthering Russian industry, arts and crafts. The Academy was instructed to publish a new technological journal, which appeared under the title of *Tekhnologicheskii zhurnal.*

Alexander also provided encouragement and financial aid for charitable institutions. Catherine had attempted in her local government reform of 1775 to establish a financial and institutional structure for the care of the sick, infirm and insane. Alexander also favoured some form of organized charity in preference to the traditional Russian practice of alms-giving. He was influenced in his thinking by his acquaintance with the work of the Hamburg Charitable Society which had performed this function since the 1770s, and whose activities Alexander had discussed with Focht, a merchant in St Petersburg, who was one of the Society's directors. Alexander gave his sanction for similar societies to be established in Russia, and gave them generous support. The Committee for Supervision of the Poor, founded in St Petersburg in 1805, received an annual state subsidy of 40,000 roubles and gifts from the Imperial family. The Medical Philanthropic Committee (also in St Petersburg), which provided free medical treatment for the poor and set up hospitals for various diseases, received a yearly state subsidy of 24,000 roubles. Alexander was to extend his philanthropic interests in the later part of his reign (see below pp. 192–3).

The early years of Alexander's reign had seen some significant reforms, in particular the restructuring of the educational system and the creation of the ministries. The hopes of some members of the court nobility and Alexander's 'young friends' that more fundamental change in the structure of government would take place had, however, been disappointed. Nor had there been any substantial alteration to the institution of serfdom. Indeed, some of Alexander's initiatives seemed to have petered out. The Commission which had been established to prepare a new code of laws was stagnating (Radishchev had committed suicide a year after its establishment). Other manifestos which had been prepared, such as the 'Charter to the Russian People' and Zubov's proposals on the peasants, had been put aside. Alexander seemed to be uncertain how to proceed and to have become out of touch with his 'young friends'. The enthusiastic and idealistic discussions of the early meetings of the Unofficial Committee had been replaced by disagreements in which Alexander appeared truculent and resentful of advice. Indeed, the Committee met less and less frequently during 1802 and 1803. Alexander had by this stage become more involved in foreign affairs and only after the Treaty of Tilsit in 1807 did he turn his attention once again to domestic matters.

. . .

NOTES AND REFERENCES

1. J.H. Schnitzler, *Secret History of the Court and Government of Russia under the Emperors Alexander and Nicholas*, 2 vols, London, 1847, I, pp. 40, 39.
2. Madame la Comtesse de Choiseul-Gouffier, *Historical Memoirs of the Emperor Alexander I and the Court of Russia,* translated by Mary Berenice Patterson, London, 1904, p. 82.
3. N. Hans, 'Tsar Alexander I and Jefferson: Unpublished Correspondence', *Slavonic and East European Review,* vol. 32, no. 78, 1953, p. 222.
4. Max M. Laserson, *The American Impact on Russia – Diplomatic and Ideological 1784–1917,* New York, 1950, p. 80.
5. A.N. Pypin, *Obshchestvennoe dvizhenie v Rossii pri Aleksandre I,* Petrograd, 1918, pp. 69, 72, 75, 112.

6. F.F. Vigel', *Zapiski*, 2 vols, Cambridge, 1974 (original; Moscow, 1928), I, p. 126.

7. Allen McConnell, 'Alexander I's Hundred Days: The Politics of a Paternalist Reformer', *Slavic Review*, vol. 28, no. 3, 1969, p. 378.

8. M.M. Safonov, *Problema reform v pravitel'stvennoi politike Rossii na rubezhe XVIII i XIX vv.*, Leningrad, 1988, p. 78.

9. A. McConnell, *Alexander I: The Paternalistic Reformer*, New York, 1970, p. 27.

10. *Memoirs of Prince Adam Czartoryski and his Correspondence with Alexander I*, edited by Adam Gielgud, 2 vols, London, 1888, I, pp. 247, 249.

11. Ibid., p. 250.

12. N.V. Minaeva, *Pravitel'stvennyi konstitutsionalizm i peredovoe obshchestvennoe mnenie Rossii v nachale XIX veka*, Saratov, 1982, p. 56.

13. Pypin, op. cit., p. 82.

14. *Memoirs of Prince Adam Czartoryski*, p. 260.

15. Pypin, op. cit., p. 66.

16. Nikolai Mikhailovich, *Graf Pavel Aleksandrovich Stroganov (1774–1817). Istoricheskoe izsledovanie epokhi imperatora Aleksandra I*, 3 vols, St Petersburg, 1903, II, pp. 40–41.

17. Ibid., p. 77.

18. M.V. Dovnar-Zapol'skii, *Iz istorii obshchestvennykh techenii v Rossii*, Kiev, 1910, p. 11.

19. *Memoirs of Prince Adam Czartoryski*, pp. 291, 294.

20. John P. LeDonne, *Absolutism and Ruling Class: The Formation of the Russian Political Order 1700–1825*, New York, Oxford, 1991, p. 107.

21. *Correspondance de Frédéric-César de la Harpe et Alexandre Ier*, 3 vols, Neuchâtel, 1978, I (1785–1802), p. 676.

22. *Memoirs of Prince Adam Czartoryski*, pp. 324–5.

23. George L. Yaney, *The Systematization of Russian Government: Social Evolution in the Domestic Administration of Russia, 1711–1905*, Urbana, Chicago, London, 1973, pp. 98–9.

24. Nikolai Mikhailovich, op. cit., p. 73.

25. Safonov, op. cit., pp. 62–3.

26. Nikolai Mikhailovich, op. cit., p. 111.

27. Ibid., pp. 231, 242–3.

28. Ibid., p. 167

29. Michael Jenkins, *Arakcheev: Grand Vizier of the Russian Empire*, London, 1969, p. 101.

30. Nikolai Mikhailovich, op. cit., p. 179.

31. James T. Flynn, *The University Reform of Tsar Alexander I 1802–1835*, Washington D.C., 1988, p. 24.

Chapter 4

THE FRUSTRATED STATESMAN: 1801–1807

. . .

RUSSIA AT PEACE

The early years of Alexander's reign are important for understanding his attitude towards foreign relations and his assumptions regarding the role that he, and Russia, should play in European affairs. During this period, Alexander lacked both a clear perception of the way foreign policy should be conducted and the military strength to impress his rather vague ideas on either his allies or his opponents, but the general lines of his thinking became apparent. The roots of later policies (such as the Holy Alliance of 1815 and the role Alexander played in the Congress System), when Russia was dominant in Europe, can be found in the years 1801 to 1807, when Russia could only play a secondary role in European affairs.

In the course of the eighteenth century Russia had become accepted as the equal of other great powers in Europe. She had increased her territory through impressive military victories. In the north, Peter I's defeat of Sweden had led to the acquisition of her Baltic provinces at the Treaty of Nystad in 1721; further territory in southern Finland had been acquired at the expense of the Swedes in 1743 during the reign of Elizabeth. In the south, Catherine II's reign marked a watershed in Russo-Ottoman relations as her two Turkish wars (1768–74 and 1788–92) established a Russian military superiority over the Turks which lasted until the collapse of the Ottoman and Russian Empires in the twentieth century. During her reign Russia

58

acquired the northern coastline of the Black Sea, the Crimea and the land between the rivers Dniester and the Southern Bug. In addition, Russian ships were given freedom of navigation in the Black Sea and permitted to pass freely through the Straits, and the Russians were allowed to build an Orthodox church in Constantinople. The change in the balance of power in Russia's favour was recognized by other European powers; the First Partition of Poland in 1772 was an attempt to divert Russian interests away from the Balkans and the British threat to attack the Russian fleet in 1791 was based on fears of Russian expansion. But the most important consequence of Catherine's foreign policy was the Partitions of Poland (1772, 1793, 1795) between Austria, Prussia and Russia with the result that the three powers now shared frontiers. Russia had gained the largest share of territory, including most of what had been the Grand Duchy of Lithuania, Courland and western Volhynia, and had extended her borders westwards into the heart of Europe. By 1801 not only were Russia's military claims to be a great European power acknowledged but she had also become an accepted and important member of the diplomatic community. Karamzin, writing in the aftermath of what he regarded as Russia's shameful capitulation at Tilsit in 1807, demonstrated his pride in Russia's eighteenth-century achievements:

> Under Catherine Russia occupied with honour and glory one of the foremost places in the state system of Europe. In war we vanquished our foes. Peter had astounded Europe with his victories – Catherine made Europe accustomed to them.[1]

Despite the apparent capriciousness of Paul's foreign policy (see above pp. 22–4), there was no reason to believe that Russia under Alexander would not play a decisive part in European diplomacy.

Before coming to the throne, Alexander had not formulated clear principles about foreign relations or thought deeply about the role of Russia in European affairs. His education had concentrated on issues which were primarily of domestic significance, such as the nature of rule and the social order. Although he had been well schooled in European languages, he had never travelled abroad, and his knowledge of other countries had come through study and through friendship with non-Russians, such as Czartoryski, or with young Russians who had lived abroad, such as Novosil'tsev and Stroganov. It is perhaps not surprising, therefore, that Alexander's early statements on foreign relations were rather naive and idealistic, and bore little relation to Russia's strength or the actual state of affairs in Europe.

His first modestly declared aim was to establish peace, not simply for Russia but for the whole world. Shortly after his accession, when the issue of the Armed Neutrality had to be addressed, Alexander wrote of his desire not only of 'pacifying the North' but also of establishing a 'continuing world peace'.[2] He told the new French ambassador to Russia, General G. Duroc, (having disconcerted him by naively greeting him as 'citoyen', a term that was no longer used in Napoleonic France) that 'I want nothing for myself, I only want to contribute to the peace of Europe'.[3] Such statements can be regarded as the idealistic dreams of an inexperienced ruler, but throughout his reign Alexander consistently maintained not only that he sought peace but also that he sought the peace of all Europe, not just Russia. A fuller statement of his principles was made in his instruction to Baron Krüdener, his ambassador in Berlin (and the husband of Julie Krüdener, who was subsequently to be Alexander's companion in Paris when the Holy Alliance was drawn up), on 17 July 1801:

> . . . [my ministers] must not at all lose sight of the fact that their sovereign never wants to abuse his power, that he respects the rights of governments and the independence of nations . . . and that his dearest wish is for the reestablishment of a peace as solid as the work of men can achieve . . . . I will never take any part in the internal disputes which trouble other states . . . . I think that real grandeur, which must be the apanage of the throne, is founded on justice and good faith . . . .[4]

Unfortunately, Alexander was hardly in a position in 1801 to bring much influence to bear within Europe to ensure the peace and happiness of mankind. His first diplomatic actions were a response to the difficult situation created by his father. The formidable British fleet was entering the Baltic in order to oppose Paul's policy on Armed Neutrality while at the same time 20,000 Cossack troops were about to set out through the inhospitable lands of Central Asia on an expedition to conquer India. Alexander's first steps were to cancel this expedition and to reach an understanding with Britain. The British ships and crews held in Russian ports were immediately released as a gesture of goodwill. A compromise was reached in the convention between the two countries signed in June 1801: the British accepted the rights of neutral ships to enter ports under blockade, and Russia recognized the right of the British navy to inspect the cargoes of ships, even when they were flying a neutral flag. The agreement was made easier as Alexander 'from notions of delicacy' avoided the issue of Malta, which had been captured by Britain in September 1798. (Alexander had declined to inherit the title of grand master of the Knights from his father but was still, formally, the protector of the Order.)

Trade between the two countries, which was important for both sides, was resumed. Russia exported raw materials to Britain such as naval supplies, iron, potash, copper and agricultural products; and imported manufactured goods, textiles and foodstuffs such as tea and coffee. Trade relations had improved since May 1801 when Alexander had cancelled Paul's prohibition on the import of many goods from Britain, including china, glassware, earthenware, steel tools, hardware, silk, cotton and linen. This was followed by further cuts in import duties on a range of other British goods. Alexander's 'young friends' had been influenced by the theories of Adam Smith and opposed mercantilism. Kochubei made some proposals in 1803, approved by Alexander, which were designed to favour the increase of the population and the growth of factories in Russian ownership but which opposed direct state intervention in the economy. Count Nikolai Petrovich Rumiantsev, the minister of commerce, who was also influenced by the ideas of Smith, firmly believed in free trade. Alexander, who never seems to have given a great deal of thought to economic matters, shared the views of his advisers at this stage and expressed his disapproval of formal commercial treaties with other nations, on the grounds that one country was always exploited. He stated in a decree on the Russian customs tariff of 1801 that he wanted 'to achieve commercial freedom and unimpeded circulation', although in fact some restrictions were retained to protect Russian industries as Alexander was also concerned to increase Russian trade. He claimed that he had the 'absolute and customary desire to furnish Russian trade with all possible advantages and free flow'.[5] The period from 1801 to 1810 saw very few formal commercial treaties signed with other nations.

At the same time as Alexander was coming to terms with Britain he was assuring General Duroc of his friendliness towards France:

> I have always desired to see France and Russia as friends; these are the great and powerful nations . . . which must agree to put a stop to the little disagreements of the continent.[6]

The early months of his reign saw a *rapprochement* with France, and a peace treaty and a secret convention were signed on 8 October 1801. Agreement was reached on the territorial settlement for the German princes who had lost land on the left bank of the Rhine to the French, and on compensation for the King of Sardinia and the rulers of Bavaria, Baden and Württemberg. Alexander had based his right to intervene in Germany on the terms of the Treaty of Teschen of 1779 which made Catherine II the mediator in the Bavarian succession conflict. The independence of the Ionian Islands was recognized and the French promised to remove their troops from Egypt and the port of Naples.

Alexander had achieved his aim of extricating Russia from her entanglements with Britain and France and had established peace for his own state, if not for the whole of Europe. This had not, however, made him entirely content. He was unhappy with the attitude shown towards him by the French government, which was in a strong position following the military victories of 1795–1801 and saw no reason to act humbly with the Russians. Napoleon concluded two favourable peace treaties with the Austrians and the British; at the peace of Lunéville on 9 February 1801, Austria had accepted French acquisition of Belgium, the left bank of the Rhine and French control of the Italian peninsula; then at the Treaty of Amiens on 27 March 1802, Britain returned most of her overseas conquests to France and gave up Malta. Kochubei reported to Count Aleksandr Vorontsov on 3 November 1801 that Alexander 'had been happy with the signature of peace with France but the tone of the first consul and that of Talleyrand did not please him', and that he referred to them as 'rogues'.[7] Alexander had shown in his treatment of the delegation from the Russian Senate in 1803 that he was very conscious of his own dignity. He was equally conscious of his position abroad, and sensitive to any real or perceived slight. Despite this, Alexander resisted the efforts of the British government to win his co-operation in action against France. He was determined that Russia should have an independent policy. As he wrote to Count Semen Romanovich Vorontsov, his ambassador in London, in November 1801:

> I have striven especially to follow a national system, that is a system founded on the benefits of the State, and not, as has often happened, on predilections for one or other power. I will be, if I should consider it useful for Russia, on good terms with France, just as the same interest inclines me now to cultivate the friendship of Great Britain.[8]

Alexander had initially put foreign affairs in the hands of Nikita Petrovich Panin, nephew of Nikita Ivanovich Panin, Catherine II's foreign minister from 1763 to 1781. Panin was hostile to France and scathing about Alexander's professed enthusiasm for revolutionary ideals which he attributed to 'the perfidious instruction of Laharpe'.[9] He believed that Russia's best interests lay in joining and playing a major part in a new coalition against Napoleon. Thus he approved of the *rapprochement* with Britain but was opposed to Alexander's conciliatory policy towards France. Alexander not only found himself at odds with his foreign minister on policy but also resented Panin's independence and refusal to accept his ideas. He was never at ease with a man who had been a member of the conspiracy which brought him to the throne, even though Panin had not been present at the murder of Paul.

By late 1801 Alexander was no longer under the

influence of the conspirators and in October 1801 Panin was replaced as foreign minister by Alexander's friend Kochubei, who was not only more sympathetic to Alexander's desire for peace but also less likely to challenge the tsar's views on foreign policy. Kochubei believed in isolating Russia from Europe so that efforts could be concentrated on domestic reform. As early as July 1801 he had expressed the view in a memorandum that 'Peace and internal reform – those are the words which should be written in golden letters in the offices of our statesmen'.[10] Czartoryski characterized Kochubei's 'system' as follows:

> . . . to hold Russia aloof from European affairs, and to keep on good terms with all foreign Powers, so as to devote all her time and attention to internal reforms. Such was indeed the Emperor's wish and that of his intimate advisers . . . .[11]

Kochubei called for the almost total isolation of Russia from Europe, with the exception only of trade agreements between countries. His views were discussed by the Unofficial Committee in early 1802, and all its members gave them general support. Alexander seemed to be in full agreement with his minister; he had stated in one of these meetings that Russia had no need of alliances with anyone. In April 1802 he repeated this assertion, but expressed the view that alliances could help Russia to influence Europe to the benefit of all.[12] This demonstrates that he was more flexible than Kochubei in his approach, but also that he was quite unrealistic about Russia's ability to influence events. Nevertheless, he rejected a proposed British alliance at this time and it seemed as if Kochubei's views had been accepted. Britain's ambassador, Sir John Warren, wrote in October 1802:

> I am extremely sorry to say that from what passed at this interview [with Count Aleksandr Vorontsov] my former opinions are realised of the system adopted by this court of withdrawing from all European connections, and confining themselves entirely, for the present, to their internal concerns.[13]

Although the tsar had supported Kochubei's proposal and was indeed occupied with proposals for domestic reforms at this time, he never lost interest in European affairs. In fact, he assumed from the very beginning of his reign that Russia should be involved in discussions with and concerning all European countries, including those which were of no obvious strategic interest to her. Alexander took a particular interest in the fate of Switzerland because it was the homeland of his ex-tutor La Harpe. In early 1802 he wrote to Napoleon supporting Swiss independence (Russia subsequently played a major part in drawing up the Swiss constitutions; see below p. 129). He also showed an interest at this time in the fate of the king of Sardinia, provoking the sharp retort from Napoleon that this affair should not concern Alexander any more than the affairs of Persia should concern Napoleon. Furthermore, Alexander showed from the start that he was determined to act independently and to pursue personal initiatives in foreign affairs rather than be the pawn of a powerful foreign minister. For example, he organized a meeting with Frederick William III, King of Prussia, in June 1802 without the knowledge even of Kochubei. 'Imagine a minister for foreign affairs who had no knowledge of this escapade',[14] wrote Kochubei, who disapproved of the whole affair. This meeting laid the basis for future close relations between the monarchs, not least because of Alexander's infatuation with the 'forme angélique' and 'l'apparition céleste' of Frederick William's young wife, Louise. (Alexander was twenty-five years old and Louise twenty-six.) At one point Alexander even claimed that the idea of the Holy Alliance of 1815 originated from the 'first embrace' of the two emperors at this meeting. By mid-1802 Kochubei was complaining that Alexander was not prepared to listen to him or to consult him ('I am still reduced to saying "The emperor wants it thus" and to the question, "Why?" I am forced to reply: "I know nothing about it; such is his supreme will" ').[15]

Kochubei was removed in September 1802, principally because Alexander had now become more interested in active involvement in European affairs than his foreign minister, to be replaced by Count Aleksandr Vorontsov. By 1804 Vorontsov favoured Russian participation in the new coalition that was taking shape against Napoleon, but in reality he had little real say in foreign policy and his ill-health meant that he could not act effectively. By 1803 foreign affairs were in practice in the hands of Czartoryski, Vorontsov's assistant foreign minister, whose aspirations concerning Russia's future role in Europe seemed to accord with those of Alexander himself, although they were expressed with considerably more elegance and intellectual coherence than the tsar was ever able to muster. At this stage Czartoryski had complete belief in Alexander. At a much later date (after he had become disillusioned with Alexander's policy towards Poland), he wrote almost wistfully in his memoirs that in 1803:

> I would have wished Alexander to become a sort of arbiter of peace for the civilized world, to be the protector of the weak and the oppressed, and that his reign should inaugurate a new era of justice and right in European politics.

In 1803 Czartoryski had drawn up a plan for the future of Russian diplomacy, 'On the political system to be followed by Russia' (ideas later developed in his *Essai sur la diplomatie*, written in the 1820s and published anonymously in 1830). His own description of his 'system', nevertheless, showed his awareness of the tsar's intellectual limitations despite his high hopes. He referred to it as:

> . . . just the one to delight Alexander in the mood in which he then was. It gave free scope to the imagination and to all kinds of combinations without requiring immediate decision or action.[16]

Czartoryski believed that all countries needed 'a free constitution founded on a solid basis' although, like the tsar, he thought that the form of government should vary according to a country's needs and level of development. He wanted constitutional change to come about gradually and carefully in order to fulfil its purpose of ensuring stable government. Like Alexander, he envisaged Europe living in perpetual peace. Czartoryski also appealed to the tsar's idealism and inflated view of Russia's role in securing Europe's happiness and reiterated his belief in Russia's role as an arbitrator and that Alexander's reign would 'inaugurate a new era in European relations . . . for the benefit of mankind'.[17] Although in general Czartoryski favoured the self-determination of nations, he also believed that peace and security would be preserved through small nations in the Italian peninsula, Germany and the Balkans forming federations under the protection of Russia or Britain.

Czartoryski's project was written at a time when Alexander had been talking freely in the Unofficial Committee about constitutions. Although nothing had been done in Russia, Alexander had already shown his interest in constitutional government elsewhere at this time. The Ionian islands were still under Russian occupation and a constitution was drawn up for them in 1803, mainly by John Capodistria, at that time Secretary of State of the islands. It planned for a legislative assembly comprising an upper and lower house which would meet every two years. Czartoryski was therefore only expressing ideas which accorded with Alexander's own at the time (although typically, according to Czartoryski, the tsar received his ideas enthusiastically but did 'not think of going more deeply into them'). However, a central assumption of Czartoryski's analysis was that Poland, his homeland, would re-emerge as an independent country under the protection of the tsar. In his memorandum he argued that the regeneration of Poland was 'in the interest of the general peace and welfare' and that the Partitions should be reversed. He suggested that either Constantine, Alexander's brother, should be made king of the newly-restored Poland or that Poland should be put under the protection of, or even be annexed by, Russia. To Russians at court at the time, it seemed that Czartoryski was putting his Polish interests before those of Russia. A more fundamental problem was that during this period neither the countries which had fallen victim to Napoleon nor the powers which opposed him looked towards Russia for ideas for a new organization of Europe, but only for the manpower of her armies (subsidized by Britain). The type of *moral* role which Czartoryski and Alexander were claiming for Russia as guarantor of peace, arbiter of Europe and protector of small states was far from the purely pragmatic assessment of the value of Russia and her army made by European statesmen.

. . .

FROM PEACE TO WAR

Hostilities resumed between Britain and France in May

1803. Alexander was as concerned as the British about Napoleon's aggression in the Italian peninsula and the potential threat posed by the French in the eastern Mediterranean. Black Sea trade in grain was becoming increasingly important for Russia in the early years of the nineteenth century and the presence of the French on the Adriatic coast was seen as a threat to the whole of the Balkans; in particular to Russia's hold on the Ionian islands (where the number of Russian troops had been increased to 11,000 by 1804). There was also a fear that the Ottoman Empire might collapse and that France would take advantage of this to increase her domination. Russia was continuing to advance in the Caucasus at this time and was therefore vitally concerned with the future of the whole Black Sea area and the Ottoman Empire. Georgia had been annexed in 1801; in December 1803 the Russians took Samegrelo (Mingrelia) under their protection, and in 1804 King Soloman II of Imeretia was forced to allow his kingdom to become a Russian protectorate.

In the summer of 1803 Alexander attempted to act as the arbiter between France and Britain, and was offended when the militarily dominant Napoleon not unnaturally rejected his suggestions for the surrender of French dominance in Germany, Switzerland, Holland and the Italian peninsula. Franco-Russian tension increased as a result of such incidents as the accusations of fomenting anti-French intrigues made against the Russian ambassador in France, A. Morkov (which forced his recall in late 1803), and the seizure of the Duc d'Enghien from neutral Baden (the homeland of Alexander's wife) and his summary execution in March 1804. Alexander formally protested about d'Enghien's execution and ordered the Russian court to go into mourning. Napoleon's response was calculated to offend. A statement was published in the official *Moniteur* asking if Russia would not have seized the English plotters of the assassination of Paul if they had been discovered no more than a league from the frontier, a pointed allusion to the conditions of Alexander's accession. In May 1804 Napoleon took the title of emperor, but the tsar not only refused to recognize the new title but also persuaded the Turkish sultan to withhold recognition, so damaging French prestige in the Balkans. Alexander still insisted that the French should withdraw from Naples and northern Germany and provide compensation for the King of Sardinia. Czartoryski supported an anti-French coalition, arguing that 'The insatiable and revolting ambition of her present chief makes any real liaison with him impossible'. He encouraged Alexander to move towards an alliance with Britain by stressing the French threat in the Balkans and by continuing to appeal to the tsar's vanity about Russia's role in European affairs:

> It is for her [Russia's] dignity and in her own interest not to neglect the occasions that offer themselves to restore Europe's lost equilibrium and reassert it on a more stable footing by rendering to states that independence without which their existence will only be precarious.[18]

The threat posed by France to the European balance of power in general and to the control of the Mediterranean in particular was responsible for the involvement of Russia in the Third Coalition. But the proposals put forward by the Russians in 1804 for an alliance with Britain also demonstrated that Alexander never saw foreign affairs in purely pragmatic terms. He proposed that Europe should become a league of liberal and constitutional states founded on 'the sacred rights of humanity . . . based on the same spirit of wisdom and benevolence', which would live in peace under the benign protection and arbitration of Russia and Britain. The King of Sardinia should be invited 'to give his people a free and wise constitution' and the neutrality of Switzerland would be strengthened by improvement of a government 'based on local requirements and on the wishes of the people'. Regional federations would be set up in Germany and Italy. Britain and Russia would determine the partition of the Ottoman Empire if Turkish rule were to collapse. This would ensure the peace of Europe 'on a solid and permanent basis',[19] as well as redrawing the political map of Europe in a way no less complete than Napoleon's. He also proposed the introduction of codes on the rights of man and on international law and the establishment of collective security. The co-operation of Britain and Russia in this paternalistic structure was appropriate because, as the proposal stated with little reference to historical reality, 'Both those powers can only ensure a durable union and prevent any trouble in the future, because for so many years there has been no jealousy between them nor any conflict of interests'.[20] In addition, there was a proposal for a new code of maritime law which would *inter alia* protect the ships of neutral nations.

The inspiration behind this document has been variously ascribed to Czartoryski (there are obvious similarities with his memorandum of 1803), Joseph de Maistre (the Sardinian minister in Russia), and Scipione Piattoli (an Italian priest who was the author of two memoranda on the reorganization of Europe and was Czartoryski's former tutor). There is no reason, however, to think that it did not accord with the tsar's sentiments, even if he were not the author. Alexander clearly saw no contradiction in proposing these solutions for Europe while at home he had only recently put aside the 'Charter to the Russian People', rejected the introduction of the principle of *habeas corpus*, and failed to introduce a constitution into Russia. Nevertheless, the proposals did envisage an alternative to Napoleonic domination based on a new system of international law and collective security, although it would have led in practice to Anglo-Russian domination instead. Alexander was only typical of his times in assuming that the great powers were best suited to determine the needs, and be the protectors, of the minor powers.

In the event, William Pitt was able to evade the more ambitious elements of the project (and, in particular, the threatening new maritime code) and make counter proposals leaving the settlement of Germany and Italy vague and the question of Malta open. (Britain had not evacuated the island despite her agreement to do so at the Treaty of Amiens in 1802.) Although the 1804 proposals were not pursued vigorously by Alexander there are obvious similarities between them and his later proposal for a Holy Alliance (see below pp. 133–6). In 1804, however, there was no reason for his proposals to be taken too seriously. Russia was not the dominant member of the coalition and needed the British alliance, and in particular British subsidies, as much as the British needed the Russian army. Russia had played a minor role in the previous campaigns against France, and Alexander had no personal experience of warfare, so Britain saw no necessity to pander to his whims. In essence, the Anglo-Russian negotiations were undertaken with the limited purpose of starting a new campaign against the strongest military power on the continent; not, as would be the case in 1815, determining the future shape of Europe following total victory. In November 1804 Russia and Austria reached agreement on the provision of troops to fight in Italy, although no specific commitments were made. In January 1805 Sweden allied with Russia. In May Napoleon created the Kingdom of Italy (from the former Cisalpine Republic) and in June annexed Genoa (the Ligurian Republic). This pushed Britain and Russia to ratify a formal treaty of alliance on 28 July, to which Austria adhered in August. Prussia (tempted by Napoleon's offer of Hanover which Britain, of course, could not match) and most of the smaller German states remained neutral, while Baden, Bavaria and Württemberg allied with France.

Czartoryski believed in the 1804 proposals, but he was also concerned to restore Poland and looked for opportunities which might arise in the course of the campaign to further this aim. During 1804 and 1805, he was entrusted with the task of bringing Prussia into the coalition, but his attempts were hindered by his own hostility to Prussia as the main obstacle to Poland's restoration. (Prussia would never willingly give up the territory she had acquired during the Partitions.) Czartoryski aimed to force Prussia to join the coalition by declaring war on her, something which was not opposed by Britain and Austria. He suggested to Alexander that he should put further pressure on Prussia by declaring himself in Warsaw as the liberator of the Poles, so making Frederick William III fearful about the reaction of his own Polish subjects and forcing him to come to terms with Russia. Czartoryski's real hope, of course, was that the enthusiasm of the Poles would induce Alexander to declare himself king of a restored Poland. Now as later, Czartoryski was to find that, despite genuine sympathies for Poland, the tsar always put his general diplomatic strategies before his sentiment for that country and friendship for Czartoryski.

Practical considerations also prevailed over sentiment in the Balkans where little was achieved in terms of the declared aim of Alexander and Czartoryski to establish freedom and good government for small nations. Before the campaign against Napoleon started, Alexander had expressed sympathy for the aspirations of the Balkan peoples for greater independence but, in practice, he did little. In December 1803 the Russian ambassador in Constantinople, A.Ia. Italinsky, had suggested to the Porte that the Greeks should be given a greater degree of autonomy; but Alexander was reluctant to give any practical help to them in case this precipitated the collapse of the Ottoman Empire, considering that a weak neighbour was too valuable to lose. The following year the Serbs revolted and appealed to Russia for assistance with arms and money, and again Alexander urged the Turks to give the Serbs greater control over their own administration but was reluctant to give anything other than diplomatic support for the revolt. In early 1805, Alexander sent a letter assuring the Montenegrin people of his goodwill; more importantly, some financial aid was provided by the Russian representative in Montenegro, S.A. Sankovsky. At the same time, Alexander agreed to the formation of a Greek-Albanian corps, which took part in the unsuccessful Russian expedition to Naples at the end of 1805. As late as May 1806 Czartoryski was putting forward a plan for an autonomous Serbia, a new state centred on Montenegro and enlarging the Ionian islands' territory by including part of the Albanian coast.

Although the British achieved a famous naval victory at Trafalgar in October 1805, the campaign on the continent of Europe was a triumph for Napoleon. He moved swiftly to defeat an Austrian force of 40,000 under General Mack at Ulm on 19 October 1805 while the advancing 40,000 Russian troops under General Mikhail Illarionovich Kutuzov were still some 270 kilometres away. Before hearing of this disaster Alexander had already abandoned the idea of proclaiming himself King of Poland in Warsaw and rallying the Poles to his cause, and had instead signed a convention with Frederick William of Prussia. The King agreed that Prussia would join the coalition if Napoleon refused to give up his conquests in Holland, Switzerland

and Naples, and Alexander promised to do what he could to obtain Hanover for Prussia. During the negotiations, a Russian army of 30,000 men under General Bennigsen was halted on the border between Russia and Prussian Poland. Frederick William finally agreed to the passage of the troops through Prussia, although, according to Bennigsen, the route which the king insisted the Russians follow delayed him so that he was unable to join up with the rest of the Russian army and the Austrians in time for the impending battle of Austerlitz. The Russian forces, without Bennigsen's troops, and the Austrians then combined. Alexander, against the advice of Czartoryski, had put himself at the head of the Russian army – the first Russian ruler to do so since Peter I. The Russians and Austrians were routed by Napoleon at the battle of Austerlitz on 2 December 1805. Along with all their artillery, the allies lost between 25,000 and 30,000 men killed, wounded or captured, out of an original force of around 60,000. French losses were between 8,000 and 9,000 men.

The defeat was all the more shaming for Alexander since he had personally contributed to it. Not only had he put himself at the head of the armed forces, but he had deliberately ignored the advice of his experienced commander-in-chief Kutuzov, who wished to delay giving battle until the arrival of reinforcements. Instead, Alexander entrusted operations to General F. von Weyrother, chief-of-staff of the Emperor Francis of Austria. When Kutuzov asked to see the plan of march for the armies, Alexander rebuffed him with the words 'This does not concern you'. Alexander's inexperience and stubbornness allowed Napoleon to improve his position. He had skilfully gained time to bring up his own reinforcements and lulled his opponents into a false sense of security by flattering Alexander with a proposal for an armistice. His proposal was probably not serious but Alexander anyway made such a course impossible by dispatching the arrogant Prince Petr Petrovich Dolgoruky to Napoleon's camp, who, according to Napoleon was 'an impertinent young puppy . . . who spoke to me as he would have done to a boyar he wished to send to Siberia'.[21] Indeed, far from performing the role of heroic commander in battle as he had hoped, Alexander almost suffered the humiliation of being captured by French forces during the disorganized and hasty retreat. He spent the night of 2 December not in triumph but on the floor of a peasant's hut suffering from violent stomach cramps.

The consequences of Austerlitz were swift and decisive. The Russian troops who had landed on the Italian peninsula had to withdraw. Austria withdrew from the coalition, signing the Treaty of Pressburg on 26 December 1805 by which she gave up her possessions in Italy and Dalmatia, the Tyrol and several cities on the passes into Germany (in all, she lost about three million of her previous population) while also having to recognize the independence of Bavaria and Württemberg. Within a month the Holy Roman Empire had been formally dissolved. Prussia, fearful of becoming a French satellite and furious about rumours that Napoleon was considering offering Hanover to George III as part of peace negotiations, now finally declared for the allies. On 14 October 1806 the Prussian forces were routed at the twin battles of Jena and Auerstädt (before Russian reinforcements could arrive). The military invincibility of Prussia, believed from the time of Frederick the Great, had been shown to be a myth; what had been regarded as the strongest European army had been destroyed. The Russian army now faced Napoleon alone.

Alexander's confidence in his abilities was shattered by the defeat at Austerlitz. Joseph de Maistre wrote that:

> The Emperor believes himself to be no use to his people, because he is not in the position of commander of his armies and this is very shaming for him . . . . He had been more defeated than his army at Austerlitz.[22]

The tsar nevertheless attempted to play a double game, negotiating for peace with France while still hoping for Prussian success. His minister in France, Baron P.J. d'Oubril, signed a preliminary treaty with France in the summer of 1806 but it was rejected by Alexander. Russian troops entered East Prussia in November 1806 but Napoleon moved into Prussian Poland, taking Warsaw and Thorn from small Prussian forces, and forced the Russian troops to pull back. Skirmishes took place between Russian and French forces, and the Russians scored a minor victory at Pultusk at the end of December (but with 3,500 Russian casualties to 2,200 French ones). On 8 February 1807 Napoleon won an expensive victory over the Russians at Eylau (both sides lost about 20,000 men killed, wounded or captured). The temperature during the battle was estimated at −26°C, and it was reported that the frost was so intense that scalpels and saws dropped from the fingers of medical orderlies. In April, Alexander and Frederick William (who had fled to East Prussia) signed a convention at Bartenstein which reaffirmed the Prusso-Russian alliance and declared the aim of restoring Prussia to her 1805 frontiers. But the decisive battle took place at Friedland on 14 June 1807 when defeat for the Russian forces involving in the region of 10,000 dead and 15,000 wounded (France lost approximately 10,000 men) persuaded Alexander that he would have to come to terms with Napoleon.

By this stage, moreover, Russia was facing a war on two fronts. The Ottoman Empire had provoked Russia in August 1806 by deposing the rulers of the Danubian Principalities of Moldavia and Wallachia and closing the Straits to Russian warships, in defiance of the terms of the treaties concluded in the reign of Catherine II at Kutchuk Kainardji in 1774 and Jassy in 1792. The Russians responded by invading the Principalities in November 1806, nominally in order to protect them but really in response to Ottoman interference in their government. After the outcome of the battle of Jena, the Turks saw their chance to inflict a defeat on Russia and declared war on 16 December 1806. Given Russia's commitments in central Europe, only a small number of troops could be released for the Turkish front. Russia won a successful but not decisive action at sea in July 1807, but the news of this victory came after the conclusion of the Treaty of Tilsit.

. . .

THE TILSIT MEETING

Pressure was put on the tsar by his generals and his brother, Constantine, to convince him that the Russian forces were not in a condition to continue fighting against the French. Alexander faced the prospect of coming to terms with Napoleon with bitterness, convinced as he was that his allies had let him down. Not only had the Russians been left to face France alone, but the British subsidies were less than he had hoped for. Napoleon, however, had no desire to pursue a lengthy, and potentially costly, campaign in Russia against an army which had been defeated but not broken. His desire was to reach a settlement with Russia which would allow him to turn his attention to the political organization of central Europe and to isolate Britain, always regarded by him as his major enemy. To achieve this, he was prepared to flatter the tsar and hinted to the Russian envoy that through an alliance the two rulers could divide Europe between them into spheres of influence. This gave Alexander the opportunity to extricate himself from a difficult situation without too much loss, either of face or territory, while convincing himself that this would also be of benefit for all Europe. Alexander's response to Napoleon's cautious approach for an alliance was a mixture of bravado, idealism, vanity and sheer cheek. He instructed General D.I. Lobanov-Rostovsky on 24 June to address Napoleon with the words:

> You tell him that this union between France and Russia has been constantly the object of my desires and that I have the conviction that this alone will ensure the happiness and tranquillity of the world. An entirely new system must replace the one which has existed up to now, and I flatter myself that we will easily reach an understanding with the Emperor Napoleon, provided that we meet without intermediaries. A lasting peace perhaps will be concluded between us in a few days.[23]

Unable to reject Alexander's offer of a meeting, Napoleon unenthusiastically proposed that they should meet midstream as neutral territory could not be found.

Negotiations took place between the two rulers on a raft in the middle of the river Niemen at the town of Tilsit on the border between the Polish lands of Prussia and Russia starting on 25 June 1807. Napoleon and Alexander tried to outdo each other in charm, amiability, hospitality, flattery and general insincerity while poor Frederick William was excluded from the conversations which *inter alia* determined the fate of his country (dismissed by Napoleon as 'a nasty king, a nasty nation, a nasty army'). Allegedly the conversation at the first meeting started with Alexander's declaration that 'Sire, I hate the English no less than you do and I am ready to assist you in any enterprise against them', to which Napoleon is said to have replied, 'In that case everything can be speedily settled between us and peace is made'. Alexander and Napoleon seemingly found much to talk about. At one point Napoleon found himself in the strange position of defending the right of hereditary succession against the liberal, almost republican, views of the tsar! Alexander had clearly changed little since Czartoryski had unsuccessfully attempted to moderate his opinions about hereditary monarchy in the 1790s. Less controversially, they enquired solicitously about each other's families and exchanged cravats and embroidered handkerchiefs. Alexander was depicted by the French historian Vandal during these conversations: 'His head slightly inclined, a pretty smile on his lips, he expressed himself in terms of perfect ease, and in his mouth the French language was modulated *à la russe* with gentle inflections, with a sweetness which was almost feminine'.[24] Napoleon responded with equal charm, if possibly even less sincerity (remarking a year later on 'the fine phrases I dropped about at Tilsit').[25]

The practical result of this pantomime was a series of treaties signed on 7–9 July 1807. Russia lost little territorially; she ceded the Ionian islands and Cattaro (in Dalmatia) but in return gained the province of Bialystok from Prussian Poland. She also had to accept French mediation in the war with the Ottoman Empire and agree to withdraw from the Principalities. On the other hand, Alexander promised to join the Continental System against Britain if she refused to come to terms with Napoleon. This meant closing Russian ports to British ships, and to British imports, and was an essential part of Napoleon's strategy to isolate Britain and cripple her economically by closing all continental ports. The Russian naval squadron in the Adriatic was in effect abandoned. Some Russian ships surrendered to the French or were sold to the Austrians, most managed to sail to Lisbon but were then captured by the British; the two ships which reached the Baltic in 1813 were the only ones to return home.

Napoleon had presented the Tilsit peace as an alliance

between Russia and France but it was clear that Russia was the junior partner. The reality was that Napoleon now dominated the continent; Prussia and Austria had been defeated and Russia had been neutralized, so allowing the emperor to concentrate his efforts on the struggle with Britain. But for the treaty to provide a stable basis for Franco-Russian relations required Napoleon to maintain this dominance and Alexander to continue to accept this subordinate role.

The real loser at Tilsit was Prussia. Alexander had encouraged Prussia to join the Third Coalition and had vowed eternal friendship at his meeting in 1805, but at Tilsit he was only able to ensure that Frederick William retained his throne (the final treaty between France and Prussia made it clear that such a concession arose 'from consideration of the wishes of His Majesty the Emperor of All the Russias'), albeit in a seriously truncated form and subject to a heavy indemnity and occupation by French forces. Prussia's territorial gains from the Partitions of Poland were reversed with the creation of the Duchy of Warsaw (which became, in effect, a French satellite) and her Rhineland provinces were lost. In all, Prussia lost one-third of her territory and almost half her population.

Alexander argued that he had made the best of a bad situation at Tilsit. He tried to convince his favourite sister Catherine, who was totally opposed to the treaty, that it was something of an achievement under the circumstances and that he had not been duped by Napoleon. He wrote from Tilsit in June that 'God has saved us: instead of sacrifices we have emerged from the contest with a sort of lustre'.[26] At home, however, the combination of humiliating military defeats (especially that of Austerlitz where Alexander was present) and having to come to terms with the enemy (Napoleon had been denounced as the Antichrist by the Russian Orthodox Church in 1806) caused Alexander's popularity to drop to a dangerously low point. Countess Edling wrote that after Tilsit 'The salons of St Petersburg reverberated with complaints, with unjust accusations, with uncalled for demands, the burden of which fell on the Emperor . . . '.[27] There was even talk of plots against Alexander's life. 'The Peace is very unpopular' wrote the Irish traveller Martha Wilmot in July 1807.[28] The memoirist

F.F. Vigel' described the mood in the country after Tilsit, which he personally felt unfairly reflected on Alexander's actions:

> In St Petersburg, even in Moscow, in all the places in Russia most touched by education, the Tilsit peace made the saddest impression: in these places they knew that the alliance with Napoleon could be nothing other than enslavement to him, an acknowledgement of his power over us. I do not possess great wisdom but in this I saw the cruel unfairness of Russians; I became ashamed for them. All that a man who was not a born commander could have done had been done by the Emperor Alexander. . . .[29]

The reaction of some of the Russian nobility to the Tilsit peace perhaps points to an ambivalence in the relationship of Russia to France, a country whose thinkers and culture both Alexander and his educated subjects had been brought up to respect. Admiration for the country and hatred for its ruler existed uneasily together. Catherine Wilmot, summed up the contradictory Russian attitude to France in 1806:

> . . . everything is shocking for dinner that is not dres'd by a French Cook, every Boy & Girl awkward who are not Educated by French People, every dress inelegant that is not Parisian etc. etc. In short, tho' this is all true & tho' French Novels are exclusively *Gobbled* by every boy & girl in Moscow, yet there is no one who does not blaspheme against Buonaparte & lament Lord Nelson.[30]

It was not a promising basis on which to build a lasting alliance.

. . .

NOTES AND REFERENCES

1. Richard Pipes, *Karamzin's Memoir on Ancient and Modern Russia: A Translation and Analysis*, Cambridge, Mass., 1959, pp. 131–2.
2. W.P. Cresson, *The Holy Alliance: The European Background of the Monroe Doctrine*, New York, 1922, p. 10.
3. N.K. Shil'der, *Imperator Aleksandr I: ego zhizn' i tsarstvovanie*, 4 vols, St Petersburg, 1897, II, p. 58.

4. Francis Ley, *Alexandre Ier et sa Sainte-Alliance (1811–1825) avec des documents inédits*, Paris, 1975, p. 40.
5. M.F. Zlotnikov, *Kontinental'naia blokada i Rossiia*, Moscow-Leningrad, 1966, pp. 89, 91.
6. Albert Sorel, *L'Europe et la révolution française*, 8 vols, Paris, 1903, VI (*La Trêve-Lunéville et Amiens 1800–1805*), p. 151.
7. Shil'der, op. cit., p. 274.
8. Charles John Fedorak, 'In Search of a Necessary Ally: Addington, Hawkesbury, and Russia, 1801–1804', *The International History Review*, vol. 13, no. 2, 1991, p. 231.
9. P.K. Grimsted, *The Foreign Ministers of Alexander I: Political Attitudes and the Conduct of Russian Diplomacy*, Berkeley, 1969, p. 70.
10. Ibid., p. 85.
11. *Memoirs of Prince Adam Czartoryski and his Correspondence with Alexander I*, edited by Adam Gielgud, 2 vols, London, 1888, I, p. 279.
12. Nikolai Mikhailovich, *Graf Pavel Aleksandrovich Stroganov (1774–1817). Istoricheskoe izsledovanie epokhi imperatora Aleksandra I*, 3 vols, St Petersburg, 1903, II, pp. 70, 200.
13. H. Beeley, 'A Project of Alliance with Russia in 1802', *English Historical Review*, vol. 49, no. 195, 1934, p. 500.
14. Grimsted, op. cit., p. 88.
15. Ibid., p. 89.
16. *Memoirs of Prince Adam Czartoryski*, II, pp. 9, 10.
17. Grimsted, op. cit., p. 124.
18. Ibid., pp. 129, 130.
19. *Memoirs of Prince Adam Czartoryski*, II, pp. 45–7.
20. M. Kukiel, *Czartoryski and European Unity 1770–1861*, Westport, Connecticut, 1981 edn, p. 47.
21. Alan Palmer, *Alexander I: Tsar of War and Peace*, London, 1974, p. 102.
22. Theodor Schiemann, *Geschichte Russlands unter Kaiser Nikolaus I*, 4 vols, Berlin, 1904, I, *Kaiser Alexander I und die Ergebnisse seiner Lebensarbeit*, p. 63.
23. Serge Tatistcheff [S.S. Tatishchev], *Alexandre Ier et Napoléon d'après leur correspondance inédite 1801–1812*, Paris, 1891, pp. 148–9.
24. Albert Vandal, *Napoléon et Alexandre Ier. L'Alliance Russe sous le premier empire*, 3 vols, 8th edn, Paris, 1914, I (*De Tilsit à Erfurt*), Paris, 1914, p. 58.
25. Palmer, op. cit., p. 137.
26. Grand-Duc Nicolas Mikhailowitch [Nikolai Mikhailovich], *Correspondance de l'Empereur Alexandre Ier avec sa soeur la Grande-Duchesse Catherine, Princesse d'Oldenbourg, puis Reine de Würtemberg 1805–1818*, St Petersburg, 1910, p. 18.

27. R. Edling, *Mémoires de la Comtesse Edling (née Stourdza) demoiselle d'honneur de Sa Majesté l'Impératrice Élisabeth Alexéevna*, Moscow, 1888, p. 29.
28. *The Russian Journals of Martha and Catherine Wilmot 1803–1808*, edited by the Marchioness of Londonderry and H.M. Hyde, London, 1934, p. 299.
29. I.A. Bychkov, 'Aleksandr I i ego priblizhennye do epokhi Speranskago', *Russkaia starina*, vol. 113, 1903, p. 233.
30. *The Russian Journals of Martha and Catherine Wilmot*, p. 216.

Chapter 5

THE UNCERTAIN CONSTITUTIONALIST AND ALLY: 1807–1812

.   .   .

SPERANSKY

The Treaty of Tilsit relieved Alexander of the immediate burden of war in the West and gave him the opportunity to turn his attention once again to reform at home. His declared commitment to governmental reform was put most severely to the test in this period; by 1809 he was not only in possession of a draft constitution for Russia but was also in the process of absorbing Finland, which had its own constitution, into the Russian Empire. Abroad, Alexander reverted to traditional eighteenth-century Russian foreign policy aims by expanding to the north and the south at the expense of Sweden and the Ottoman Empire. In the process, however, it became clear that Napoleon had no intention of allowing Russia to extend her influence in any area where France also had interests. The Tilsit treaty, moreover, was unpopular at home and committed Russia to the Continental System which harmed her own economic interests. Furthermore, the creation from the lands of Prussian Poland of the Duchy of Warsaw, nominally independent but in practice a satellite of France, threatened Russia's western border. Alexander had been forced to abandon, for the time being at least, his more grandiose visions of becoming the arbiter of Europe or even of having any influence over territory or events west of the Russian border. As relations between Russia and France deteriorated it became clear that Tilsit had not provided a stable basis either for friendship between the two powers or for European peace.

The man to whom Alexander turned for domestic reform proposals was Mikhail Mikhailovich Speransky, the son of a village priest, who had already demonstrated his ability through his work in the Ministry of Internal Affairs during the early years of the reign. He became state secretary (in effect, prime minister) and accompanied Alexander to the meeting with Napoleon in Erfurt (discussed below) in 1808. In the years from 1807 to 1811 Speransky turned his hand to a number of important internal matters. In late 1807 a Commission was set up to reorganize education in the seminaries and Speransky (himself, of course, a product of ecclesiastical education) was appointed to head the commission. By the summer of 1808 the commission had completed its work and a new simplified and more rational structure of ecclesiastical schools was set up, which paralleled the structure of secular schools established in 1803–4 (see above pp. 52–4). The curriculum of the primary and secondary church schools was modernized by the introduction of new subjects, such as modern languages and natural sciences, while new courses were added to the upper classes of seminaries and ecclesiastical academies. The quality of instruction in seminaries was often low. In an attempt to tackle this problem it was specified that teachers should have their qualifications tested before appointment and standards should be set for them to achieve. Speransky's restoration of the church's monopoly of the sale of wax candles ensured that sufficient capital could be accumulated to fund the new schools.

The concern Speransky showed in raising the standards of teaching is a reflection of his general awareness of the low calibre of many Russian officials and of the need for more, and better, training and education. This was a view shared, of course, by Alexander, who had made scathing comments about the calibre of the Russian bureaucracy early in his reign. Speransky's encouragement of the establishment of a new lycée for fifty sons of the Russian aristocratic élite, and his interest in the curriculum of the school, showed his concern to provide the proper intellectual foundations for the education of the country's future leaders. Alexander took a personal interest in the new lycée, commissioning the architect Vasilii Stasov to build it in a wing of the imperial palace at Tsarskoe Selo and insisting that the pupils should be provided with attractive gardens, part of which they were allowed to cultivate themselves. The real problem, however, lay not with the level of education of the élite but with the training of the nobles who filled the middle and lower posts in the bureaucracy. Speransky attempted to force an improvement in standards of education and in performance of duties. Two decrees in 1809 addressed this issue and led, not surprisingly, to hostility from those who were affected by them. The first required nobles at court who held the title of gentlemen of the chamber either to perform the appropriate duties for this rank or to transfer to another branch of the military or civil service; and the second required that officials should be examined in several subjects, including Russian, mathematics, modern languages and Latin, before being promoted to the eighth rank (the rank which gave the holder hereditary nobility). Alexander, as has been seen, had no great affection or respect for the nobility as an estate, and was therefore sympathetic to Speransky's approach. His minister, however, alienated many influential nobles at court by these policies and made himself very vulnerable in the process. His survival thereafter depended entirely on maintaining the tsar's favour.

Alexander put Speransky in charge of two other areas of domestic reform which needed urgent attention: the drawing up of a law code and the improvement of state finances. The Commission which had been set up in 1801 to codify the Russian laws had made little progress. Speransky's appointment to the Commission in 1808 greatly speeded up proceedings and resulted in the preparation of a law code in 1812. Speransky had used Napoleon's Civil Code of 1804 as a framework for a Russian code (something which did nothing to endear him to his enemies). The result was a rather hurried piece of work in which Russian laws were often artificially fitted into the appropriate paragraphs of the French Code with little regard to legal history or tradition, but Speransky was under pressure to produce something quickly and which would easily be understood by Alexander. The code was accepted by the Permanent Council but never put into effect.

Speransky's attempts to restore firm foundations to Russian finances (in a parlous state after military campaigns and further weakened by the Continental System) were more successful. The government's remedy for dealing with vastly increased expenditure during the war of the Third Coalition had been to print more and more paper money, or assignats, which in turn meant a depreciation in their value. In 1810 Speransky issued a decree which promised to redeem assignats and to issue no more (in fact, the effect of the 1812 campaign meant that this promise was not kept and the issue of assignats vastly increased). The administration of finance was improved, however, by a rationalization of the duties of the Ministry of Finance and through the establishment of annual budgets. More revenue was raised through the sale of state land and increases in taxation, including a temporary tax on the nobles which further fuelled their resentment. Many nobles had been prepared to contribute financially to the war effort as good patriots but objected to this formal obligation, particularly when it was put forward by the son of a priest.

While these reforms were important, Speransky's significance stems from his far more ambitious designs for the reform of the whole internal government of Russia. This was laid down in the plan presented to Alexander in 1809, and kept secret from all but a few trusted advisers. Speransky envisaged a transformation of Russia's central and local administration and proposed the formal separation of functions between the executive (headed by the Ministries), the judiciary (for which the Senate would be the highest court of appeal) and the legislature (a State Duma); the whole structure to be presided over by the tsar and a Council of State. At local level, property owners in each township (*volost*) were to elect a township duma every three years, from which deputies were to be elected to a district (*uezd*) duma, from which in turn deputies were to be elected to a provincial (*guberniia*) duma. These dumas were to meet once every three years and had no rights to initiate legislation. The State Duma was to meet once a year and was to be made up of representatives selected by the tsar from lists prepared by the provincial dumas.

In his influential biography of Speransky, the historian

Marc Raeff presents his subject as a cautious, conservative reformer who wished to establish orderly, efficient government based on the rule of law, but who was not prepared to give any real legislative power to the State Duma and was essentially socially conservative. Raeff points out that the proposed Duma could be dissolved by the tsar and was given no control over the budget or policy making. Although a complicated structure for election to local and provincial dumas was proposed, this did not include the serfs who were to have no part in the representative process. (It did, however, include state peasants, who would send one elder from every 500 to the township dumas, the lowest level of representation.) Speransky's own explanation, written in a letter to Alexander from Perm', has been cited in support of this view of him as a conservative reformer:

> In the very beginning of your reign, after the many hesitations of our government, Your Imperial Majesty set Yourself as goal the establishment of a firm administration based on law. From this single principle gradually developed all Your major reforms. All these studies, perhaps a hundred talks and discussions with Your Majesty had finally to be made into an unitary whole. In essence, it [the Plan] did not contain anything new, but it gave a systematic exposition to the ideas which had occupied Your attention since 1801.[1]

This, however, was written not in 1809 but in January 1813; that is, after Speransky had been exiled in disgrace and after his plan had been discredited.

The publication in 1961 of Speransky's earlier writings and the first draft of his plan of 1809[2] has changed historians' perceptions of the extent of his radicalism and of the nature of his relationship with Alexander. In fact, Speransky had made his abhorrence of serfdom clear in his writings in 1802 and 1803. Not only, in his view, did it lead to the degradation of the peasantry but also to the degradation of the nobility who were no better than the serfs in their slavish dependence on the state. He wrote in 1802 that:

> I find in Russia two classes: the slaves of the sovereign and the slaves of the landowners. The first call themselves free only in

relation to the second; there are no truly free people in Russia, apart from beggars and philosophers.[3]

This led him to believe that not only should the serfs be given civil rights, but that Russia needed a new type of property-owning nobility; an English-style squirarchy, whose political role would be to 'mediate' between tsar and people. At this time, he proposed that serfs should be freed in stages. Their obligations to their masters should first be codified and limited so as to diminish their personal dependence; their right to move freely would then be restored. At this time, of course, Alexander was expressing equal abhorrence of serfdom and had also proposed ways of gradually dismantling the system. Yet serfdom was not mentioned in the 1809 plan.

Furthermore, it is clear from these early writings that Speransky found unlimited autocracy incompatible with the existence of fundamental laws, and that he believed formal limitations on the Russian form of absolutism were essential for the rule of law to prevail. Russia, in his view, lacked clear, permanent and fundamental laws and government was therefore arbitrary and lawless. The most important task was the establishment of these laws, which in turn would limit despotism. Alexander had also stressed the need for the rule of law, without, however, reflecting on the potential consequences of this for his own authority. Speransky took the argument a stage further. As the government was founded on the will of the people, so he believed there should be an elected legislative body to which the government would be accountable. Speransky did not draw back from this position in 1809. Although his proposed State Duma had only limited powers and could not initiate legislation, all laws and taxes were to be submitted to it nevertheless, and it was given the right to make representations if it felt that the fundamental laws had been broken and to call ministers to account. The Duma would also have had the right to reject a law proposed by the ruler if it were thought to be harmful: 'A law acknowledged by the majority of voices to be inappropriate remains without effect'. This would have given the Duma the crucial power of veto, although only in these particular circumstances.

What accounts, then, for Speransky's neglect of the question of serfdom in 1809 but his bolder attempt to limit, albeit in a modest degree, the power of the ruler? His plan started with a long historical introduction, clearly written for Alexander's benefit, in which he put Russian development in the context of the general development of European states and tried to convince the tsar that the time was now ripe for fundamental political reform in Russia. (In contrast, in 1802 he had written of the Russian government under Paul that '. . . the provinces were governed in a European manner, but higher [central] government was completely Asiatic'.)[4] That the reform would result in limiting the power of the ruler could not be disguised but Speransky perhaps hoped that at this point in his career, with his intimacy with Alexander so firmly established, he would be able to persuade Alexander that this was the moment for Russia to take this step. Equally important, it is possible that he hoped to succeed by flattering Alexander, portraying him as the potential instigator of a step which would result in a great advance in civilization for Russia. Speransky, in his words, had 'perhaps a hundred talks and discussions' with Alexander on his proposed constitution. Alexander, as we have seen, was adept at pleasing his listener, but presumably Speransky had the impression that his commitment to constitutional change was genuine and that it was conceivable that his plan would be implemented if it were properly explained to the tsar.

In earlier drafts of the 1809 plan Speransky also proposed granting civil rights to the serfs, and improving their economic position, in definite stages, but the final version only made a vague reference to a possible emancipation if appropriate measures were taken. The reason for this remains unknown but Speransky must have become aware of Alexander's caution on the matter during their 'talks and discussions'. Speransky had decided to concentrate in 1809 on political reform and to postpone his radical proposals for the eradication of serfdom until the time was ripe to do so. He held that the establishment of a proper framework for a government based on law was, in any case, a necessary prerequisite for the emancipation of Russian society. Such an approach accorded with his conviction that reform could only be implemented in stages. After he had been sent into exile he outlined the process he had favoured:

> Cleanse the administrative part. Then introduce permanent laws, that is, political freedom and then by degrees approach the question of civil freedom, that is, the freedom of the serfs. That is the present course of affairs.[5]

In 1809, Speransky clearly felt the time was right for fundamental progress in political reform, but not for the next stage of reform of the social structure.

Speransky's high hopes of Alexander were not to be realized. The only part of the plan which the tsar agreed to was the establishment of a new Council of State (which replaced the Permanent Council) and additional Ministries, but without the supporting pyramids representing the executive, judicial and legislative power. The whole structure envisaged by Speransky was abandoned. One can only speculate on the reasons why Alexander chose not to adopt the plan. Although he had no reason to feel threatened by Speransky (there was no question of the 1809 plan being implemented without Alexander's approval, and Speransky, far from representing a 'party', was unpopular at court), it is clear that he was aware of the potential challenge posed by the plan to his own authority. Alexander had already shown that he was sensitive to any attempt to challenge his prerogatives and, although Speransky deliberately tempered some of his views in 1809, the fact that his plan envisaged limitations on the power of the tsar could not be hidden from Alexander. Speransky may have believed through his conversations with Alexander that he would not be hostile to this development, but Alexander frequently showed an inability to appreciate the logical consequences for his own power of his expressed desire for rule based on law and the elimination of arbitrariness. Furthermore, unlike his minister, Alexander might well have felt that the time was not right for such a radical change. He was aware that his own position was rather vulnerable (the Tilsit treaty was regarded as shameful by many members of the nobility and there was talk of plots against the throne) and that therefore it would be rash to embark on such fundamental change at this time.

The new Council of State was given authority over ministers, who required its sanction, and the Senate, whose resolutions were referred to it before being submitted to the tsar. Ministers were not made *ex officio* members of the Council (as they had been in the Permanent Council), but the heads of the four departments of the Council (Laws, Military Affairs, Civil and Religious Affairs, State Economy) were *ex officio* members of the Committee of Ministers. (This Committee had never formally been created by decree; it functioned from about 1805, examining ministers' reports and anything Alexander saw fit to put before it, but seldom met until 1812.) The constitutional historian B. Nol'de saw the Council of State as a triumph for the principle of the separation of powers and asserted that the Council had been given far greater powers than the French Council of State under Napoleon, in that it could participate in civil and criminal legislation, codes of law and that the budget had to be submitted to it. As the tsar, however, still had to sign all decisions taken by each department of the Council of State and his approval had to be given on all matters, in practice the Council had no real independence and was essentially an advisory body. Further reform of the central adminstration followed. The Ministries, which had been set up in 1802, were reorganized and their functions redefined and redistributed in 1810. A new Ministry of Internal Affairs was set up, military and naval affairs were brought under one Ministry and economic matters put under the authority of a new Department of State Economy. All matters concerning commercial and industrial development had to pass through this Department before being passed on to the appropriate Ministry (Ministry of Finance, Ministry of Commerce or Ministry of Internal Affairs). Police matters were removed from the responsibility of the Ministry of Internal Affairs by the creation of a new Ministry of Police. This reorganization failed to eliminate overlapping jurisdictions between Ministries entirely, and was followed in 1811 by a General Instruction to the Ministries which defined areas of responsibility and laid down administrative procedures. From 1812, ministers were instructed to submit reports to the Committee of Ministers during Alexander's absences from Russia.

Speransky fell from power in March 1812. It is not certain why he suddenly lost Alexander's support. The specific charge of treason cannot be believed (Alexander commented to Novosil'tsev that he was not a traitor) but there was no doubt that he had been sympathetic to certain aspects of Napoleonic France, and had drawn upon Napoleonic practice in his law code and plan of 1809. As war with France became ever more likely such sympathies made his position increasingly vulnerable. Alexander had shown himself to be stubborn in the past and had previously supported his minister on such matters as the introduction of examinations for the civil service and taxation policies despite the opposition of many members of the court nobility. Notwithstanding Alexander's comments to Count Karl Nesselrode (later his foreign minister) that Speransky was loyal and devoted but that 'only present circumstances could force me to to make a sacrifice to public opinion',[6] it is unlikely that he would have dismissed his closest adviser if this had been completely against his wishes. Speransky had been indiscreet and had made hurtful comments which found their way back to Alexander, who was always sensitive to any slight. Speranksy had commented to General Aleksandr Dmitrievich Balashev, minister of police:

> You know the suspicious character of the Emperor. Whatever he does he does by halves. He is too feeble to reign and too strong to be governed.[7]

Furthermore, Alexander was not above making a scapegoat of his minister to rally support on the eve of the forthcoming conflict with France.

Alexander had also been conscious of the potential threat to his authority posed by Speransky's plan. We do not know what passed between the two men at their last meeting but shortly before his dismissal Alexander told the police official Ia.I. de Sanglen that Speransky's suggestion that in the event of war the tsar should transfer responsibility to a specially convened *boyar* duma 'convinces me that he and his Ministries were indeed intriguing and intriguing against the autocracy which I cannot and I do not have the right voluntarily to abandon to the disservice of my heirs'.[8] Alexander was not, of course, at odds with his other advisers regarding the ruler's retention of full powers and in seeing this as perfectly compatible with major reform. The members of the Unofficial Committee had earlier put their faith in the reforming power of the tsar rather than in an institution like the Senate. When something of Speransky's plan was made known, Alexander's friend Aleksandr Golitsyn demonstrated that he shared this distrust of giving powers to institutions. He commented on Speransky's proposal not to allow appeals against resolutions passed by the Senate that: 'The general opinion in Russia is that only the influence of the sovereign alone over all parts of the administration and courts can determine the correct resolution of cases'.[9] Speransky, for all his intelligence and his closeness to Alexander, had not fully realized the intellectual divide not only between himself and the tsar, but also between himself and many other educated Russians.

A fully developed challenge to Speransky's view of the path which should be taken by the Russian state can be found in the *Memoir on Ancient and Modern Russia* by Nikolai Mikhailovich Karamzin, the official historiographer of the Russian Empire. This was shown to Alexander in 1811 (that is, after the establishment of the Council of State but before Speransky's fall from power) and posited an alternative path for Russia's development. One of the severest critics of the Tilsit treaty had been Alexander's sister, Catherine. She had married George of Oldenburg, who had been made governor of the provinces of Tver', Novgorod and Iaroslavl'. To counteract the boredom of life in the provincial town of Tver' (approximately one hundred miles north-west of Moscow) Catherine created her own salon which prominent writers and thinkers, including Karamzin, were invited to attend. It seems that it was Catherine who supplied the initiative for Karamzin to put his thoughts on paper in the form of the *Memoir*. Karamzin met Alexander in Tver' and held discussions with him; he, too, apparently found himself in the position of defending autocracy against the tsar during after-dinner conversations. Catherine in the meantime had read Karamzin's manuscript and, to his understandable consternation, had privately given it to her brother.

Unfortunately, it is not known whether Alexander read the *Memoir*. The original manuscript is lost; the version known to us is a copy which was found in the papers of Arakcheev. Certainly, Alexander never made any reference to it and there is no evidence that it had any influence on Speransky's fall from favour, but as a summary of the resentments and concerns of an educated member of the nobility, and presumably as a reflection of the tenor of discussions in the salon in Tver', the *Memoir* is a useful commentary on the mood of the time and of the intellectual atmosphere in which Speransky had so confidently put forward his bold constitutional project.

The principles behind the *Memoir* are stated in the conclusion:

> The gentry and the clergy, the Senate and the Synod as reposi-
> tories of laws, over all – the sovereign, the only legislator, the
> autocratic source of authority – this is the foundation of the
> Russian monarchy, which the principles followed by the rulers
> can either strengthen or weaken.[10]

The first part of the book was a historical survey of Russian history intended to demonstrate that the principle of absolute monarchical power was responsible for the creation, preservation and happiness of the Russian state (in other words, quite different from Speransky's historical introduction to his 1809 plan which tried to persuade Alexander that the time was ripe for fundamental change to the structure of tsardom). Karamzin's criticisms of attempts to reform governmental institutions under Alexander were based on the same premise. He criticized unnecessary changes, the concentration of power in the hands of ministers and in particular the Council of State; and the corresponding diminution in the power of the Senate, and the increase in bureaucratization as a result of the introduction of Ministries. (Speransky's project of 1809 was not made public and Karamzin's criticisms, therefore, were based only on those reforms which were enacted.) Karamzin saw danger as well as wasted effort in these reforms, not just because all change was potentially threatening but because he detected the influence of foreign (particularly, Napoleonic) institutions on Russia which, in his view, had adequate traditions and structures of her own. If indeed Alexander did read the *Memoir* it is doubtful whether he would have been grateful for Karamzin's 'spiritual fortitude' in making known to him the causes of dissatisfaction in the country as he saw them. The tsar was criticized for involving Russia in a war which held no advantage for her instead of maintaining peace, and his new universities were condemned for relying on foreign professors, for their inappropriate curricula and their inadequate financial organization. Karamzin criticized Speransky for policies which Alexander had approved, such as the introduction of examinations for officials and fiscal measures, and, on dubious and historical and legal grounds, defended the institution of serfdom which Alexander had expressed loathing for.

Even while Speransky was at the peak of his influence, moreover, Alexander still valued the friendship of a very different man, Arakcheev, whom he had previously entrusted with the reform of the artillery. Arakcheev had been made minister of war and inspector of the infantry and artillery in January 1808. After the formation of the Council of State in 1810 he had resigned his position, possibly because he feared that he would be made subordinate to the new Department of Military Affairs in the Council. Arakcheev's importance to Alexander was shown by the fact that the tsar refused to accept his resignation and brought him back as president of the newly formed Department. His letter to Arakcheev demonstrated how much he valued his service:

> I cannot accept the reasons that you give . . . . You alone, on whose co-operation I was above all relying, you who have repeated so often to me that apart from your devotion to the nation you are motivated by personal affection for myself, you alone despite all this are forgetting your value to the Empire and are hastening to give up the sector you direct at a time when your conscience must tell you how impossible it will be to replace you.[11]

It was Arakcheev who was able to persuade the tsar not to stay with the army in 1812.

· · ·

WARS WITH SWEDEN AND THE OTTOMAN EMPIRE

The Tilsit peace put an end for the moment to Russian influence in central Europe but gave Alexander the opportunity to advance Russian interests in the north against Sweden and in the south against the Ottoman Empire. In the process, he was faced with constitutionalism again through his acquisition for Russia of Swedish-controlled Finland. Sweden had refused to join the continental blockade against Britain, and Alexander used this as justification for attacking her in 1808. Alexander was not so much concerned with economic matters as with the strategic threat which Sweden could pose to Russia in the Baltic if she were to maintain her alliance with Britain. Napoleon was quite content for Russia to be diverted to the north, particularly as, at least nominally, it was in defence of his Continental System. He even offered to assist Russia with French troops, but in the event (and probably to Alexander's relief) French troops were too occupied in the war in Spain from the summer of 1808 (see below p. 106) to be involved elsewhere.

Russian troops quickly overcame the Swedes in Finland (approximately 24,000 Russian troops faced about 20,000 Swedish and Finnish troops, but the latter were poorly equipped and ill-prepared for war). They were held up only by the garrison of the fortress of Sveaborg (Suomenlinna), which commanded the entry by sea into Helsinki. When this fortress surrendered in May, amidst accusations of treachery, the way to Helsinki was clear and Alexander announced the incorporation of Finland into the Russian Empire. However, partisan warfare in Finland frustrated the Russians and only a daring attack on Stockholm over the frozen Baltic in early 1809, which resulted in the overthrow of King Gustavus IV, ensured Swedish capitulation. At the Peace of Fredrikshamn (Hamina) in September 1809, Finland and the Åland islands (of strategic importance in the Baltic) were ceded outright to Russia while Sweden also agreed to join the continental blockade against Britain. Alexander wrote to his sister Catherine on 18 September, perhaps trying to regain her approval after her criticisms of the Tilsit treaty:

This peace is perfect and absolutely what I had wanted. I cannot sufficiently thank the Supreme Being. The cession of all of Finland up to the Torneo [river] with the Åland islands, the adherence to the continenal system and closure of ports to England, finally peace with the allies of Russia; all of this concluded without intermediaries. There is something to sing a beautiful Te Deum Laudamus for; also our own tomorrow at Isaac [cathedral], with all the military ceremony, to do things in style![12]

The war had been a success, but it was not popular in Russia. It seemed to many Russians that Alexander had simply been the pawn of Napoleon and had allowed himself to be diverted from the real concerns of Russia with the fate of central Europe and the Balkans. To many, Finland did not seem to be a valuable prize and the attack on Sweden, with whom Russia had maintained good relations, was criticized by some as unjust and unnecessary.

Even before the peace treaty with Sweden, Alexander had announced that Finland would be united with Russia as the Grand Duchy of Finland, with the Russian tsar as Grand Duke. He convened the Finnish diet at Borgå (Porvoo) where he confirmed the rights, privileges, religion and fundamental laws of Finland according to its constitution. This act led to controversy later in the nineteenth century between Finnish and Russian lawyers and historians about the status of the Finnish state within the Russian Empire, a controversy which was largely based on disagreements over the semantics of Alexander's manifestos, speeches and correspondence. (The issues were made more complicated by the fact that the language of these statements often lacked legal precision and there were differences between the Russian and Swedish texts.) The Finns claimed later in the century that by guaranteeing their 'constitution' Alexander was consciously giving a concession to the Finnish people, as a result of the weakness of the Russian forces, which assured them a degree of autonomy. Certainly, the Russian army was harassed by Finnish guerrilla forces at the time and Alexander was keen to bring the campaign to a successful conclusion as rapidly as possible, but there is no evidence that he was under any pressure which obliged him to make a 'deal' with the Finns from a position of weakness. The diet did not form of its own accord in order to demand concessions; Alexander summoned it. But Alexander's policy towards the Finns is of great interest as a further indication of his attitude towards constitutionalism.

By guaranteeing the Finnish constitution Alexander was accepting the rights and forms of government which Finland had enjoyed under Swedish rule. This was essentially an *ancien régime* style constitution: the structure of the Diet – one chamber in which all four estates were represented – is typical of the type of representative bodies in Europe before the French Revolution. Alexander, in other words, did not *introduce* a constitution into Finland, let alone create one which incorporated ideas such as 'the rights of man', but rather he simply confirmed the *status quo*. This then was not so different from his confirmation at the beginning of his reign of the rights and privileges of the Baltic provinces. Alexander in practice, however, showed little respect for the rights of the Finnish Diet. He did not respond to the requests from Finnish representatives in St Petersburg that he should summon another meeting of the diet after 1809; in fact the next Diet was not convened until 1863 in the reign of Alexander II. The delegates at the diet in 1809 were ordered not to discuss a project which attempted to define the Finnish constitution. What the tsar required of the Diet was not decrees 'but only its opinion', commented Speransky on 9 July 1809. [13]

Furthermore, Alexander made changes to the administrative structure of Finland without consultation with the Diet or any reference to Finnish rights or the 'constitution'. Alexander's main aim was to achieve administrative efficiency. His attitude was pragmatic; he saw no reason fundamentally to alter the administrative structure of Finland if it functioned effectively. In 1811, Alexander reunited the lands of the Duchy with the Finnish territory north of St Petersburg (known as 'Old Finland') which had been won from the Swedes in the course of the eighteenth century, and in which Russian institutions had been established during the reign of Catherine II. There was an element of the 'grand gesture' about his action; he could project himself both to the Finns and to foreign states as a magnanimous ruler. There were also, however, pragmatic reasons for this policy. Neither the administration nor the economy of the provinces of Old Finland operated satisfactorily and it was hoped that the situation would improve if these lands were joined with the Duchy.

Alexander's policy in the Baltic provinces and Georgia in the early years of his reign (see above pp. 49–51) had already shown that he was content to allow the continued existence of local institutions if they functioned efficiently. Russification in the sense of the forced imposition of the structure of Russian local government was not pursued as a policy, and in this respect Alexander differed from Catherine II who had deliberately introduced the same forms and structures of administration throughout the Empire. His policy in Finland has to be seen in these terms rather than as a stage in the development of his thinking on constitutionalism. Alexander did, however, put Speransky in charge of Finnish affairs in 1809, just at the time when he was preparing his project for a constitution for Russia. This has led some Finnish historians to suggest that Speransky was influenced by the content of the Finnish constitution in his writing and used Finland as a testing ground for reforms in Russia. It is true that there were some similarities between the Finnish Diet and the Diet which Speransky proposed for Russia – representation was to be by social estates as in Finland, for example – but this does not mean that Finland was the model for Russia. Speransky was influenced by the views of several writers and the practice of government in England and France and had formulated many of his ideas before being given responsibility for Finnish affairs. Although Speransky recognized the separate status of Finland within the Russian empire ('Finland is a state and not a province' he wrote in 1811[14]), he never saw Finland, or the Finnish diet, as having any real independence. He envisaged that after the reforms of the Russian government and administration, which in 1809 he thought he was going to introduce, Finland would merge fully into the Russian state.

The success enjoyed by Russian troops in their campaign in the north was not repeated in the south against the Ottoman Empire. War had broken out between the two countries in 1806 (see above p. 75) and Russian forces had made only slow progress against the Turks in the Danubian Principalities (Moldavia and Wallachia) and in the Caucasus. In accordance with one of the secret clauses of the Treaty of Tilsit Alexander had to accept French mediation in this conflict. Napoleon and Alexander had talked vaguely at Tilsit about the possibility of dividing the Ottoman Empire between them. But in practice, Alexander's position in the eastern Mediterranean had been weakened by his cession of the Ionian islands to France at Tilsit, and Napoleon never intended that Russia should have a free hand, let alone increased influence, in the Balkans. Franco-Russian relations in the Balkans after 1807 demonstrated the incompatibilty of their foreign policy aims and the essential instability of the Tilsit agreement. Napoleon's tolerance, and even encouragement, of Russia's expansion at the expense of Sweden to the north was not matched by an equal acceptance of her ambitions in an area where France also had commercial and strategic interests.

In February 1808 Napoleon suggested a combined expedition of 50,000 French and Russian troops ('including perhaps a few Austrians') to conquer India via the Levant and Egypt. Alexander's response to Napoleon was straightforward: 'Take all you want in Asia, except that which borders on the Dardanelles',[15] making his own interests clear. Alexander had to promise at Tilsit, and then later at the armistice with the Turks in August, to evacuate the Principalities on the understanding that they would not be reoccupied by the Turkish forces until a peace treaty had been signed. This would have deprived Russia of her territorial advantage and, in consequence, the Russian government used various pretexts to refuse to ratify the agreement and keep the troops in place. Napoleon's proposed alternative which he put to Alexander in late 1807 – that Russia should retain the Principalities on the condition that France gained Silesia – was no more attractive. At the same time that Napoleon was promising Alexander support in Sweden he was also warning the Austrians about Russian ambitions in the Balkans and putting forward the idea of a Franco-Austrian alliance to restrain Russia in this area.

At Erfurt in 1808 (see below pp. 106–7) Napoleon

recognized Russia's right to annex the Principalities, in return for Russia's vague expressions of support for France in the event of a conflict with Austria, but by now both sides had abandoned the idea of dividing the Ottoman Empire. By this time Russia was in control of the Principalities and seemed to be in a strong position (Russian forces took the important fortresses of Rustchuk and Giurgevo in late 1810). Still peace negotiations with the Turks dragged on. As relations deteriorated with France, Alexander realized that he could no longer afford to have so many troops tied down in the south and in the autumn of 1811 he ordered the commander-in-chief, Kutuzov, to start peace negotiations with the Turks on the basis that Russia would abandon Wallachia and retain Moldavia. The Turks were not unnaturally reluctant to come to terms while the international situation remained unclear. In the Caucasus, Russian forces had taken Poti, Sukhum-kale and Akhalkalaki from Turkish and Persian forces. By the beginning of 1812, the outbreak of war between France and Russia was almost certain (see below pp. 106–9) and Napoleon approached the Ottoman Empire and sought an alliance against Russia. The Turks, however, had been exhausted by the long war and were finally prepared to agree terms with the Russians. A hasty peace was concluded on 28 May 1812 at Bucharest in which Russia abandoned her demands for the Principalities and settled for the cession of Bessarabia up to the river Pruth. In the Caucasus, Poti and Akhalkalaki were returned to the Turks. Russia had also been at war with Persia in the Caucasus, and the Persians were forced to come to terms after the peace with the Turks. Russia acquired most of the territory she had sought north of the Aras and Kara rivers (Alexander claimed that 'this barrier is necessary to prevent the incursions of barbarian people who inhabit the land')[16] with the exception of Erevan and Nakhjavan. There had been some rewards for a long and costly campaign but Russia had gained far less territory than she had hoped for or indeed seemed likely to acquire earlier in the campaign.

The Russo-Turkish war had raised the aspirations of the Balkan peoples for some degree of independence. The Serbs were most active in this respect and sought an independent 'Serbian Kingdom', with a constitutional monarchy, under Russian protection. The question of an independent government for Serbia was raised in the peace negotiations with Turkey in 1810 but at the Treaty of Bucharest Serbian demands were not met in full. An amnesty was granted to rebels and agreement was reached on administration and taxation which allowed Serbia some autonomy but these measures fell far short of political independence. Even while the treaty was being ratified, Admiral P.V. Chichagov proposed to Alexander that Russian troops in Moldavia under his command should raise rebellion throughout the Balkans and make their way to Dalmatia, the Adriatic and Switzerland appealing to the oppressed populations to rise against Napoleon. The ultimate aim of this proposal was to establish a Slav empire in the Balkans under Russian protection. The plan was clearly unrealistic (although no more so than Czartoryski's earlier plan for a Balkan federation under Russian protection) but Alexander gave Chichagov his support. He was quite prepared to pose as the protector of the Balkans and the champion of pan-Slavism to achieve his aims, but less willing to commit himself in practice. He instructed Chichagov on 21 April 1812 that 'You must use all means to raise the spirit of Slavonic peoples towards our aim, such as the promise to them of independence, the establishment of a Slavonic kingdom, the rewarding of people . . . '.[17] In reality by this stage Alexander's main concerns were with the forthcoming struggle against France and neither he nor Napoleon envisaged, or wanted, the total disintegration of the Ottoman Empire and the disorder and complications which would follow it. War between Russia and France was imminent, and Alexander used the threat of Chichagov's plan to frighten the Austrians so that they would not assist Napoleon in Russia. Only when the Austrians agreed to keep their forces in reserve if Napoleon attacked Russia did Alexander formally abandon the scheme. He also contemplated using the plan as a basis for a diversionary campaign against France in the Balkans; a Russian negotiator was sent to Serbia in June 1812 to discuss this but it came to nothing.

THE BREAKDOWN OF FRANCO-RUSSIAN RELATIONS

Napoleon had made it clear that he was opposed to Russian expansion in the Balkans. Conflicting ambitions in this area damaged relations between the two countries, but even without this dispute the Tilsit alliance proved to be unsatisfactory to both sides. This was exposed in the years after 1807 by disagreements in two main areas: the question of Poland and the Continental System.

The creation of the Duchy of Warsaw in 1807 from the lands of Prussian Poland always posed a potential threat to Russia. Alexander feared that the Duchy could be the nucleus of a newly-formed independent Polish state, allied to France, whose aim would be to regain the lands lost to Russia during the Partitions in the late eighteenth century. At the treaty of Schönbrunn in October 1809 (see below p. 107) the Duchy was expanded by the return of Western Galicia from Austria and this increased Alexander's concern. He played a double game. On the one hand, he held conversations with Czartoryski about the possibility of establishing a Polish administration in the lands Russia had acquired through the Partitions. Czartoryski wrote to Pavel Stroganov from St Petersburg in late 1809 that:

> A short time after my arrival here the Emperor spoke to me of his former project on Poland, and spoke to me with more interest than he had ever shown before; he demonstrated with the strongest arguments the advisability of this project.[18]

At the same time, Alexander sought formal assurance from Napoleon that a Polish state would never be restored in name. A convention between Russia and France on Poland was prepared in 1810 but never ratified. The sticking point was that Napoleon was not prepared to accept the first two articles which had been proposed by the Russians. The first article read that 'the kingdom of Poland will never be re-established'. The second article read: 'The contracting parties undertake to ensure that the names of *Poland* and of *Poles* are never applied to any of the parties which already constitute this kingdom, not to their inhabitants, not to their troops, and will disappear forever in all official or public acts, of whatever nature they are' – a far cry from Czartoryski's vision in 1806 of Alexander as the champion of Polish independence. Yet in April 1812, on the eve of tha Napoleonic invasion, Alexander wrote to Czartoryski assuring him that he still held to his 'favourite ideas for the regeneration of your country' and that the only question was to determine the most appropriate time to put these ideas into effect.[19]

Alexander's position on Poland was not as contradictory as it seemed. In essence, he was opposed to the establishment of an *independent* Poland, but a Poland dependent on Russian will (like Poland before the Partitions) was far preferable to a truly independent state or, even worse, to one linked with French interests. The strategic interests of Russia and her relationship with France always predominated over any sentimentality about the fate of Poland. Alexander's suspicions of Napoleon's intentions were further aroused when the French increased the army of the Duchy to 60,000. In 1810 and 1811, Alexander toyed with the idea of seizing the initiative and trying to win the loyalty of the Poles in a conflict with France by offering to restore Poland to her former size, with himself as King, in return for Polish support against France. At the same time he also spoke about the possibility of creating a separate kingdom of Lithuania (the lands acquired by Russia in the Partitions were mostly from the old Grand Duchy of Lithuania). But Alexander could not alter the fact that Napoleon had done more in practical terms for the Poles than any Russian ruler.

After 1807 Napoleon was in a position to attempt to close all continental ports to Britain, a policy which, if successful, would have had a devastating effect on her trade and prosperity. The Continental System was never popular in Russia, which relied on the export of naval supplies to Britain and imported a variety of manufactured goods and textiles. Alexander had placed restrictions on British traders in Russia even before Tilsit, as he fully realized the value of the Russian trade to them and wished to encourage domestic industry. Early in 1807 British traders were obliged to acquire new certificates to trade in Russia and were forced to register formally in Russian guilds and pay tax on their declared capital. Alexander had agreed at Tilsit to join the Continental System in December 1807 if Britain had not concluded an armistice by then, but already in October he had announced an embargo on British ships, although this was not implemented vigorously. The formal adherence to the Continental System was far more serious, however, and meant the closure of Russian ports to British ships and the sequestration of British property. Goods continued to enter Russia through Finland and even through Afghanistan and trade continued, not only on neutral ships (in particular, on American ones – 120 docked in St Petersburg alone in 1810) but also on British and Russian vessels throughout the period. A Russian merchant in London reported in 1810 that Russian hemp and grain were reaching Britain and that the Thames 'was full of' Russian ships.[20] Commissions to examine the authenticity of neutral ships were established in St Petersburg and Archangel. In 1809 these commissions confiscated 25 ships and 36 cargoes, mostly in the port of Riga (13 ships and 25 cargoes). It was also a source of irritation to the Russian government that France continued to import goods from Britain carried in neutral ships.

The Continental System resulted in the setting up of some Russian industries, and was popular among some merchants. In Moscow, for example, more cotton spinneries were set up and in 1812 a number of Moscow industrialists requested the banning of all imported manufactures. In general, however, Soviet research has shown that Russian industry was insufficiently advanced to benefit from the withdrawal of British competition. For example, despite the increase in the number of cotton-spinning mills, the Russian textile industry as a whole suffered because the factories needed English yarn and could not compensate for this through cotton imports from the United States. Russian exports fell from a yearly average of 54.1 million silver roubles in the period 1802–6 to 34.1 million in the period 1808–12. In the same periods imports fell from a yearly average of 40.8 million silver roubles in 1802–06 to 20.6 million in 1808–12. Exports of wood, hemp, flax, grain, tallow, copper, potash and iron were especially hard hit. Amongst the restricted imports was lead which was needed for the artillery. Trade with France did not increase to compensate for the collapse of British trade; on the contrary, the volume of trade with France fell after 1811. The rouble also dropped in value: the paper rouble fell from 50 silver copecks in 1808 to 43 in 1809, 35 in 1810 and 23.5 in 1811. State revenues from customs also suffered: the income in 1805 was 9.1 million silver roubles, but this collapsed in 1808 to 2.9 million, and only rose gradually to 3.7 million in 1810 and 3.9 million in 1811. The nobility in St Petersburg and Moscow particularly resented the Continental System as the prices of imported luxuries rose (the price of sugar and coffee rose from about 18 to 20 roubles a *pood* – about 36 pounds – in 1802 to between 100 and 115 roubles a *pood* in 1811). Merchants also resented the loss of generous credit facilities provided by Britain.

On 31 December 1810 Alexander in effect withdrew from the Continental System when he announced that the following year he would impose heavy duties on goods arriving by land (such as French luxury goods, and, in particular, French wine) and lighter duties on goods arriving by sea, which favoured neutral American ships carrying British goods. At the same time, duties on the wines of France and her allies were increased to double the duty imposed on wines from south-east Europe. The manifesto accompanying the new tariff and new rules on neutral ships justified this action because 'having seen the present situation of our trade, that the import of foreign goods has obviously harmed internal industry and, with the deliberate fall of monetary circulation, unfairly exceeds the export of Russian products, and wishing, as much as is possible to restore appropriate equilibrium' rules were to be established on neutral shipping 'the aim of which is to obstruct the increase of excessive luxuries, to curtail the import of foreign goods and to encourage, as much as possible, the production of internal trade and industry'.[21] During 1811 more and more British vessels delivered their goods in Russia without hindrance. Napoleon himself estimated in August 1811 that 150 ships sailing under the American flag but carrying British goods had been received in Russian ports. The duties were decreased on the raw materials which Russian industries needed and, despite the disruptive effects of the Napoleonic invasion, the number of factories, and workers in factories, in Russia grew after 1812: from 2,332 factories in 1812 (2,399 in 1804) to 3,731 in 1814; and from 119,000 workers in 1812 (95,000 in 1804 and 137,800 in 1811) to 170,600 in 1814.

Incompatibility of interests meant that conflict between France and Russia was always likely and had only been postponed by Napoleon's other commitments. In the summer of 1808, revolt had broken out in Spain and large numbers of French troops were committed to resist guerrilla warfare (300,000 French troops were in Spain by 1812). In August 1808 Britain sent an expedition to Spain; by 1813 there were in the region of 100,000 British troops confronting Napoleonic forces in the peninsula. Encouraged by the French army's difficulties in Spain, and in the belief that there was opposition to Napoleon within France, Austria threatened to resume military action. Napoleon summoned a congress in Erfurt in September 1808 in order to force Alexander to restate his commitment to the alliance with France. Alexander decided to attend, convinced by this stage that Russia needed a breathing space to prepare herself for any future struggle. On his way to Erfurt he visited the Prussian king and queen and was urged by the Prussian chief minister, Baron H.F.K. vom Stein, to take the lead in a coalition against the French. At Erfurt, the affability of Tilsit was still maintained between the two rulers on the surface. But Napoleon found Alexander less easy to deal with than at Tilsit (although he wrote to Josephine of Alexander that 'If he were a woman, I think I would make him my mistress')[22] and Alexander was openly cynical about Napoleon. He wrote to his sister Catherine from Weimar on 8 November 1808 that 'Bonaparte pretends that I am nothing but a fool. *He who laughs last laughs longest!* and I put all my hope in God'.[23] Alexander refused to commit himself to support France in the event of Austrian aggression. He only gave Napoleon verbal assurances of support for his campaign in Spain and promised vaguely to make 'common cause' with the French if Austria attacked her; in return, Napoleon had to recognize Russia's acquisition of Finland and support her proposed annexation of the Principalities. Alexander felt his position further enhanced by the disloyalty of the French ambassador to Russia, General A.-A.L. Caulaincourt, and the foreign minister, C.-M. de Talleyrand, who flattered him by secretly urging that he should resist Napoleon's ambition for the sake not just of Russia but of Europe.

In Austria, pressure from the anti-French foreign minister J.P. Stadion and the new Empress, and unwarranted optimism about Napoleon's problems in Spain and at home, led Emperor Francis I to declare war on France on 9 April 1809. This was despite warnings from his generals about the Austrian armed forces' lack of preparation and despite Alexander urging caution. The Austrian army was decisively defeated by the French at the battle of Wagram on 6 July (Napoleon had occupied Vienna in May). By the terms of the humiliating Treaty of Schönbrunn of 14 October, Austria was obliged to cede her gains from the Polish Partitions to the Duchy of Warsaw, her strip of the Dalmatian coast to the Kingdom of Italy and parts of Upper Austria to Bavaria. Also imposed were a restriction on the numbers of her forces, adherence to the Continental System and an indemnity of 85 million francs. Alexander had delayed giving the French any substantial military help (when the French ambassador Caulaincourt asked if the Russian army was marching on Olmütz, Alexander replied with deliberate vagueness that 'Elle marchera dans la direction d'Olmütz')[24] and he secretly assured the Austrians of his neutrality. He then infuriated Napoleon by complaining when Russia was only rewarded at Schönbrunn with the acquisition of the small region of Tarnopol in Eastern Galicia. Russia had suffered all of two casualties in the campaign.

Relations were further strained by Napoleon's unsuccessful attempt to marry into the Russian royal family in 1810 after his divorce from his first wife, Josephine. Alexander first caused resentment by hindering Napoleon's attempts to marry one of his sisters, but then was resentful in turn when Napoleon instead took an Austrian bride. By early 1810 both sides were seriously contemplating armed conflict. In March of that year, Napoleon's foreign minister, J-B. de Nompère de Champagny, drew up a plan for an anti-Russian coalition which assumed that war was inevitable. Both Napoleon and Alexander approached

Austria with offers of territorial gain in return for an alliance, but Austria prudently resisted these overtures. Tension was increased when Napoleon followed his annexation of Bremen, Hamburg and Lübeck with the annexation of the Duchy of Oldenburg on 22 January 1811. Alexander's favourite sister, Catherine, was married to the Duke of Oldenburg who was heir to the Duchy and the annexation was in clear violation of the Treaty of Tilsit.

In the spring of 1811 Alexander was still able to write to Napoleon that:

> Russia has no need of conquests and perhaps possesses too much territory. For the rest, coveting nothing from my neighbours, liking France, what interest would I have in wanting war? Moreover my self-respect is attached to the system of union with France.

He conveyed to Napoleon via Caulaincourt that:

> I want the alliance, I want it as a man and as a ruler: as a man because I believe that it can save a lot of blood; as ruler because I think that, better than any other political combination, it can keep the peace of Europe in a way *geographically* useful to both states. I add also that I want it because I am attached to your emperor and to your nation: believe me, it is the truth.[25]

Napoleon responded to his 'très cher ami et frère' protesting equally firm friendship. But despite the rhetoric, both sides saw that by now armed conflict was inevitable. In August 1811, on the occasion of his birthday, Napoleon gave the Russian ambassador Prince Aleksandr Borisovich Kurakin a public dressing down, complaining about all aspects of Alexander's foreign policy and threatening a campaign against Russia; it was clear that he had resolved on war. Alexander assured the French ambassador, Jacques Lauriston, on 10 April 1812 that he had 'the sincere desire not to wage war' and proclaimed himself to be 'the friend and most faithful ally of Napoleon'. 'The tears welled up in his eyes' commented Lauriston dryly.[26] This conversation took place on 10 April; on 21 April Alexander departed for Vil'na.

In fact the only remaining issue was the position of other

countries in the forthcoming struggle. Frederick William was forced to agree to commit 20,000 Prussian troops to Napoleon's army, although he secretly assured Alexander that these troops would do as little as possible. Russian-Austrian negotiations resulted in an assurance from Metternich that Austrian troops would not play an active role in the campaign, although formally Austria was in alliance with France. Sweden signed a mutual defence treaty with Russia in April 1812, and the Treaty of Bucharest assured Turkish neutrality. The interests of France and of Russia had proved to be incompatible. As the two countries had been unable to work together the stage was now set to determine which one would predominate on the Continent.

.   .   .

NOTES AND REFERENCES

1. Marc Raeff, *Michael Speransky: Statesman of Imperial Russia 1772–1839*, The Hague, second edn. 1969, p. 167.
2. M.M. Speranskii, *Proekty i zapiski* edited by S.N. Valk, Moscow-Leningrad, 1961. This was published four years after the first edition of Raeff's biography of Speransky in 1957; no substantial changes were made to the second edition, in 1969, although Raeff consulted Valk's volume.
3. Ibid., p. 43.
4. N.V. Minaeva, *Pravitel'stvennyi konstitutsionalizm i peredovoe obshchestvennoe mnenie Rossii v nachale XIX veka*, Saratov, 1982, p. 112.
5. M.V. Dovnar-Zapol'skii, 'Politicheskie idealy M.M. Speranskago' in *Iz istorii obshchestvennykh techenii v Rossii*, Kiev, 1910, p. 123.
6. M. Korf, *Zhizn' grafa Speranskago*, 2 vols, St Petersburg, 1861, II, p. 25.
7. N.K. Shil'der, *Imperator Aleksandr I: ego zhizn' i tsarstvovanie*, 4 vols, St Petersburg, 1897, III, p. 35.
8. Ibid., p. 38.
9. A.V. Predtechenskii, *Ocherki obshchestvenno-politicheskoi istorii Rossii v pervoi chetverti XIX veka*, Moscow–Leningrad, 1957, p. 265.
10. Richard Pipes, *Karamzin's Memoir on Ancient and Modern Russia: A Translation and Analysis*, Cambridge, Mass., 1959, p. 204.
11. Michael Jenkins, *Arakcheev: Grand Vizier of the Russian Empire*, New York, 1969, p. 136.
12. Grand-Duc Nicolas Mikhailowitch [Nikolai Mikhailovich],

Correspondance de l'Empereur Alexandre Ier avec sa soeur la Grande-Duchesse Catherine, Princess d'Oldenbourg, puis Reine de Würtemberg, (1815–1818), St Petersburg, 1910, p. 25.

13. K. Ordin, *Pokorenie Finliandii. Opyt opisaniia po neizdannym istochnikam*, 2 vols, St Petersburg, 1889, II, supplements, p. 88.

14. *Sbornik Imperatorskago russkago istoricheskago obshchestvo*, XXI, p. 456.

15. Albert Vandal, *Napoléon et Alexandre Ier. L'Alliance Russe sous le premier empire*, 3 vols, 8th edn, Paris, 1914, I, *de Tilsit à Erfurt*, p. 299.

16. Muriel Atkin, *Russia and Iran 1780–1828*, Minneapolis, 1980, p. 101.

17. I.S. Dostian, *Rossiia i balkanskii vopros: iz istorii russko-balkanskikh politicheskikh sviazei v pervoi treti XIX v.*, Moscow, 1972, pp. 75–6.

18. Nikolai Mikhailovich, *Graf Pavel Aleksandrovich Stroganov (1774–1817): Istoricheskoe izsledovanie epokhi imperatora Aleksandra I*, 3 vols, St Petersburg, 1903, II, p. 413.

19. Grand-Duc Nicolas Mikhailowitch [Nikolai Mikhailovich], *L'Empereur Alexandre Ier: essai d'étude historique*, 2 vols, St Petersburg, 1912, I, pp. 363–4.

20. M.F. Zlotnikov, *Kontinental'naia blokada i Rossiia*, Moscow-Leningrad, 1966, p. 172.

21. Ibid., p. 239.

22. Alan Palmer, *Alexander I: Tsar of War and Peace*, London, 1974, p. 159.

23. Nicolas Mikhailowitch, *Correspondance de l'Empereur Alexandre Ier*, p. 20.

24. Albert Vandal, *Le Second mariage de Napoléon. Decline de l'alliance*, 3 vols, 8th edn, Paris, 1918, II, p. 77.

25. Serge Tatistcheff [S.S. Tatishchev], *Alexandre Ier et Napoléon d'après leur correspondance inédite 1801–1812*, Paris, 1891, pp. 551, 563.

26. Albert Sorel, *L'Europe et la revolution française*, 8 vols, Paris, 1911, VII, *Le Blocus Continental – Le Grand Empire, 1806–1812*, p. 566.

Chapter 6

THE SAVIOUR OF EUROPE: 1812–1815

· · ·

NAPOLEON IN RUSSIA

Napoleon's Grande Armée of between 400,000 and 500,000 men, of whom less than half were French (the rest being predominantly Germans, Poles and Italians) crossed the river Niemen into Russian territory on 23–24 June 1812 and rapidly moved eastwards. Napoleon hoped for a quick, decisive battle in which he would reassert his superiority over Alexander. This would allow him to force Alexander to conform with the terms of the Tilsit treaty, including his adherence to the Continental System, and to accept his subordinate position in an alliance with France. Such an outcome would achieve the isolation and defeat of Napoleon's real enemy, Britain. The Russian forces, however, were in no position to confront the enemy. The armies were divided – 90,000 at Vil'na under Field-Marshal Mikhail Bogdanovich Barclay de Tolly, 60,000 further south under General Petr Ivanovich Bagration and reserve armies of 45,000 at Volhynia under General Aleksandr Tormassov and 35,000 in Moldavia under Field-Marshal Kutuzov – and the total number of troops did not match that of the French forces. Alexander was at a ball in Vil'na, dressed in the uniform of the Semenovsky guards 'which became him well' and charming the ladies, when the news of the invasion reached him. He later confided 'that he had suffered intensely in being obliged to show a gaiety which he was far from feeling'.[1] Yet he had done little to help the Russian position, seeming unsure about whether to approach Britain for an alliance and failing to draw up a clear plan to counter the forthcoming invasion.

The Russian forces had little choice, or plan, other than to retreat before numerically superior forces and the French entered Vil'na on 28 June, Vitebsk on 26 July and were at the gates of Smolensk by the middle of August. The retreat seems to have had the general approval of the tsar although Bagration appealed to him: 'I pray you to start the offensive . . . . One simply must not trifle with this country . . . . It is not for Russians to flee . . . . We have become worse than the Prussians . . . . It's shameful'.[2] The French army, in the meantime, was already being weakened by desertions, disease and loss of equipment as it pursued the retreating Russians on inadequate roads in poor climatic conditions.

Napoleon had been disappointed when the decisive battle which he sought took place neither at Vil'na nor at Vitebsk, but he was confident that the Russians would not abandon the 'sacred city' of Smolensk without a fight. The French forces at Smolensk outnumbered the Russians by 185,000 to 116,000. After a two-day assault by the French on 16–17 August Barclay de Tolly ordered the Russian forces to retreat and abandon the city (both sides had suffered approximately 10,000 casualties) and on 18 August the French 'began creeping like mice through every breach in the wall'.[3] The loss of Smolensk was met with an outcry from Alexander's other generals and from advisers who were safely distant from the battlefield, such as Arakcheev; but for Napoleon, the retreat of the Russian forces was deeply frustrating and, ultimately, crucially damaging. He had planned on going no further than Smolensk and had hoped that the taking of this historic city would force Alexander to come to terms. The French armies had entered Russia better supplied than for any other campaign. Provisions had been stockpiled at Danzig to supply 400,000 troops and 50,000 horses for fifty days, and the Grande Armée entered Russia with supplies for twenty-four days. This meant that the army should have established winter quarters in Smolensk while further supplies were brought up. But the city had been deliberately set on fire by the Russians, and most of the inhabitants had fled, so that neither adequate shelter nor additional provisions were to be found. Throughout the presence of French forces in Smolensk (from 18 August to

14 November) it proved impossible to administer the town effectively and to procure sufficient supplies from the surrounding countryside. In the event, Napoleon spent only six days there before moving eastwards in the hope of forcing the Russians to commit themselves to a decisive battle. Lieutenant Vossler summed up the French predicament:

> . . . we were embarked on a strenuous campaign entailing frequent forced marches along abominable roads, either smothered in sand or knee-deep in mud and frequently pitted by precipitous gulleys, under skies alternately unbearably hot or pouring forth freezing rain . . . many regiments had no more than three days' supply of rations, which, because of the total devastation of the countryside, could never be adequately replenished. Four-fifths of the army subsisted on the flesh of exhausted, starving cattle . . . our drink consisted – not even of inferior spirits or at least wholesome water, but of a brackish liquid scooped from stinking wells and putrid ponds . . . within two or three days of crossing the Niemen the army, and in particular the infantry, was being ravaged by a variety of diseases, chief among them dysentry, ague and typhus . . . . Inexorably the whole vast host seemed to be moving ponderously to disaster . . . .[4]

The friction between Barclay de Tolly and Bagration obliged Alexander to appoint another commander. Barclay's policy of retreat was widely resented in the army, and Alexander was prepared, not for the first time, to sacrifice individuals accused by others of being traitors to Russia. The unanimous choice of his advisers was Kutuzov. Alexander had no liking for Kutuzov, whose presence reminded him all too painfully of his own failings at the battle of Austerlitz, but he was too conscious of the perilous position of Russia to risk ignoring the popular choice. 'The public wanted his appointment, I appointed him: as for me, I wash my hands of it', he commented to General-Adjutant Komarovsky.[5] Alexander had been persuaded by Arakcheev and by his sister Catherine not to assume personal control of the army ('you have not only the role of captain to play but also that of ruler' she wrote in June and 'in God's name do not choose to command yourself in person', more bluntly, in August).[6] Rather, they believed he should attempt to consolidate support in the country for the war and to rally the nation. Alexander seemed to have no coherent plan for the defence of Russia and seemed content to leave strategy to his generals, but he had shown some awareness of possible public reaction to the invasion in Russia and elsewhere in Europe. On hearing of the crossing of the Niemen, he promptly drafted a stirring manifesto in which he promised not to lay down his arms until 'not a single enemy soldier remains in my empire',[7] and his proclamation to the troops called down the wrath of God on Napoleon: 'I shall be with you and God will be against the aggressor'.[8] He also sent a last message to Napoleon, expressing his willingness to maintain the alliance if Napoleon were to withdraw immediately, but threatening that peace would not be made until the 'soil of Russia was purged entirely of the enemy presence'.[9] Alexander made this plea in the sure knowledge that it would be ignored, but aware that it would firmly demonstrate to other European countries that Napoleon was the aggressor.

Alexander was greeted enthusiastically in Moscow, where he arrived in July, and he wrote to Catherine from there that spirits were excellent. Donations of three million and eight million roubles were received from the Moscow nobility and merchants respectively. Certainly the patriotic response within Russia to the invasion cannot be doubted. A six per cent government treasury bond had been issued in April but donations were still essential to supply the army. The evidence suggests that all sectors of society with some wealth – nobles, merchants, townspeople and clergy – donated large amounts of money and goods to the cause. The eleven town dumas in Kaluga province, for example, donated between them 239,652 roubles, while the clergy donated 9,204 roubles and ten pounds of silver vessels. In the country as a whole over 82 million roubles were collected in the period from 1812 to 1815. Yet it was hard for Alexander to maintain his personal popularity in face of the retreat. He admitted to his sister from St Petersburg, where he arrived on 3 August, that 'Here I have found spirits less high than in Moscow and in the interior'.[10]

Kutuzov had continued the policy of withdrawal and by 3 September the Russian forces had retreated as far as

Borodino, 72 miles west of Moscow. Here Kutuzov had to make a stand, but by this time the French forces were already depleted by illness and much equipment had been abandoned (135,000 men and 587 canon were deployed by Napoleon at Borodino). The battle of Borodino took place on 7 September. In a costly encounter Napoleon's forces prevailed, but with the loss of 40,000 men (including 14 lieutenant-generals, 33 major-generals, 32 staff officers, 86 aides-de-camp and 37 regimental colonels). The Russians lost approximately 50,000 men, many passive victims of the French artillery. Ségur, a participant in the battle, recorded the extent of the slaughter:

> The latter [Russian infantry] advanced in compact masses in which our cannon balls cut wide and deep swathes. . . . Those inert masses simply let themselves be mowed down for two long hours, without any motion than that of falling. The massacre was frightful; and our artillerymen, knowing the value of bravery, admired the blind, motionless, resigned courage of their enemies.[11]

Nevertheless, the Russian forces were able to retreat in good order. Against the advice of most of his generals, Kutuzov decided not to attempt a further assault on the French, but to retreat to the south on the road to Kaluga and leave Moscow open to the invaders. The first news to arrive in St Petersburg on 11 September was that the Russians had won a great victory at Borodino; next day the rumours started that this was not the case. The French entered Moscow on 14 September, but found that most of the population had fled. Fires raged for five days, probably started by Count Fedor Vasil'evich Rostopchin, the governor-general of Moscow, so that the French found the city devastated.

Rumours that Moscow had been taken reached St Petersburg on 21 September although the disaster was only formally announced on 29 September. When Alexander attended a service in the Kazan' cathedral in St Petersburg on 27 September, to celebrate the eleventh anniversary of his coronation, he felt it necessary to travel in a closed carriage rather than on horseback because he had been made aware of the hostility of the populace. The imperial party had to enter the cathedral before a silent crowd.

Catherine, ever the harbinger of bad news and not one to spare Alexander any pain, informed her brother from Iaroslavl' in September that:

> The taking of Moscow has brought the feelings of exasper-
> ation to a climax; the dissatisfaction is at the highest point,
> and your person is far from being immune . . . . You are
> accused loudly of the misfortunes of your Empire, of its ruin
> in general and in particular, and finally of having lost the hon-
> our of your country and of your person.[12]

In these distressing times Alexander found solace in religion. His education had not entirely neglected religion but, under La Harpe's influence, the emphasis had been on moral education rather than religious instruction. In June 1810 Joseph de Maistre, the Sardinian minister, reported Alexander as saying that 'Christians are honest people but they serve no purpose'.[13] Even before the invasion, however, Alexander had come into contact with mystical ideas through his friend the senator Rodion Aleksandrovich Koshelev. As early as March 1811 he had written to Koshelev that 'Like you I put all my confidence in the Supreme Being'.[14] He was already, therefore, predisposed to these ideas, but the trauma of the invasion provided the catalyst for a major change in his thinking. The popular story (which has several variations) of his spiritual conversion is that while in St Petersburg he asked his friend Aleksandr Golitsyn (later Minister for Religious Affairs) how he managed to remain so calm during such a crisis, and received the reply that it was because of his trust in God and the Holy Scriptures. At this point Golitsyn's Bible fell to the floor and opened at Psalm 91. Golitsyn then presented his personal copy of the Bible to Alexander. Later the tsar attended a service at the cathedral for departing troops and heard the reading of the same Psalm, and was told by the priest that he had been directed by God to choose this reading. Alexander then called for a Bible and started his study by reading this Psalm.

This was a time of intense religious activity in Russia in response to the shock of the invasion and, more specifically, to the attack on churches by Napoleon's troops. The Russian Orthodox Church had already denounced Napoleon as the Antichrist in 1806. Ségur, serving in the

Grande Armée, accused the Orthodox clergy of inciting the peasants against the French by telling them that the French were a 'legion of devils commanded by the Anti-christ, infernal spirits, horrible to look upon, and whose very touch defiled'.[15] Another French participant commented that:

> It is certain that the hate which they directed against Napoleon was further excited by the priests themselves and by other ministers of religion, who only saw in the person of the Emperor [Napoleon] a blasphemer who wanted to overturn one by one all the religions.[16]

In this respect, Alexander experienced the emotions of many of his subjects. As he wrote to Frederick William III:

> . . . the burning of Moscow at last illumed my spirit and the judgement of God filled me with a warmth of faith I had never felt before. From that moment I learned to know God, such as He is revealed by the Bible, from that moment I tried to comprehend, as I now do comprehend, His wish and His law, from that time I became another man, and to the deliverance of Europe from ruin do I owe my own safety and deliverance.[17]

For many Russian subjects, the religious frenzy excited by the French invasion passed with the departure of the enemy, but for the Russian ruler the experience had long-lasting consequences. Before 1812, Alexander had based his beliefs on the ideal organization of Europe and the conduct of future international relations on secular principles, albeit hazily expressed; after 1812 his religious experience coloured all his statements.

Despite his military successes, Napoleon was now in an impossible position in Moscow. He had penetrated into the heart of Russia but still could not force Alexander to sue for peace. He toyed with the idea of marching on St Petersburg, but this was never a practical possibility, given the depletion of his forces and the disruption of his supply lines. He also contemplated the total destabilization of the Russian social order by proclaiming the freedom of the serfs. While in Moscow, Napoleon ordered material relating to the Pugachev revolt (the last great Cossack revolt of 1773–4 in which serfs turned on their masters) to be brought to him from archives and private libraries. He expected to be petitioned by peasant delegations but this failed to happen. The Russian government, however, had taken the precaution of stationing extra troops in the provinces to counter any peasant unrest. After his return to France, Napoleon gave a speech to the Senate in which he asserted that only the prospect of a bloodbath between serfs and masters had prevented him from taking this step. In exile in St Helena he expressed regret that he had not done so. But emancipation was never a realistic policy. Napoleon did not seek to overthrow the social order in Russia; rather he wanted Alexander to come to terms with him. The unleashing of social warfare would make any agreement with Alexander impossible, and chaos in the country would not have brought Napoleon any military benefits. Without sufficient supplies of their own, the Napoleonic armies were already relying on requisitioning goods by force from the countryside; social disorder would not improve the situation.

Napoleon, in fact, was helpless in Moscow. As harassment of the French forces by partisan groups and by peasants grew his army and his supplies diminished. In an increasingly weak position he was forced to rely on Alexander coming to terms of his own volition. Alexander, however, demonstrated considerable fortitude and determination at this time of crisis. The hesitations he had shown when it came to planning the campaign against the French were replaced by a stubborn refusal to consider any terms. He wrote to Count Christoph Lieven, the Russian ambassador in London, that:

I will not make peace until I have driven the enemy back across our frontiers, even if I must, before succeeding in this, withdraw beyond Kazan'. As long as I am defending Russian territory I will only ask for munitions and arms from England. When, with the aid of Providence, I have repulsed the enemy beyond our frontiers, I will not stop there, and it is only then that I will reach agreement with England on the most effective assistance that I can ask for to succeed in liberating Europe from the French yoke.[18]

Of course, Alexander was also aware that, given the hostility shown by the nobility after the Treaty of Tilsit and the discontent which arose from the fall of Moscow, any attempt to reach a compromise with Napoleon would be totally unacceptable to the army and the nobility and would put his own throne at risk. Napoleon seems never to have appreciated this. His letter to Alexander offering peace went unanswered.

The Grande Armée left Moscow on 19 October. Napoleon had hoped to return through the fertile provinces south of his invasion route, but his losses at the battle of Maloiaroslavets on 24–25 October forced him to retrace his steps through country which had already been devastated by the passage of Russian and French troops. The onset of the very severe Russian winter and harassment by partisan groups and peasant bands helped to demoralize his army. One memoirist recounted that peasants could conduct 'a pitiless war against transportation, attack couriers, massacre the sick and wounded returning to Smolensk, and isolate permanently all the French army'.[19] On 9 November the first French troops re-entered Smolensk. The troops had hoped to find much-needed supplies but they were to be bitterly disappointed. Smolensk had been devastated: only 350 out of 2,250 buildings remained. The remnants of the army crossed the Berezina river on 26 November; only the successful deception of the Russian forces and the skill of the French sappers prevented total disaster (Alexander never forgave Kutuzov for his miscalculation which permitted this), and reached Prussian territory by crossing the Niemen on 13–14 December. Of the Napoleonic army of at least 400,000 less than 40,000 returned. It was a devastating military blow from which Napoleon never recovered. On 24 December 1812, his birthday, Alexander announced to his generals that 'You have saved not only Russia, you have saved Europe'.[20]

. . .

THE DEFEAT OF NAPOLEON IN EUROPE

Alexander now reassumed personal command of the Russian armies and returned in triumph to Vil'na on 23 December. He was, nevertheless, still capable of expressing an idealistic and naive vision of international relations, putting the question to Madame Choiseul-Gouffier 'Why could not all the sovereigns and nations of Europe agree among themselves to live like brothers, aiding each other in their need and comforting each other in their adversity?'. According to her account, Alexander's 'angelic soul' was further illustrated by his action in sending home some Spanish prisoners of war at his own expense.[21] But in reality, Alexander was on the verge of being able to do more than merely indulge in wishful thinking about foreign relations. As the conqueror of Napoleon he had suddenly become the potential liberator of Europe.

In January 1813, Russian troops crossed into Prussia. Alexander ordered the advance against the advice of Kutuzov, who thought that the Russian army was not in a fit state to continue the campaign and wished to wait for the arrival of more recruits and the onset of spring. Prussia was still formally an ally of France, but a minor Prussian commander, Count von Yorck, on his own authority abandoned Napoleon and made an agreement with the Russian general I.I. Diebitsch at Tauroggen to remain neutral. Now that the myth of Napoleon's invincibility had been shattered in Russia, and with French forces continuing to experience difficulties in Spain where British forces were advancing, the total defeat of Napoleon seemed at last to be a possibility and a new coalition began to take shape. At Kalisch (Kalisz) in former Prussian Poland, Alexander was supported by Freiherr vom Stein, who had been a Prussian cabinet minister and whom Alexander now made head of a provisional government to administer the territories of Prussia in the wake of the departing French armies. Alexander shared Stein's desire to restore Prussia to her former status (although not necessarily her former borders). In January 1813 Alexander wrote magnanimously to Frederick William III assuring him that 'According to my religion and my principles I like to repay wrong with right and I will not be satisfied until Prussia has regained its splendour and its power'.[22] However, the view previously taken by some German historians that Stein was instrumental in persuading Alexander to carry the war against Napoleon into Europe, thereby freeing Germany, has been convincingly challenged. Alexander showed no reluctance to take this step (he had shown he was prepared to do so against the advice of his commander-in-chief) and Stein was in no position to exert such authority. He recalled, showing a clear appreciation of his weakness and also of the tsar's intellectual limitations, that '. . . I had influence without authority, influence on very imperfect human beings, who were to be used as tools for the attainment of high purposes. Alexander lacked depth and the ability to concentrate'.[23]

In late February 1813 Alexander and Stein prepared the text of a military alliance between the two countries which was signed on 28 February by Frederick William in Breslau, where he had fled from Berlin. The treaty committed 150,000 Russian and 80,000 Prussian troops against France and declared that neither side would conclude a separate peace. More controversial secret clauses promised Prussia a territorial link with East Prussia, which implied that she might not regain her Polish territories (which had formed the Duchy of Warsaw) and gave rise to the suspicion that Russia coveted this area. On 22 February, Alexander had issued a proclamation in which he promised to assist the German people: 'Profiting from our victories we extend a helpful hand to oppressed people'. At Kalisch, Alexander stated that 'the time will arrive when treaties will no longer be dreams, where they can again be observed with this religious faith, this sacred inviolability on which the esteem, the power and the maintenance of empires depends'.[24] By this stage Alexander was not thinking merely in terms of alliances which would assist in the defeat of French forces. Rather, the French invasion, and his own religious experience, had convinced him that he had a mission to save Europe and Europe's oppressed people (including the French) from the tyranny of Napoleon. Alexander, of course, had made earlier idealistic statements about his desire to see people living in liberty and peace, albeit without this religious turn of phrase, but he had never been in a position before to ensure that such sentiments were endorsed by his allies by being expressed formally in proclamations and alliances. The time when the tsar's more grandiose ideas could be safely ignored or evaded had passed. In March, Prussia formally declared war on France. Shortly afterwards a joint declaration by Prussia and Russia called on the German 'princes and people' to help to liberate German lands from Napoleon. In April, Britain agreed to provide a subsidy of two million pounds for the

Prussian and Russian troops (two-thirds of which was allocated to Russia).

The Russian and Prussian armies moved swiftly through central Europe. The French had committed large forces to Spain and Napoleon had to form an army from veterans and inexperienced youths, but, nevertheless, he was able to check the advance with victories at Lützen, on 3 May, and Bautzen, on 20 May 1813. Alexander's choice of the irresolute General Ludwig Wittgenstein to command both Russian and Prussian forces (Kutuzov had just died) was partly responsible for these setbacks. The tsar had on several occasions proved himself to be a poor judge of military commanders. His usual recourse after military setbacks was to dismiss his chosen commander, which he duly did on this occasion by recalling Barclay de Tolly (whom he had dismissed after the abandonment of Smolensk). Austria, nominally France's ally (Napoleon had married the Habsburg archduchess Marie Louise) then proposed an armistice, which both sides accepted and signed at Pläwitz on 4 June, mainly with the intention of using this breathing space to rebuild their forces. In Austria, the state chancellor Clemens von Metternich was suspicious of the messianic tone of the Kalisch agreement which seemed to be proposing a German national crusade against Napoleon. He also feared the consequences of the triumph of Russia and distrusted Alexander's ambitions in Poland and the Balkans. Therefore, Metternich favoured some attempt at a negotiated peace which would keep Napoleon, or his son, on the throne and keep France sufficiently powerful to act as a counterweight to Russian ambitions in central Europe. However, the refusal of Napoleon to negotiate and Wellington's defeat of the French army at Vittoria in Spain persuaded the reluctant Metternich that Austria's best interests lay in joining the coalition, despite his reservations about Prussian and Russian plans for the reorganization of central Europe.

At Alexander's headquarters at Reichenbach on 27 June 1813, Austria, Prussia and Russia signed a convention to restore Prussian and Austrian possessions, to recreate independent German states and formally to dissolve the Duchy of Warsaw and its constitution. Napoleon attempted to counter these moves by seeking Austrian armed mediation and succeeded in extending the armistice period, but, as French weakness had become apparent to Metternich, these ploys were fruitless and Austria declared war on France in August 1813. In late August the allies unsuccessfully attempted to recover Dresden and were repelled by French forces. Alexander had shown yet again his lack of tactical understanding by insisting that the attack should go ahead against the advice not only of the Austrians but also of his own generals. On 9 September 1813, Russia, Prussia and Austria signed the Treaty of Teplitz, which committed each of the signatories to keep 150,000 men in the field against the French and not to accept a separate peace. The treaty also agreed on the restoration of the independent German states and dissolution of the Confederation of the Rhine, and on the joint determination of the fate of the Duchy of Warsaw. Metternich, however, would not commit himself on the future settlement of Europe or rule out a negotiated settlement with Napoleon. Sweden joined the alliance, giving the allies a numerical superiority: they now had approximately 490,000 men while Napoleon could muster about 440,000.

The costly victory (both sides lost approximately 30,000 men on the first day alone) of the three powers over Napoleon at Leipzig (the 'Battle of the Nations') on 16–19 October marked the end of France's power in Germany and saw her forces retreat over the Rhine. Alexander played an active part in the battle, directing the field and participating himself in a Cossack attack on the French cuirassiers (when requested to move to a safer place he responded that 'there are no bullets for me here'). The shame of his performance at the battle of Austerlitz was finally erased. At this point, however, it looked as if the alliance would break up as neither the Austrians nor the Prussians were prepared to carry the campaign into France itself. Despite Napoleon's critical shortage of troops and munitions, and the resistance within France to further recruitment, they were not keen to risk their own forces on French soil. Alexander alone was determined to pursue the campaign to its bitter end and remove Napoleon from power. Only his threat to march on Paris without his allies and then the arrival of Viscount Castlereagh, the British

Foreign Secretary, in February 1814 with new proposals prevented the coalition from disintegrating. At the beginning of February the allies gained their first victory on French soil but by the middle of the month they were encountering fierce resistance and had to pull back. This forced Alexander to come to terms with his partners and accept Castlereagh's proposals. On 9 March 1814 the Treaty of Chaumont committed all the members of the coalition to the total defeat of France and called for a confederated Germany and an independent Holland, Switzerland, Italy and Spain. A decision was not reached on the more problematical questions of the future of Poland and who would rule France. Britain provided subsidies of five million pounds, divided equally among the allies.

Russian troops entered Paris on 31 March 1814, with Alexander at their head. Determined as he had been to defeat Napoleon completely, Alexander could now afford to be magnanimous in his hour of victory. He had always stressed that Napoleon alone was his enemy, and that he felt no hostility towards the French people whom he regarded as victims of the emperor's evil rule. He announced to the citizens of Paris that 'I come not as an enemy. I come to bring you peace and commerce'[25] and informed a delegation which met him before he entered the city that:

> I esteem France and the French, and I hope they will give me the opportunity to do good for them. Please tell the Parisians, Gentlemen, that I am not entering their walls as an enemy, and it is for them to accept me as a friend; also, that I have but one enemy in France and with that one I am irreconcilable.[26]

Napoleon abdicated on 6 April and on 20 April was aboard a ship sailing to the island of Elba. Alexander was left in Paris to exert his charm upon French dignitaries and the ladies; he graciously declined an invitation to change the name of the Pont d'Austerlitz to something with less painful memories and delighted the former Empress Josephine during his frequent visits to her. (Alas, for Josephine, Alexander's charms had fatal consequences; she contracted a bronchial disorder during a picnic at which he was present and died at the end of May.)

As Alexander accompanied his army across Europe he

did not neglect his new spiritual interests. He wrote to his friend Koshelev in January 1813 asking him to pray for him so that he could achieve his task which was 'to make my country happy, but not in the ordinary sense: it is to advance the true reign of Jesus Christ that I invest all my glory'.[27] The ideas that were later expressed in the Holy Alliance of 1815 took root during the campaign of 1813–14 in Europe. Alexander later claimed that the Alliance originated at a meeting with the King of Prussia and Emperor of Austria after the victory of Leipzig. (His memory, however, cannot be trusted on this issue; he also asserted that inspiration came from his first meeting with Frederick William in 1802 (see above p. 65) and, on another occasion, that the idea was only formulated at the Congress of Vienna (see below p. 136).) He also continued his spiritual reading and became familiar with the works of contemporary mystics. He had met the German pietist Johann Jung-Stilling during the passage of the Russian armies through southern Germany in July 1814. During this year he also corresponded with the mystic Madame Julie de Krüdener, a Lutheran from Livonia who had married Baron Krüdener, a Baltic nobleman who served in the Russian diplomatic corps. Madame Krüdener pursued Alexander to his headquarters in Heilbronn in 1815 and managed to arrange a meeting with him on 4 June. This, according to the account by the evangelical minister Empaytaz, was an emotional encounter; Madame Krüdener harangued the tsar for three hours during which 'Alexander could scarcely articulate a few broken words; his head held in his hands, he wept copious tears'. The tsar then immersed himself in the reading of the scriptures but did not become so obsessed with his own inadequacies as to forget his mission to Europe. He prayed for his enemies and asked 'that God might grant me the favour of procuring the peace of Europe; I am ready to lay down my life for that end'.[28]

Alexander followed his triumphal entry into Paris with visits to Holland and England (the first Russian ruler to do this since Peter the Great), where he was acclaimed by the crowds as a popular hero. Unfortunately, he did not achieve the same success with the political leaders of Britain. Castlereagh was wary of the consequences of

Alexander appearing too popular and had deliberately arranged that other 'heroes' such as Frederick William III and the Prussian General Gebhard von Blücher should be invited at the same time; for, as he wrote to the Earl of Liverpool, the British Prime Minister, 'the [Russian] Emperor has the greatest merit, and must be held high, but he ought to be grouped, and not made the sole feature for admiration'.[29] Alexander's sister Catherine, who had recently been widowed, preceded him, and had already succeeded in alienating many influential people by her ungracious manners and love of intrigue. In the event, Alexander managed to infuriate the Prince Regent by upstaging him with the crowds and by displays of sheer tactlessness (for example, bowing to the Regent's estranged wife at the opera, so forcing him to do likewise); after a week the Regent was 'worn out with fuss, fatigue and rage'. He also deliberately courted the Whig opposition, but without impressing anyone. 'A vain, a silly fellow' was the verdict of Lord Grey.[30]

Alexander revelled in the honours which he duly received. He had the degree of Doctor in Civil Law by Diploma conferred upon him by the University of Oxford, as did Frederick William. The eulogistic poems specifically addressed to him on this occasion included the gratifying lines:

> Reviving Europe breathes at last,
> And hails in him, th' immortal CZAR,
> The pure and steadfast ray of Freedom's morning star.[31]

The speech addressed to Alexander by the Corporation of London must have made even more pleasant hearing, designed as it was to please him most:

> In the accomplishment of these happy and beneficial results to the World, we have contemplated in the august Person of Your Imperial Majesty a Monarch followed by a brave and loyal People in arms to the redress of injuries the most wanton, unprovoked, and barbarous, that baffled Ambition could conceive, or profligate Cruelty perpetuate – a Hero, by inflexible perseverance in his object, traversing whole regions, and pursuing to the Capital of France a discomfited Tyrant, not for purposes of retribution, not in vindictive fury to raze or to

destroy, not to subdue but to deliver a misguided People, to unbind their chains, to bring peace to their hearts and prosperity to their homes – a Hero, to the astonishment, and amidst the acclamations of the vanquished, holding out in his victorious hand graces, favours, and immunities, and evincing, in the proudest hour of triumph, the confidence, magnanimity, and clemency of a Christian Conqueror.[32]

At least publicly, Alexander had received the recognition of his role as the magnanimous saviour of Europe. He was probably unaware of the poor impression he made on Britain's political leaders, unused as he was to dealing with anyone other than reigning sovereigns.

During his visit to England Alexander continued in his new religious interests. In June 1814 he had met members of the British and Foreign Bible Society and Quakers, and had attended a Quaker meeting which he found very moving. Alexander invited William Allen, Stephen Grellet and John Wilkinson, all prominent Quakers, to visit him in his hotel the day after the meeting. According to Allen, the tsar expressed himself with seriousness and humility:

> On the subject of worship, he said, he agreed entirely with Friends, that it was an internal and spiritual thing; he said that he was himself in the habit of daily prayer . . . . He remarked, that divine worship consisted not in outward ceremonies or repetition of words, *which the wicked and hypocrite might easily adopt,* but in having the mind prostrate before the Lord . . . .[33]

This serious conversation, it must be remembered, took place amidst the far more frivolous entertainments which had been laid on for the royal visit. Alexander expressed a wish to visit a Quaker family while he was in Portsmouth but the arranged visit, to the family of John Glaisyer in Brighton, could not take place because of the size of the enthusiastic crowd which surrounded the tsar's carriage. On the road to Dover, Alexander surprised a couple in Quaker dress at the roadside by descending from his carriage and asking if he and his sister could spend a short time with them. He was shown round the house and dairy and, according to a historian of the Quakers, made a favourable impression:

On parting he stooped to kiss Mary Rickman's hand, to the surprise of the Quaker lady; throughout he and the Duchess behaved with the utmost simplicity and friendliness, and left the farmer and his wife greatly puzzled by their attention but entirely captivated by their gracious manner.[34]

. . .

THE EUROPEAN SETTLEMENT

Having paraded himself abroad as the conqueror of Napoleon, Alexander now turned his attention to the future shape of Europe. The peace settlements took place in three stages: in May 1814 the First Peace of Paris dealt with containment of France in the West; the Congress of Vienna, which met between November 1814 and March 1815, dealt with the frontiers of central and eastern Europe. Napoleon returned to France on 1 March 1815, deposed the French king, Louis XVIII, and had reinstalled himself as ruler of France by 20 March. British and Prussian forces defeated his army on 18 June 1815 at Waterloo, a battle in which Russian troops took no part. The Second Peace of Paris of November 1815 further penalized France following these events. Alexander appeared at the peace congresses as the 'saviour' and 'liberator' of Europe and assumed a leading role in the proceedings.

In general, the great powers were able to reach agreement on the territorial settlement of the West without much difficulty. France was reduced to her 1792 frontiers by the First Treaty of Paris of 30 May 1814. Buffer states contained France in the north (through a united Belgium and Holland), the east (by the Prussian acquisition of parts of the Rhineland) and the south-east (through an enlarged Piedmont-Savoy). England acquired Tobago, St Lucia, Mauritius, the Dutch Cape of Good Hope and Malta. After the battle of Waterloo, Napoleon abdicated for a second time and was exiled to the island of St Helena. France was punished for this episode in the Second Treaty of Paris on 20 November 1815 by the further reduction of her frontiers to those of 1790 (which meant the loss of the Saarland to Prussia and part of Savoy to Piedmont) and by the imposition of a large indemnity of 700 million francs. She had also to accept an army of occupation for five years (later reduced to three years).

The main source of dispute in the West arose over the new ruler and nature of the government for France. Alexander was personally hostile to Louis XVIII (when Louis had earlier appealed to Alexander he addressed him as 'Monsieur, mon Frère et Cousin'; the tsar coolly replied to 'Monsieur le Comte') but was persuaded to accept the Restoration. Although Alexander reluctantly accepted the restoration of the Bourbons, it was through his insistence that Louis returned not as an absolute monarch but as a constitutional monarch with a formal constitution or 'Charte'. It is of some interest, therefore, to note the nature of the Bourbon constitution which Alexander not only approved but was partly responsible for creating. It guaranteed equality before the law and religious toleration, and retained Napoleon's Civil Code and Concordat with the Pope. Executive power was given to the king and a bicameral assembly was established, based on a restricted franchise. This assembly had limited legislative power, with no right to initiate legislation but with the right to reject, not amend, a bill proposed by the king.

Alexander had frequently expressed his belief in constitutions, and the peace process of 1814 to 1815 gave him several opportunities to insist that they should be established in various countries other than his own. He had always shown a special interest in the fate of Switzerland, the birthplace of his tutor La Harpe. In 1814 he sent John Capodistria, a native of Corfu, to try to resolve the complexities of establishing a federal constitution for Switzerland after the departure of the French, something which he achieved despite many difficulties by the time of the peace conferences. (Alexander wrote to La Harpe in January 1814 of Capodistria that 'He comes from Corfu, and is therefore a republican; and what led me to choose him was the knowledge of his principles.')[35] Capodistria, however, was not rewarded for his labours by Alexander's support for the independence of the Ionian islands as he had hoped – these were put under British protection. The German states had looked to Alexander as their protector but the tsar, although he showed some interest in their territorial and constitutional arrangements, was mainly concerned that there should be a central European barrier to France whose creation would not cause too great disruption to existing states. He wanted, he instructed Count Karl Nesselrode, his state secretary for foreign affairs since August 1814, to 'adhere to simpler principles and unsettle things as little as possible'.[36] After many minor territorial adjustments a new German Confederation was established of thirty-eight states (there had been over 300 states before the the wars) with a Federal Diet at Frankfurt.

The settlement in the East proved to be far more contentious because of the question of Poland. The Russians had no reason to feel generous. Napoleon had hoped that the Polish and Lithuanian nobility within the Russian Empire would rally to the French cause in 1812. Although this did not happen to any significant degree, approximately 100,000 Poles from the Duchy of Warsaw had joined the invasion of Russia. Many of them envisaged a restored Poland which would include at least the lands acquired by Russia as a result of the Partitions and possibly absorb part of the Ukraine (Malorossiia). The popular perception of the behaviour of Polish troops in Russia (Russian memoirists consistently put the blame for most atrocities in western Russia on the Poles rather than the French or other nationalities in Napoleon's multinational army) further inflamed Russian public opinion against the Poles.

Alexander's statements on the Poles remained conciliatory. He had written to Czartoryski on the eve of the invasion asking when it would be most appropriate to raise the question again of restoring Poland, and he saw no reason now to change his approach. He reassured Czartoryski in January 1813 that 'vengeance is a sentiment that is unknown to me'.[37] Alexander issued a manifesto in Vil'na forgiving the Poles for their actions against him. He later released Polish prisoners of war in Russia and gave safe passage for the Polish army in France to return home. In May 1814 he wrote to the Polish rebel Tadeusz Kosciuszko (who had led the Poles in a rebellion against Catherine II in 1794 after the Second Partition of Poland) that:

> My dearest wishes have been fulfilled. With the assistance of the All-Powerful, I hope to effect the regeneration of the brave and respectable nation which you belong to . . . . A little

more time, and with a wise course, and the Poles will recover their true name and I will have the pleasure of convincing them that the man who they believed to be their enemy will, having forgotten the past, fulfil all their desires. How much it will please me, General, to have your assistance in these beneficial labours![38]

Later, in Paris, Alexander held several conversations with Kosciuszko in which he broached the possibility of returning to Poland the lands lost at the Partitions. At the same time, he held conversations with C.A. Pozzo di Borgo (a Sardinian who had been in Russian service since 1805) in which he restated his view that great injustices had been done to Poland which needed to be rectified by the restoration of the country, including the provinces incorporated into Russia (something opposed by his listener). On the other hand, he found Czartoryski's suggestion for an enlarged kingdom of Poland, to be ruled by Alexander's brother Michael, to be impractical at this stage. He also informed Czartoryski, contradicting his statements to Kosciuszko and Pozzo di Borgo, that he regarded the lands acquired by Russia as a result of the Partitions as permanent possessions. Not surprisingly, Czartoryski was left in ignorance of Alexander's true view on Poland. He commented in June 1813 at Reichenbach that it was 'impossible to discern whether he is frank or deceiving; there is ample reason for thinking the latter'.[39]

It was the issue of Poland which was to prove most contentious in the peace negotiations of 1814–15. Alexander now proposed that the whole of what had been Prussian Poland should become a new kingdom, bound dynastically to Russia through the tsar of Russia being at the same time the king of Poland. Prussia was to be compensated for the loss of her Polish territories by the acquisition of Saxony. The Austrians were not surprisingly hostile to these plans which would strengthen both Prussia and Russia. Neither they nor the British were impressed by Alexander's assertions that Poland would be independent or that Russia would return some of the territory which she had acquired at the Partitions; in their eyes the tsar's proposal simply envisaged the aggrandizement of Russia. A secret defensive agreement designed to check the Russian advance was reached on 3 January 1815 between Austria,

Britain and France, and deliberately leaked to the Russians. This forced Alexander to reach agreement with Britain and Austria, and a compromise was reached in February by which Russia ceded some of what had been the Duchy to both Prussia and Austria and Prussia received only two-fifths of Saxony. The new Congress Kingdom of Poland was 127,000 square kilometres in size with a population of 2.5 million.

The Polish constitution of 27 November 1815 bound Poland to Russia through the person of the tsar, who was also the constitutional King of Poland. Although Polish historians understandably compare this constitution unfavourably with the Polish constitution of 1791, Poland was given an elected lower house (the *Sejm*) which had to be called every two years, the rights of *habeas corpus*, freedom of religion and the press, a separate army (which could not be used outside Poland) and a promise that the Polish language should be used in all official business and that public offices would be reserved for Poles. The bicameral *Sejm* had limited powers; it had no authority to initiate legislation, and was called, prorogued and dismissed by the authority of the king, who also had the power of veto over its resolutions. Furthermore, the most important post in Poland was that of viceroy, and Alexander appointed his brother Constantine to this post. Czartoryski, who had laboured so hard for a restored Poland, was given no effective power. The electoral base in Poland, however, was wider than that of France in 1814 – between 106,000 and 116,000 Polish citizens were enfranchized compared with 80,000 French citizens in a country with over ten times Poland's population. On paper, at least, the Poles were in a more advantageous position than the Finns after 1809, whose existing 'constitution' had been confirmed but who were not given a formal written document establishing their rights. The Poles had also been given something which so far, of course, had been denied to the Russians.

Alexander's statements and actions towards Poland between 1812 and 1815 are full of contradictions (although, admittedly, no more so than his statements in 1806 or between 1807 and 1812), but it seems that he was motivated by a mixture of pragmatism and idealism. In

November 1812 he stated in a conversation with M. Oginski that 'I will re-establish Poland . . . I will do it because it accords with my conviction, with the sentiments of my heart, and also with the interests of my Empire . . . '.[40] It was certainly advantageous to Russia to extend her borders westwards and to have control over most of Poland. But Alexander had also been influenced by his friendship with Czartoryski, and by conversations with Poles such as Oginski and Kosciuszko, and had often expressed the view that a great injustice had been perpetrated by Catherine II. He was not, of course, prepared to tolerate the creation of an independent state which could pose a threat to Russia – this had been made clear after 1807 – but only a state which was subordinate to and dependent on Russia. Alexander demonstrated yet again his stubbornness by his determination to proceed with this plan against the advice of his diplomats and advisers; these feared that his actions would only increase Polish ambitions and that a constitution would be a dangerous inspiration for Russian youth.

The 1815 settlement was to be maintained, and the containment of France was to be insured, by the continuation of the Quadruple Alliance formed at Chaumont. The allies furthermore agreed to meet 'at fixed intervals'. Alexander, however, saw this alliance in more than simply pragmatic terms and wanted formally to incorporate into it his new religious convictions. In a note to the plenipotentiaries of Austria, Britain and Prussia in December 1814, he suggested the reform of the Quadruple Alliance on the new basis of 'the immutable principles of Christian religion' as the 'only foundation of the political order and of the social order with which sovereigns, making common cause, will refine their principles of state and guarantee the relations between the peoples entrusted to them by Providence'.[41] With the enthusiasm and insensitivity of the newly-converted, Alexander clearly assumed that his convictions were shared by all his allies.

The following year Alexander presented his project for a Holy Alliance to Francis I of Austria and Frederick William III of Prussia, who duly signed it on 26 September 1815. The Holy Alliance asserted that the three rulers were part of the same Christian nation and agreed to act in brotherly union taking as 'their sole guide' Christian principles; 'namely, the precepts of justice, Christian charity, and peace, which, far from being applicable only to private concerns, must have an immediate influence on the council of princes and guide all their steps . . . '. The three sovereigns pledged to act together in this spirit of fraternity and to provide mutual assistance. Alexander was a frequent nocturnal visitor at Madame Krüdener's salon at this time but the evidence suggests that the text of the alliance was his alone. It seems that he gave the text to Madame Krüdener just before he presented it to the rulers of Austria and Prussia, but it is unlikely that she made anything other than minor textual amendments. Later, she stated that 'God and the Emperor did everything . . . I approved his projects and devoted myself to the service of that great work which had been undertaken by him'.[42] By this stage, a certain coolness had entered their relationship after a member of Krüdener's group had gone into a trance in Alexander's presence supposedly to make a striking prophecy, which turned out to be a divine request for some money to establish a small group near Heilbronn.

The Holy Alliance was dismissed scathingly at the time. Castlereagh called it a 'piece of sublime mysticism and nonsense' and asserted that 'the Emperor's mind is not completely sound'. Although Metternich referred to the Alliance as a 'loud sounding nothing' he took it seriously enough to alter the wording and make it less dangerous. He took out the reference to the brotherhood of 'subjects' and the statement that the European armies were 'part of the same army summoned to protect peace and justice'. He had earlier shown equal concern about the dangerous wording of the declaration of Kalisch. Russia was the dominant continental European power in 1815 and, unlike in 1804, it was now impossible to ignore Alexander's proposals, even if they were not taken very seriously. Only the Prince Regent in Britain and the Pope refused the invitation to sign the alliance (Castlereagh was prepared to humour Alexander but the Prince Regent refused to sign, although he did send Alexander a personal letter sympathetic to its aims); the Turkish Sultan was not invited.

It has been argued by some historians that the Holy Alliance was a clever ruse by Alexander to disguise his ambitions by the use of high-minded Christian phrases (see below p. 141). But the emotional upheavals which Alexander had experienced since 1812 – his spiritual awakening, the horror of the Napoleonic invasion (he told Madame Choiseul-Gouffier that it had aged him ten years), his reading of the Scriptures and mystical works, his meetings and conversations with foreign mystics and his friendship with Golitsyn and Koshelev – all suggested that the Holy Alliance reflected his present way of thinking and was not coldly calculated. Earlier statements at Kalisch and on the Quadruple Alliance already pointed in this direction. It was also a reflection of the spirit of the time, and of contemporary writings. For example, Adam Müller's work, *Elemente der Staatskunst*, published in 1809, argued that Christianity should be the means to bind Europe in some sort of federation; and in 1814 and 1815 Alexander received memoranda from the German Catholic theologian, Franz Xavier von Baader, which posited a Christian theocracy and European union. In a more general sense, the emphasis in the Alliance on a supranational community of peoples, the 'moral situation of peoples', the image of a 'great European family' reflect the tendency, in the wake of the French Revolution, to address the 'people' as well as rulers. Alexander had already done this in his proclamation on the peoples of Germany in 1813. Metternich's suspicion of the possible implications of this approach had accounted for his hesitation in joining the Fourth Coalition and then led to his alterations to the text of the Holy Alliance.

There is also evidence that Alexander took the Alliance seriously. He ordered that it should be read out in churches throughout his empire (interestingly enough, in its original version, before Metternich's editing) not just in 1815 but on an annual basis on the anniversary of the signing of the Alliance; a practice which continued until the reign of Nicholas I. In March 1816, Alexander enthused about the Alliance in a letter to Lieven, with a confidence which was typical of his statements during this period:

> My allies and myself . . . had the intention of applying more effectively the principles of peace, of concord and of love, which are the fruit of religion and of Christian morality, to the

civil and political relationships of states . . . one cannot flatter oneself to work usefully for the well-being of the people without an absolute return to these same principles, without a solemn declaration which will serve to determine the epoch and which will submit to this constant rule the mutual relations between sovereigns and the nations with which they are entrusted.[43]

In 1822 he told Golitsyn that the Alliance had been formulated by him at the Congress of Vienna and was 'to crown his work there', but that only after Napoleon had been defeated at Waterloo was he able to 'realize the plan which I had cherished since the Congress'.[44]

This does not mean, of course, that Alexander had a clear idea about how such sentiments were going to be applied to actual problems after 1815, or indeed what relationship he envisaged Christian monarchs having with their people if the people acted against what the monarch perceived to be their best interests. It remained to be seen how Alexander would use his new authority in Europe and whether his Russian subjects would receive the benefits of the type of constitution he had given the Poles and favoured for the French.

. . .

NOTES AND REFERENCES

1. Madame la Comtesse de Choiseul-Gouffier, *Historical Memoirs of the Emperor Alexander I and the Court of Russia*, translated by Mary Berenice Patterson, London, 1904, pp. 92, 94.
2. Michael and Diana Josselson, *The Commander: A Life of Barclay de Tolly*, Oxford, 1980, p. 102.
3. Ibid., p. 122.
4. H.A. Vossler, *With Napoleon in Russia*, translated by Walter Wallich, London, 1969, pp. 51–2.
5. N.K. Shil'der, *Imperator Aleksandr I, ego zhizn' i tsarstvovanie*, 4 vols, St Petersburg, 1897, III, p. 98.
6. Grand-Duc Nicolas Mikhailowitch [Nikolai Mikhailovich], *Correspondance de l'Empereur Alexandre Ier avec sa soeur la Grande-Duchesse Catherine, Princess d'Oldenbourg, puis Reine de Würtemberg 1815–1818*, St Petersburg, 1910, pp. 76, 81.
7. Shil'der, op. cit., p. 83.
8. Choiseul-Gouffier, op. cit., p. 94.
9. Grand-Duc Nicolas Michailowitch [Nikolai Mikhailovich], *L'Empereur Alexandre Ier: Essai d'étude historique*, 2 vols, St Petersburg, 1912, I, p. 97.

10. Nicolas Mikhailowitch, *Correspondance de l'Empereur Alexandre Ier*, p. 82.
11. Philippe-Paul de Ségur, *Napoleon's Russian Campaign* translated by J.D. Townsend, London, 1959, pp. 76–7.
12. Nicolas Mikhailowitch, *Correspondance de l'Empereur Alexandre Ier*, p. 83.
13. Francis Ley, *Alexandre Ier et sa Sainte-Alliance (1811–1825) avec des documents inédits*, Paris, 1975, p. 45.
14. Nicolas Mikhailowitch, *L'Empereur Alexandre Ier*, II, p. 1.
15. De Ségur, op. cit., p. 51.
16. Armand Domergue, *La Russie pendant les guerres de l'Empire (1805–1815): Souvenirs historiques*, Paris, 1835, pp. 338–9.
17. Judith Cohen Zacek, *The Russian Bible Society, 1812–1826*, unpublished PhD thesis, Columbia University, 1964, p. 19.
18. Albert Sorel, *L'Europe et la révolution française*, 8 vols, 1st edn, Paris 1903, VII, *Le Blocus Continental – Le Grand Empire 1806–1812*, pp. 591–2.
19. Constantin de Grünwald, *La Campagne de Russie*, Paris, 1963, p. 252.
20. Shil'der, op. cit., p. 134.
21. Choiseul-Gouffier, op. cit., pp. 138, 147.
22. Sorel, op. cit., 1st edn, Paris 1904, VIII, *La Coalition, les traités de 1815. 1812–1815*, p. 56.
23. Hans A. Schmitt, '1812: Stein, Alexander I and the Crusade against Napoleon', *Journal of Modern History*, vol. 31, no. 4, 1959, p. 328.
24. Ley, op. cit., pp. 63–4.
25. Shil'der, op. cit., p. 212.
26. A.A. Lobanov-Rostovskii, *Russia and Europe, 1789–1825*, New York, 1968, p. 323.
27. Nicolas Mikhailowitch, *L'Empereur Alexandre Ier*, II, p. 7.
28. H.L. Empaytaz, *Notice sur Alexandre, Empereur de Russie*, Geneva, 1828, pp. 13, 28.
29. Wendy Hinde, *Castlereagh*, London, 1981, p. 217.
30. Ibid., p. 218.
31. *An Account of the Visit of His Royal Highness the Prince Regent and Their Imperial and Royal Majesties the Emperor of Russia and the King of Prussia to the University of Oxford in June MDCCCXIV*, Oxford, 1815, p. 57.
32. *An Account of the Visit of His Royal Highness The Prince Regent, with their Imperial and Royal Majesties the Emperor of all the Russias and the King of Prussia, to The Corporation of London, in June 1814*, London, 1815, pp. 83–5.
33. W. Allen, *Life of William Allen with Selections from his Correspondence*, 3 vols, London, 1846, I, pp. 197, 198.

34. Richenda C. Scott, *Quakers in Russia*, London, 1964, p. 56.
35. C.M. Woodhouse, *Capodistria: the Founder of Greek Independence*, London, New York, Toronto, 1973, p. 84.
36. Enno E. Kraehe, *Metternich's German Policy*, 2 vols, Princeton, New Jersey, 1983, II, *The Congress of Vienna, 1814–1815*, p. 135.
37. Nicolas Mikhailowitch, *L'Empereur Alexandre Ier*, I, p. 115.
38. Shil'der, op. cit., pp. 236–7.
39. M. Kukiel, *Czartoryski and European Unity 1770–1861*, Princeton, 1955, p. 109.
40. M. Oginski, *Mémoires de Michel Oginski sur la Pologne et les Polonais, depuis 1788 jusqu'à la fin de 1815*, 4 vols, Paris, 1827, III, p. 251.
41. Jacques-Henri Pirenne, *La Sainte-Alliance: Organisation européenne de la paix mondiale*, 2 vols, Neuchâtel, 1946, I, *Les traités de paix*, p. 165.
42. V.K. Nadler, *Imperator Aleksandr I i ideia sviashchennago soiuza*, 5 vols, Riga, 1892, V, p. 629.
43. Nicolas Mikhailowitch, *L'Empereur Alexandre Ier*, I, pp. 171–2.
44. W.P. Cresson, *The Holy Alliance: The European Background of the Monroe Doctrine*, New York, 1922, p. 29.

Chapter 7

THE MASTER OF EUROPE: 1815–1825

. . .

FROM VIENNA TO AIX-LA-CHAPELLE

The new authority of Russia, and of its ruler, in the wake of Napoleon's defeat was recognized by contemporaries. Napoleon wrote from exile in St Helena warning that '. . . within ten years all of Europe could be Cossack or all could be republican' and that 'Russia is encroaching by nature'. In 1819 the French bishop and political commentator Dufour de Pradt wrote that Russia, with her great population, would:

> . . . achieve the conquest of the world. One hundred million Russian peasants . . . present an outlook which makes one tremble. . . .

In 1828 he characterized the situation as one in which, 'England rules the sea and Russia the land: such is the real division of the world'. The American Alexander H. Everett gave a historical analysis of the growth of Russian power in 1828, concluding that the tsars:

> . . . having finally . . . raised their subjects, in point of civilization, to a level with the rest of Europe, these princes . . . now took their places, not so much in it as over it. Russia became at once not merely a leading, but in substance and effect the ruling state.[1]

Alexander was at the height of his power and confidence in the period from the Congress of Vienna to the Congress of Aix-la-Chapelle in 1818; his confidence only seriously began to wane in the early 1820s. He had already articulated grandiose views of how he thought Europe should be organized, and of Russia's leading role within this, at a time when he was in no position to affect events. Before the defeat of Napoleon, it had been possible for other statesmen to ignore or deflect such ideas. In the years after 1815, however, Alexander was at last in a position to insist on a proper response from the other powers to his proposals.

Alexander had asserted on many occasions that he sought peace. The French ambassador, Comte J. de Noailles, reported that it was difficult to 'penetrate to the essence of this sovereign's thought' but, nevertheless, his judgement on Alexander in late 1816 was that:

> I do not believe that the Emperor Alexander contemplates conquests: in conserving his enormous army he only wants to continue to play the role of the arbiter of Europe . . . .

In February of the following year he summarized his understanding of Alexander's aims as follows:

> The Emperor continues to follow with the same interest everything which concerns the cohesion and details of his army. The internal administration is also an object of particular attention. If one looks in addition to these for other things which concern his mind one must rejoice in seeing him absorbed in religious ideas. They take a greater hold on him each day and this moral disposition, happily for His Imperial Majesty in Europe, gives him a new guarantee of the fidelity of Russia to maintain her commitments and his love of peace . . .[2]

Alexander's actions, however, in the years after the Vienna settlement suggest that he wished to take a more positive role in European affairs than this statement suggests. Far from having little interest in foreign policy, he was concerned to exercise his new authority and to ensure that his views on European peace, and on the methods and institutions which he considered were best suited to achieve this, were well known and received general acceptance. Alexander was not purely altruistic or idealistic; indeed his foreign policy demonstrated that he had a clear understanding of where Russian interests lay. A shrewd assessment of Alexander's vanity but also of his determination to oblige other powers to acknowledge Russia's importance was made in a *mémoire* given to Metternich in 1818 by the Austrian ambassador in Russia: 'His [Alexander's] aim is that the peace of Europe should be the work of his hands and that Europe should recognize that the maintenance of this peace depends on him'.[3]

Although Alexander was conscious of his new strength, he had also been made painfully aware at the Congress of Vienna that the combination of Britain, Austria and his previous enemy France had isolated Russia and forced him to make concessions on Poland. He was conscious that Britain had retained a flexibility in pursuing her ambitions overseas which had been denied to the continental European powers, territorially bound as they were by the terms of the Vienna settlement. He was also aware that the Anglo-Austrian friendship could be used again within the Quadruple Alliance to thwart Russian ambitions. In the years from the Congress of Vienna to the Congress of Aix-la-Chapelle Alexander pursued several lines of policy which attempted to deal with this situation. Some historians have suggested that the Holy Alliance was a deliberate attempt by Alexander to set up an alternative to the Quadruple Alliance, in order to counter British power. There is no evidence, however, that Alexander assumed, or hoped, that Britain would not join. He had hoped that the United States would adhere to the alliance, but as this did not happen, the consequences for the balance of power in the Atlantic of drawing the United States into a general European alliance which in effect excluded Britain cannot be gauged. In fact, the Holy Alliance in the form of an alliance of almost all European states, large and small, was never invoked by Alexander against the Quadruple Alliance. In general, Alexander assumed, like other rulers and ministers of large states at the time, that decision-making should be the province of the major European powers alone.

Of more significance were the approaches that Alexander made to France after 1815. The restoration of France to her position as a great power accorded with his desire to appear as the main instrument behind the preservation of European peace and harmony. It could

141

demonstrate his magnanimity to a former enemy, his Christian forgiveness ('revenge is a sentiment unknown to me' he had declared to Czartoryski), and his personal role in restoring stability to Europe. He had frequently asserted his personal goodwill towards France and her people (he had always made it clear that his enemy was Napoleon, and not the French population) and his desire to establish good relations between the two countries. It was also important that a restored and rehabilitated France should act as a counterweight to the informal alliance of Britain and Austria against Russia. Therefore, Alexander pressed for a reduction of France's reparation payments and for the end of her military occupation. His comment in 1816 to the French ambassador, de Noailles, was pragmatic as well as appealing to the vanity of the French king who, of course, was as eager as the Russian tsar to re-establish France's position in Europe:

> The union of my country with yours can only be useful to both countries. We cannot collide with each other, we cannot have demands on each other: on shaking hands we will ensure the peace of Europe.[4]

Alexander also demonstrated how idealism could be blended with a realistic awareness of Russia's limitations in his proposals to Britain in 1816 for 'a simultaneous reduction of the armed forces of all kinds which the Powers have brought into being to preserve the safety and independence of their peoples'. He expressed the hope that Britain and Russia would 'be able to bring about in common, and by methods best adapted to the present situation and the relations of the various Powers, the reduction of armed forces of all kinds whose maintenance on a war footing weakens the credit of existing treaties and must lay a heavy burden on every people'. Europe had been left in little doubt about the strength of the Russian army in the final campaign against Napoleon. Alexander's proposals for some reduction of forces have sometimes been seen as a cynical ploy to allow him to pose as a lover of peace but in reality to reduce the strength of his potential enemies while disguising his own huge forces by keeping them in reserve in his so-called military colonies (see below pp. 179–85). Such an interpretation ignores the devastating financial consequences for Russia of the 1812 invasion and Alexander's desperate need to reduce the huge expenditure on the army. In 1816 he had pointed out to the Austrian ambassador that his troops had to be so widely distributed throughout his empire that he could put less men in the field than Prussia. In September 1816 the recruit levy was suspended for a year. In fact, the tone of these proposals was similar to that of 1804 – expressing the tsar's desire for peace but assuming, as always, that the great powers (and in particular Britain and Russia) would be the instruments for enforcing this policy. Not surprisingly, neither Britain nor Austria was enthusiastic about accepting a Russian proposal to weaken their own naval and military forces, and Alexander failed to receive a positive response to his overtures.

At Vienna Alexander had expressed approval for 'moderate and wise' constitutions which he thought would ensure the stability of Europe, and had supported the establishment of such constitutions in France, the German states and Poland. In March 1818, he opened the first session of the Polish *Sejm* in Warsaw. Alexander foresaw no conflict of interest between himself and his new Polish subjects at this date. Furthermore, he hinted that such constitutional arrangements as had been introduced into Poland could also be made available to his Russian subjects (see below pp. 166–8). He certainly did not expect that this would lead to a political challenge to his power. When the *Sejm* dared to complain about illegalities in the Kingdom's administration, his cold response to what he regarded as the impertinence of the deputies was that:

> According to article 154 of the constitution the Sejm does not have the right to indict the government or to make re-proaches to it; it must deliver its views only on those matters which the government communicates to it.[5]

Nevertheless, Alexander approached the Congress of Aix-la-Chapelle in 1818, shortly after his Warsaw speech, still confident about the future of Europe and still believing that moderate constitutional reform was beneficial to the preservation of peace and stability. He used the Congress to assert his views in general about European organization and, more specifically, to put into effect his plans to rehabilitate France as a great power. He proposed replacing the Quadruple Alliance with a new five-power alliance which would include France. Alexander naturally disclaimed any self-interest in such a proposal. Instead it was projected typically as a move which would benefit all Europe. As Capodistria reported, Alexander, with customary modesty, promoted this policy 'not for myself, nor for Russia, but in the interest of the entire universe'.[6] The proposal was presented in support of the principle of legitimacy in that France, as a restored monarchical regime (Alexander referred to the French monarchy as 'légitime et constitutionelle'), would contribute to the monarchical solidarity of the great powers, and thus to the stability of Europe, something which Austria, in particular, would find hard to oppose. Alexander was also aware, of course, that France could provide a useful counterweight to the combination of Britain and Austria within the present four-power alliance. He further argued that the departure of allied troops from France would help ensure peace. The tsar also tried unsuccessfully to have Spain admitted to the Congress, which would have had the effect of diluting the four-power alliance further.

Alexander attempted, moreover, to change the whole nature of the Quadruple Alliance so that it accorded more with the principles he had expressed in the Holy Alliance. He wanted it to establish the precise obligations of the allies and to be formally institutionalized as the structure which would guarantee the European order. He suggested, for example, that the powers should reach agreement over what constituted circumstances requiring the powers to put into effect their treaty obligations, on the military measures which the allies could take and on the frequency of congresses and the participation of other states in them. He made his own views about the obligations of the allies clear:

> . . . it is necessary that the principle of the general coalition should be established and developed by regulations for all contingencies. It is necessary, in the second place, that the coalition should be able to act and that the four courts should be able to count on the unanimous co-operation of all the states in Europe should the occasion arise.[7]

This was Alexander at the zenith of his power – confident that he could not only gain a practical advantage for Russia by admitting France to the alliance, but daring to mould the alliance to accord with his own views and sentiments about European organization. Not surprisingly, his broader aims were met with suspicion and hostility by the other powers. Alexander's attempt to establish some general guarantee ('les garanties morales' in his words) of the European settlement, which would include signatories from countries other than the four victors, was resisted. Neither Metternich nor Castlereagh wanted to commit themselves to defend the constitutions of individual states. Nor, understandably, was his proposal for a maritime league or an international army greeted with any great enthusiasm by Britain. There was little sympathy for the proposals of 'ce terrible Empereur Alexandre' from Metternich either. He complained to the Emperor Francis in August 1818, before the Congress opened, that:

> . . . the emperor Alexander and his cabinet let themselves go further and further in the desire to practise moral and political proselytism. Hence all intrigues, small and large, which baffle us, us and so to speak all governments; hence a storm-cloud of emissaries and apostles . . . .[8]

Alexander's views, however, could not now be ignored completely. The final outcome of the Congress of Aix-la-Chapelle was a compromise, both in the treatment of France and in the response to Alexander's more ambitious proposals. Russian support ensured that the army of occupation was withdrawn and the question of French reparations was settled. Although France was readmitted to the congresses as a great power, to Alexander's satisfaction, the Quadruple Alliance was renewed at the same time, thus reasserting the commitment of the allies to uphold the settlement of 1815 and thereby ensuring the continuation of restrictions on French ambitions. Although the other powers resisted Alexander's attempts to introduce a general guarantee and to broaden the scope of the alliance, he did win a partial victory in that the very language of the Aix-la-Chapelle protocol affirmed at least the spirit of the Holy Alliance:

They [sovereigns] formally recognize that their duties to God and to the people whom they govern prescribe them to give to the world, as much as possible, the example of justice, of harmony and of moderation: happy to be able to devote henceforth all their efforts towards protecting the arts of peace, to augment the internal prosperity of their states and to revive the sentiments of religion and of morality which the evils of the age have so diminished.[9]

This emphasized that the great powers accepted some community of interests and went some way towards establishing the principle of collective action.

Alexander had even managed to impress the astute and normally cynical Friedrich von Gentz, Metternich's aide, with the sincerity of his desire for peace and his concern for Europe which went beyond Russia's own particular interests:

. . . he [Alexander] considered the very thought of a rupture of the Quadruple Alliance as a crime and a betrayal of Europe; that he wanted to maintain the peace, observe treaties and support the political system which the great powers had adopted and followed for three years. These declarations, made with the expression of the very noblest enthusiasm for the general good, for religion, for morality, for everything which is the most elevated in the actions of men, produced the most immediate and strongest impression. The doubts and the fears died away . . . . Throughout the congress he [Alexander] was distinguished by his wisdom, his conscience and his moderation. His august person was the centre of the Congress of Aix-la-Chapelle: he was the instigator, the inspiration, the hero.[10]

This from the man who three years earlier had scathingly referred to the Holy Alliance as 'a monument to the eccentricity of men and princes in the diplomatic code of the nineteenth century'.[11]

Alexander was in no mood in 1818 to be modest about his achievements. When he wrote to Count Christoph Lieven, his ambassador in London, from Aix-la-Chapelle on 21 November, he claimed that:

The meeting of Aix-la-Chapelle whose labours are coming to an end is a decisive epoch for the endurance and the stability of the European system. The results which it has produced characterize the second period of this grand political era, which started from the moment when the sovereigns became brothers for the cause of religion and of good order, of justice and of humanity . . . .[12]

In an audience with Thomas Clarkson, the English Quaker who was campaigning against the slave trade, Alexander expressed his commitment to peace, reportedly saying '. . . *I am sure* (laying his hand upon his heart) that *the Spirit of Christianity is decisive against War*' and his belief that peace was now assured in Europe:

> At Present he could see nothing in Europe that was likely for years to come to be productive of War . . . . He had looked here and there and everywhere as far as he could for Causes for War, but could not find any. It was his intention as the different Sovereigns were now well acquainted with each other to propose a meeting every three years among themselves during which they might talk over the affairs of Europe *entirely* with the *view* of *preventing future Wars,* and he hoped if his Plan were acceded to, that such an Effect would be produced.[13]

. . .

REVOLTS AND CONGRESSES IN THE EARLY 1820s

Within two years, Alexander's confidence was shown to have been sadly misplaced. In March 1819 August Kotzebue, a German dramatist whose work Alexander admired and who had long worked for the Russian intelligence service, was murdered in Mannheim by a student. Metternich used this as the pretext to introduce the repressive Carlsbad Decrees in the summer, to root out what he saw as subversion in German universities and to increase press censorship. The Carlsbad measures at the same time served to challenge the influence of Alexander as the self-styled protector of the constitutions of the German states which were established in 1815. The first half of 1820 saw the outbreak of revolts in the Iberian and Italian peninsulas. In March King Ferdinand VII of Spain was forced to restore the liberal constitution of 1812. Revolt broke out in Naples in July and was of particular concern to Metternich as it threatened the stability of Austria's Italian provinces and the dominant position in the peninsula which she had acquired in 1815.

Metternich had already warned Alexander of the threat of revolution at Aix-la-Chapelle. He was now keen to make use of the tsar's high-minded statements about the great powers' community of interests, which he had expressed in 1818, to appeal to this unity for support in suppressing revolution. Austria had relied on British support to restrict Russian ambitions in 1815, but when Castlereagh made it clear that Britain had no intention of letting the Quadruple Alliance be used to suppress revolution, Metternich was forced to turn to Russia for help. Although Metternich could appeal to Alexander's own sentiments about collective action by the great powers, his purpose was to manipulate the sentiments expressed by the tsar at Aix-la-Chapelle in two important respects. First, he needed to establish the principle not of collective action by the great powers against smaller states but of collective *approval* by the powers for Austria's unilateral action in an area which threatened her. Second, he needed to convince Alexander (who had publicly favoured moderate constitutions, at least outside Russia) that such constitutional demands, in particular in Naples, were in themselves subversive and a threat to the European order. This required Alexander to appreciate that Europe indeed faced a revolutionary threat, and Metternich applied himself with vigour to convincing the tsar of this fact.

Alexander was by now much more susceptible to Metternich's arguments. He was shocked by the assassination of Kotzebue and had begun to suspect that revolutionary ideas were once again emanating from France. As a result his friendship for France cooled, as did his belief that the 'wise constitution' in France guaranteed stability. The French ambassador, Auguste de La Ferronays, noted that events abroad had brought about a change in Alexander's attitude as early as February 1820 (that is, before the granting of constitutions to Spain and Naples). This resulted in a shift away from the tsar's desire, expressed at the opening of the Polish *Sejm*, to extend constitutions to Russia:

> . . . what has happened in Germany, the perpetual state of fermentation which is assumed to exist in France, the excessive abuses of the freedom of the press, all this has succeeded in considerably diminishing his taste for liberal

ideas and in persuading the Emperor to delay indefinitely all the projects which one credited to him and which the aim had to be to give up a part of his power.[14]

Alexander's growing disillusionment with constitutional government was increased by the behaviour of the deputies in the second Polish *Sejm*, which met in September 1820. The deputies, and in particular the Niemojowski brothers, far from being grateful to Alexander for graciously granting them a constitution, dared to challenge the government in his presence. The *Sejm* had the temerity to reject government proposals to extend the prerogatives of the public prosecutor, to introduce closed court hearings and also a statute for the Senate. The Niemojowskis specifically attacked what they regarded as the government's unconstitutional behaviour. When Novosil'tsev made Alexander's position on the constitution absolutely clear with the blunt words 'You will bear in mind gentlemen, that you have been granted the constitution and that it is possible to take it away from you', W. Niemojowski replied: 'Then we will become revolutionaries'. This was hardly likely to endear his Polish subjects to Alexander. His speech which closed this turbulent meeting was very different in tone from his opening address in 1818 and contained a distinct threat that it was the duty of governments to eradicate any revolutionary disorder in the state. He ordered the deputies to:

> Interrogate your consciences, and you may know if in the course of your discussions, you have accorded to Poland all the services that she expects of your wisdom, or if, to the contrary, carried away by the seductions so common to our days and giving up a hope that would have been realized by a foresighted confidence, you have not retarded in its progress the work of the restoration of your fatherland.[15]

It was in this atmosphere, so different from two years before, that the great powers met again. The question of the right to intervene to suppress revolutions was central to the Congresses of Troppau (October to December 1820), Laibach (January to May 1821) and Verona (October to December 1822). Alexander presented two proposals to the

Congress of Troppau, both drawn up by Capodistria, who shared responsibility for foreign affairs at this time with Nesselrode. The first one asserted the general principle that all five powers had the right to intervene in the internal affairs of all states. This displeased the British and served to heighten their disagreement with Austria. It was in Alexander's interests to undermine Anglo-Austrian friendship, but it was in keeping with his statements at Aix-la-Chapelle to assume that there was a common interest shared by the great powers. His second proposal was to tolerate internal reforms within small states provided the five powers assented to these changes. This, of course, was quite unacceptable to Metternich. Alexander, however, was not being entirely disingenuous as he only gradually abandoned his belief that moderate constitutions could serve a useful purpose in ensuring stability. His first reaction on hearing of the revolt in Madrid was to advise Ferdinand VII to accept the constitution proposed by the rebels. This was the Spanish constitution of 1812, a radical constitution based on the French constitution of 1791, but one which Alexander had recognized in 1812 at the height of the conflict with Napoleon. Even when Alexander rapidly came to see that such a policy was impracticable, he favoured the establishment of 'un régime sagement constitutionel' rather than the rejection of a constitution out of hand. He also initially supported Capodistria's proposal that Naples should have a 'national constitution'. Metternich, however, had no intention of making any concessions in Naples and moved to secure Russia's support for the first proposal at the cost of sacrificing his relationship with Britain, on the understanding that Austria alone had the obligation to intervene in the Italian peninsula. The British were opposed to accepting a general right of intervention and the French were not willing to abandon their own interests in Italy by giving support to unilateral action by Austria.

Metternich steadily worked on Alexander in private tea-drinking sessions to convince him of the spread of secret societies which undermined the social and political order. When in November Alexander learnt of the so-called mutiny which had taken place the previous month in the prestigious Semenovsky Guards (see below p. 216) he was therefore easily persuaded that this was a symptom of a Europe-wide revolutionary conspiracy. Metternich commented that Alexander 'came to the point where he believed that only the radicals could have perpetuated this disturbance in order to intimidate him and compel him to return to St Petersburg'.[16] In a letter to Princess Sofiia Meshcherskaia on 4 November, Alexander suggested that the allies were confronting the power of the devil:

> We are occupied here with a most important but a most difficult task. It concerns producing a remedy against the empire of evil which is spreading with swiftness and by all the occult means used by the satanic genius which directs it . . . . The Saviour alone through his Divine word can furnish the means.[17]

The consequence of Alexander's extreme anxiety was that he joined the rulers of Austria and Prussia in signing the Protocol of Troppau on 19 November 1820, which asserted the right of the alliance to intervene in any state which had suffered an 'illegal' change in government, in order to protect the ruler from disorder. This gave Austria a free hand to intervene in Naples (the Austrian army was to be accompanied by representatives from the other allied powers) but it also exposed the divisions between the great powers. The refusal of Britain and France to accede to the Protocol effectively discredited Alexander's assumption that there was a community of interest between the allies. The split also heralded a new alignment of the powers; the informal Austrian-British and Franco-Russian friendship was replaced by an alliance between the three eastern powers and the isolation of Britain and France.

The congress moved from Troppau to Laibach (Ljubljana in present-day Slovenia) at the beginning of January 1821. The next month revolts broke out in Piedmont and, still shaken by the Semenovsky revolt, Alexander wrote to Golitsyn about the 'enemy' which threatened Christian religion. The pupil of La Harpe added that 'In a word, this is only the putting into practice of the doctrines preached by Voltaire, Mirabeau, Condorcet and by all the bogus *philosophes* known under the name of Encyclopedists'.[18] Certainly the perception elsewhere was that Alexander had now radically changed his attitude.

Thomas Jefferson, the President of the United States, wrote to his ambassador in St Petersburg, Levett Harris, in 1821 that:

> I am afraid our quondam favourite Alexander has swerved from the true faith. His becoming an accomplice of the soi–disant Holy Alliance, the anti-national principles he has separately avowed, and his becoming the very leader of a combination to chain mankind down eternally to oppressions of the most barbarous ages, are clouds on his character not easily to be cleared away.[19]

Nevertheless, Alexander could still advocate the establishment of constitutions, although he now suggested that perhaps not all nations were equally suited to enjoy such benefits. He commented to the French ambassador La Ferronays on events in the Iberian and Italian peninsulas that:

> I love constitutional institutions and think that every decent man should love them, but can they be introduced indiscriminately for all peoples? Not all peoples are ready to the same degree for their acceptance. Of course, freedom and law which can be enjoyed by an enlightened nation such as yours does not suit other ignorant peoples of both peninsulas.[20]

Alexander had rarely made his views on constitutions so clear; his current perception of the readiness, or otherwise, of countries to receive these benefits had implications not only for his reaction to constitutional change abroad but also for developments within Russia.

. . .

THE GREEK QUESTION

At the beginning of March 1821, a more immediate threat to Russian interests occurred when Alexander Ypsilantis, a Greek with a commission in the Russian army, raised a revolt against the Turks in the Principalities of Moldavia and Wallachia. Even before this incident, Alexander had had to balance his irritation with the dilatoriness of the Turks in implementing the terms of the Treaty of Bucharest (1812) with his other foreign policy aims. The Russians accused the Turks of failing to implement the conditions which would ensure the full autonomy of the Principalities and of not renouncing their claims to territory in the Caucasus. But until 1821, Near East concerns had been subordinated to his more general European concerns; in 1817 Count G.A. Stroganov, the Russian ambassador to Constantinople, was ordered not to let disputes over the Bucharest treaty lead to war because Alexander 'subordinated the success of the negotiation in Constantinople to the general good of the European alliance'.[21] Alexander would have liked to use the Congress of Aix-la-Chapelle to establish a general European guarantee of the Russo-Turkish settlement, but sacrificed this aim in favour of propping up the alliance with the Western powers. Negotiations between Russia and the Ottoman Empire continued without success through 1819 and 1820, with the Russians holding to their insistence that the Treaty of Bucharest should be the basis for discussion. On the eve of the Greek revolt, therefore, tension was already high.

Ypsilantis made the situation more difficult for Alexander by directly appealing to him as protector of the Greek Orthodox faith ('. . . Sauvez nous, Sire; sauvez la réligion de ses persécuteurs'). Alexander, however, remained true to Metternich's position on rebels which he had adopted at Troppau, and informed Ypsilantis that he could never approve of the attempt to win liberty by armed force. If Ypsilantis had genuinely hoped to receive Alexander's approval then his revolt was untimely, to put it mildly. In an almost hysterical outburst to his friend Golitsyn, Alexander made his abhorrence of rebellion at this time clear:

> There is no doubt *that the stimulus behind this insurrectional movement could only have been given by the same central committee directed from Paris*, with the intention of making a diversion to help Naples and to hinder us from destroying one *of the synagogues of Satan, established solely to spread and extend his anti-Christian doctrine.*

The secret societies, he added, aimed to '*paralyse the results of the Christian principles professed in the Holy Alliance*'.[22] Alexander was convinced by now that revolts were part of a Europe-wide plot emanating from France. As he told the

Quaker William Allen:

> . . . this rebellion against the Turks was organized at Paris, by the revolutionists, who wished, above all things, for a war, and to make the Greeks the means of embroiling the Powers of Europe . . . .[23]

Metternich was concerned that Alexander should maintain his opposition to rebellion against legitimate authority, which he had secured at Troppau, but was also determined that Russia should not be permitted to intervene single-handedly in the Balkans, in the way that Austria had been allowed in the Italian peninsula. He took the line that Ypsilantis's revolt should be dealt with entirely by the collective policy of the great powers, an approach which, of course, he had rejected in 1820 for Austria. Just as he had attempted to restrain Russian advances into central Europe in 1815, he now intended to restrict Russian expansion in the Balkans. Britain shared Austrian fears of Russian advancement in this area, and both countries feared that Russian intervention in the Balkans would give France the justification she sought to intervene militarily to put down the revolt in Spain. The Anglo-Austrian *entente*, so recently breached, formed again in opposition to the Protocol of Troppau being applied by France and Russia in the way it had been applied by Austria. At the Congress of Laibach (January to May 1821), the Austrians and the Russians reached an understanding to regard the Greeks as rebels, but this did not extend to helping the Turks to crush the revolt.

Ypsilantis's revolt had no chance of success without Russian support; on 7 June his forces were defeated and he took refuge in Austrian territory; in consequence, he spent the next seven years in an Austrian prison. In the meantime, a second rising had taken place in the Morea peninsula which rapidly spread to the Greek islands and soon threatened Turkish control of the whole area. Turkish policy towards the rebels now became a matter of direct concern to the Russians. Russia had treaty rights to protect co-religionists and Turkish desperation led to savage attacks on Greek Christians – in April, the Greek Patriarch Gregory was hanged in Constantinople and in the following year over 20,000 Greeks were murdered on the island of Chios. Much sympathy was expressed at the court in St Petersburg and among army officers for the Greek cause. Capodistria, a native of Corfu and still one of Alexander's most influential advisers, not surprisingly urged action against the Turks on behalf of the Greeks. Attacks on Russian shipping in the Black Sea, and consequent damage to the Russian grain trade (the value of goods exported by sea from Odessa fell from 4,739,000 silver roubles in 1820 to 3,745,000 silver roubles in 1822), further exacerbated relations between the two countries.

The problem for Alexander, however, was that the legitimate authority which was being challenged was the Ottoman government. In the summer of 1821 he briefly considered the possibility of Russian unilateral military action against the Turks. He also approached France with tentative proposals for an alliance which would result in the partition of European Turkey. But at the same time he was assuring La Ferronnays that 'I have not and can never have any ambition other than to preserve and maintain peace: this is my most beautiful title, the one for which I would sacrifice all manner of glory'.[24] By the late summer Alexander had decisively resolved against unilateral action and determined to seek collective action ('it is a very complicated affair and, I repeat, Europe will not extricate herself except by remaining united' he commented to La Ferronays).[25] This signalled the failure of Capodistria's influence at court; he remarked with some bitterness that Alexander had sacrificed Russian interests for the sake of strengthening the European alliance.

In reality, however, Alexander was never in a desperate dilemma over this issue. He had never shown any great personal devotion to the cause of fellow Orthodox Christians in the Balkans or, for that matter, any great interest or sympathy for the Orthodox religion in Russia. At the time he was closely involved with the work of the Protestant Bible Society in Russia and expressing his own sympathies with Quakerism. Nor was he eager at this stage to become involved in another military campaign, particularly without support from other countries. The Napoleonic Wars had been costly in manpower and Russia had been financially crippled by the additional military expenditure and the effect of the 1812 invasion. Although it had been many years since the Ottoman Empire had been able to inflict defeat on the Russian forces, she had been a stubborn opponent and it had proved difficult for either Catherine II or Alexander to translate military success in the field into territorial gains. Furthermore the tsar was not prepared to jeopardize his position with the other powers, or to compromise the stand on the importance of collective action which he had been asserting since the Congress of Vienna. Therefore, on both pragmatic grounds and on principle, he sought a peaceful and collective solution to the Eastern crisis, and only at the very end of his reign did he show signs of deviating from this course. Alexander showed more consistency in his principles on the subject of revolts and held a more genuinely 'European' view about the obligations of the great powers in these circumstances than Metternich, whose attitude was always determined by the particular interests of Austria.

The Congress of Verona (October to December 1822) was preoccupied with the consequences of the Spanish revolt of 1820. Alexander, with the Greek issue in mind, supported the principle of collective action and offered to send 150,000 troops to assist the French in suppressing the revolt. His generous offer was not surprisingly greeted with little enthusiasm either by Metternich or the French. Alexander, of course, had throughout his reign expressed his views on developments in European states which had little strategic significance to Russia, but now he not only had the physical means to intervene directly in other countries but could also justify such action on the grounds of the general principles established at Troppau. The other powers had no desire to see Russian troops cross Europe yet again but Metternich's negative response exposed his contradictory position of supporting armed suppression of revolts when they threatened Austria but opposing both unilateral and collective military action by the powers in Greece and Spain. Metternich tried to maintain the semblance of great power unity by suggesting that all the powers should simultaneously send notes protesting to the constitutional government in Spain (Ferdinand VII had accepted the constitution) that it should restore absolutism. But he was not able to gain the co-operation of Britain, and when in April 1823 the French sent an army of 100,000 men into Spain to crush the revolt there was nothing the Austrians or the British could do to prevent it. The Congress System effectively came to an end at this step.

Little progress was made at Verona on the Greek question. In August 1822 diplomatic relations between Russia and the Ottoman Empire had been broken off and the task of presenting Russian demands to the Turks lay with the British ambassador, Viscount Strangford, who was pro-Turkish. He presented the Sultan with three Russian demands which were not opposed by the other powers: guarantees of future good government in Greece; reduction of Turkish forces in the Principalities; and re-establishment of the freedom of shipping in the Black Sea. By the end of September, Strangford had obtained satisfaction on the third demand. The other powers accepted that Russia had some rights of protection over co-religionists in the Balkans. This was of limited value to Alexander, but his statement at the Congress to François René, Vicomte de Chateaubriand (the French foreign minister), was not only a re-expression of his principles on collective action but also an attempt to reassure the other powers that Russia had no ambitions for herself in this area:

> It is not possible anymore to have an English, French, Russian, Prussian or Austrian policy; there is only one general policy, which must, for the good of all, be accepted in common by both peoples and rulers. It is I who proved to be the first to be convinced of the principles on which I founded the alliance . . . What need have I of augmenting my empire? Providence has not given me eight hundred thousand soldiers in my command to satisfy my ambitions, but to protect religion, morality and justice and to ensure the reign of the principles of order on which human society rests.[26]

Despite Alexander's rhetoric and diplomatic activity, negotiations with the Turks stagnated. Castlereagh had committed suicide in August 1822 and in March 1823 his successor as Foreign Minister, George Canning, recognized the Greeks as belligerents. This was provocative to both Austria and Russia. In January 1824 a Russian plan proposed the creation of three autonomous principalities in Greece with a status similar to that enjoyed by the Principalities of Moldavia and Wallachia. Alexander's grandiose assumptions about the aims and achievements of the alliance in settling the Greek question were expressed with that lack of modesty which typified his statements after 1815:

> To assure the rights of humanity without the shedding of blood, to lay down rules for long-term relations . . . , to paralyse the influence of revolutionaries in all of Greece; to complete and consolidate the peace of the world: such has been the work of the alliance, and its glory could have been one of the most useful and most beautiful that divine Providence could have given to monarchs and their governments.[27]

Ungenerously, the British failed to appreciate the potential benefits to mankind and the glory which would accrue to the allies if Alexander's plan were accepted (Canning commented that 'when a plan consists of many and complicated parts, it is absolutely foolish and of very little help'),[28] and instead feared that it would give Russia too much power in Greece. Canning, therefore, opposed the proposal, and in this he was backed by Austria.

The subsequent conference of powers at St Petersburg in June 1824 only lasted for two meetings as neither the Greeks nor the Turks were prepared to accept the proposal for autonomous principalities; the Greeks because it offered too little and the Turks because it offered too much. The attitude of the British and the Austrians made even Alexander aware of the shortcomings of collective policy, although he still adhered publicly to his principles. He commented to La Ferronays that '. . . I have proved again that I do not wish to act except in agreement with my allies . . . I would not take up arms except with all my allies, or at least I would not act except in agreement with them'.[29] Canning sarcastically commented on Alexander's generosity of spirit that 'The Emperor would have no objection to help us in Ireland, so general and purely philanthropic are his principles of occasional intervention with unruly subjects, whether of his friends or neighbours'. The breach with Britain could not be healed, and Canning recalled his ambassador, Sir Charles Bagot, from St Petersburg. Alexander made it clear that he was annoyed by the British attitude. Canning wrote on January 17 1825 that:

> The Emperor of Russia seems to be in a passion. . . . For the present he contents himself with directing Count Lieven to send to me a despatch, the amount of which seems to be that 'he will be d – d if he ever talks Greek to us again'.[30]

The second St Petersburg Conference in 1825 took place without British representation. The conference failed to agree on any action. France and Austria opposed any type of intervention, either collective or unilateral. Metternich tried to produce a stalemate by suggesting the recognition of Greek independence, which he knew Alexander would be reluctant to do. Alexander achieved limited success with a protocol in April, which established that collective intervention would follow if the Ottoman Empire refused to make concessions. But Metternich's reluctance to commit himself to any type of military intervention made this meaningless. By the end of the conference Alexander was beginning to abandon his support for the principle of collective action, which he had maintained since the outbreak of Ypsilantis's revolt, disillusioned with the actions of his allies, and in particular furious with Metternich for his lack of co-operation.

Canning hoped to exploit the deadlock over Greece to realign the great powers, and in particular to encourage Alexander to break with Austria. He used the services of Countess Dorothea Lieven (wife of the Russian ambassador in London and, since 1818, mistress of Metternich), who travelled to St Petersburg and became an unofficial intermediary between himself and Nesselrode (Nesselrode had had sole responsibility for foreign affairs since the fall of Capodistria in the summer of 1822). On the eve of her departure from St Petersburg for England, at the end of August, Lieven was received by Nesselrode, who told her about a conversation which he had held with Alexander the evening before. The tsar had expressed the view that:

> The Turkish power is crumbling; the agony is more or less long, but it is stricken with death. I am still here, armed with all my power, but strong in my known principles of moderation and disinterestedness. How will it not profit me,

with my aversion from any project of conquest to reach a solution of the question which is incessantly disturbing Europe? . . . My people demand war; my armies are full of ardour to make it, perhaps I could not long resist them. My Allies have abandoned me. Compare my conduct to theirs. Everyone has intrigued in Greece. I alone have remained pure. I have pushed scruples so far as not to have a single wretched agent in Greece, not an intelligence agent even, and I have to be content with the scraps that fall from the table of my Allies. Let England think of that. If they grasp hands [with us] we are sure of controlling events and of establishing in the East an order of things conformable to the interest of Europe and to the laws of religion and humanity. That should be the foundation of the instruction to Madame Lieven.[31]

Alexander had made a spirited, if rather petulant, defence of his own innocence and disinterest and had roundly accused his allies of perfidious behaviour; but he was also still speaking of his intention to act for the European good through the actions of the great powers. Collective action having proved impossible, he now turned back to Britain, as he had done in 1804, as the power which should most appropriately act together with Russia to maintain the well-being of Europe.

By this stage, however, Alexander seems also to have been seriously contemplating armed action against the Turks in the following spring if they refused to retreat from the Principalities. As Alexander left St Petersburg for what was to be his last journey south to the Crimea in September 1825, his armies began to concentrate on the borders of Moldavia and Wallachia. It was only Alexander's death in Taganrog in December which postponed further action.

. . .

ALEXANDER AND RUSSIAN TRADE

Alexander's awareness of Russia's interests and her new strength after 1815 was also shown in his commercial policies with other European countries after 1815, and, in particular, with Britain. Alexander never demonstrated great interest in, or understanding of, economic affairs, but he had been made aware after 1807 of the unpopularity of the Continental System which he had been forced to join at Tilsit. The System, of course, had been intended to ruin

British trade and after the failure of the French invasion of Russia the British merchants had naturally hoped that their trading privileges would be fully restored. But although trade formally resumed between the two countries in 1811, Alexander made no move to abolish the duties on British goods or to overturn the obligation imposed on British merchants in 1807 to join Russian guilds and pay the same taxes as Russian merchants. In 1816, he passed a new tariff law which removed some prohibitions on imports and lowered duties on a variety of goods, but in practice protective duties remained and free trade was never fully established. In the same year measures were taken to try to restrict smuggling of goods through Finland. Alexander's shift in policy was made in response to pressure from other powers at the Congress of Vienna (in particular, Prussia) rather than on any philosophical basis, although the free traders within Russia celebrated the less restrictive tariff as a victory for the views of Adam Smith. A moderate tariff was introduced in the following year for goods from Asia, where, of course, Russia faced little direct competition.

The designation of Odessa as a free port in 1818 and a new schedule of lower tariffs in 1819 led to a great increase in imports, from 155,454,992 roubles in 1819 to 227,349,564 roubles in value in 1820. Alexander responded by raising tariffs in decrees of 1822 and 1824, showing his essentially pragmatic approach to this issue. The 1822 tariff coincided with warnings that the tax on spirits (regulated by a new code in 1817) was not yielding as much revenue as had been expected. Alexander's tariff policy showed an awareness of the needs of Russian industry; British printed cottons were heavily taxed to protect the domestic textile industry, while cotton twist and unprinted calicoes were admitted without duty so that they could be used in Russian factories. He also showed, in his refusal to respond to complaints by British merchants, that he was no longer prepared to accept a subordinate role for Russia in trading relations with Britain. He believed that Russia should be acknowledged as an equal in economic matters in the same way as the great powers now had to recognize her importance in diplomatic matters.

In contrast, the trading activities of the Russian-American Company on the west coast of North America were never of paramount interest to Alexander, and were subordinated to the establishment of good relations with the government of the United States. In 1818–19 Alexander declined to support the proposal by the Russian-American Company to annex Hawaii. In 1821, in response to pressure from the Company, Alexander declared that the Alaskan territory north of the 51st parallel was 'exclusively' Russian and that foreigners were prohibited from trading there. He also claimed exclusive use of the waters within a hundred miles of the coast and the right to confiscate the cargoes of foreign ships. He was nevertheless sensitive to the reaction of the government of the United States, and its outraged response to these claims meant that this decree was never implemented. In 1824 a negotiated settlement was reached which opened Russian possessions to American traders and fishermen for a ten-year period. The complaints by the Russian-American Company that this violated its privileges and was a threat not only to its welfare but to its very existence went unheeded. Alexander made it plain that he did not welcome initiatives by the Company which could harm relations with the United States. In 1825, the Company proposed establishing another settlement along the Copper River. Alexander responded by calling the directors of the Company 'to strictest account for the impropriety of the proposal itself and to indicate that they must unfailingly abide by the decisions and plans of the government without going beyond the boundaries of the merchant estate'.[32] The merchants had received a dressing-down for their impertinence which mirrored that handed out to the senators who had tried to assert a degree of initiative in 1803 and the deputies of the Polish *Sejm* who dared to challenge his authority in 1820.

A mood of depression had overtaken Alexander by the time the powers met in Verona in 1822. By this stage his confidence in the stability of Europe following the defeat of Napoleon had been shattered by revolts in Europe and disturbances at home. It had become clear that the threat of revolution had not been eliminated by the victory of the allies and that the great powers faced further challenges. The differences between the allies and the incompatibility of their interests were exposed by the revolts in the Italian and Iberian peninsulas and in the Balkans. Nevertheless, Alexander persisted in seeking a collective solution, with the co-operation of all the great powers, to the Greek revolt until almost the very end of his reign. There were pragmatic reasons for his stand, but Alexander was not motivated purely by military or financial considerations. He genuinely believed in the right, and indeed the obligation, of the great powers to determine collectively the fate of smaller powers in order to benefit all Europe. It was a paternalistic view, but not essentially at odds with the generally accepted assumptions of rulers and statesmen about the relationships between strong and weak nations.

Alexander, of course, envisaged that Russia would play a leading, if not *the* leading, role in determining the new European order. This had been clear in his proposals to Pitt in 1804. In the period from the Congress of Vienna to the Congress of Aix-la-Chapelle such a role for Russia, now coloured by the sentiments expressed in the Holy Alliance, had seemed feasible within the context of Congress diplomacy and had generally, if reluctantly, been accepted by the other powers. The revolts of the early 1820s shook Alexander's faith in the stability of the new Europe he had helped to create; the response of his allies to his attempts to solve the Greek crisis eventually shook his faith in the ability of the great powers to act collectively for the good of all Europe. But his approaches to Britain at the very end of his reign demonstrate that he had not changed his vision of Russia's role in European affairs. Although he was now turning away from the idea of collective action he still wanted to act with another power to settle the Greek crisis with the same broad and ambitious aim of conforming with 'the interests of Europe and to the laws of religion, and humanity'. The military strength which Russia had shown she possessed by defeating Napoleon meant that by the time of Alexander's death no-one could doubt that Russia had the ability and the right to play an important part in all aspects of diplomatic decision-making. In this respect, Russia's position as a European great power had been transformed during Alexander's reign.

NOTES AND REFERENCES

1. Dieter Groh, *Russland und das Selbstverständnis Europas: Ein Beitrag zur europäischen Geistesgeschichte*, Neuwied, 1961, pp. 125, 126, 130, 136.
2. Grand-Duc Nicolas Mikhailowitch [Nikolai Mikhailovich], *L'Empereur Alexandre Ier: Essai d'étude historique*, 2 vols, St Petersburg, 1912, II, pp. 250, 259.
3. Jacques-Henri Pirenne, *La Sainte-Alliance: Organisation européenne de la paix mondiale*, 2 vols, Neuchâtel, 1949, II, *La rivalité Anglo-Russe et le compromis autrichien 1815–1818*, p. 391.
4. Ibid., p. 257.
5. Frank W. Thackeray, *Antecedents of Revolution: Alexander I and the Polish Kingdom, 1815–1825*, New York, 1980, pp. 52–3.
6. W.P. Cresson, *The Holy Alliance: The European Background of the Monroe Doctrine*, New York, 1922, p. 70.
7. Maurice Bourquin, *Histoire de la Sainte Alliance*, Geneva, 1954, p. 231.
8. Francis Ley, *Alexandre Ier et sa Sainte Alliance (1811–1825)*, Paris, 1975, p. 215.
9 Pirenne, op. cit., p. 379.
10. Nicolas Mikhailowitch, op. cit., I, pp. 201–2.
11. P.K. Grimsted, *The Foreign Ministers of Alexander I: Political Attitudes and the Conduct of Russian Diplomacy*, Berkeley, 1969, p. 58.
12. N.K. Shil'der, *Imperator Aleksandr I: ego zhizn' i tsarstvovanie*, 4 vols, St Petersburg, 1898, IV, p. 497.
13. *Thomas Clarkson's Interview with the Emperor Alexander I of Russia at Aix-la-Chapelle, as told by himself*, Wisbech, 1930, pp. 10, 21, 22–3.
14. Nicolas Mikhailowitch, op. cit., II p. 289.
15. Thackeray, op. cit., pp. 76, 77.
16. Kenneth R. Whiting, *Aleksei Andreevich Arakcheev*, unpublished Ph.D. thesis, Harvard University, 1951, p. 238.
17. Shil'der, op. cit., IV, p. 470.
18. Nicolas Mikhailowitch, op. cit., I, p. 222.
19. Nikolai N. Bolkhovitinov, *The Beginnings of Russian-American Relations, 1775–1815*, translated by Elena Levin, Cambridge, Mass. and London, 1975, p. 144.
20. S.M. Solov'ev, *Imperator Aleksandr pervyi: politika i diplomatiia*, St Petersburg, 1877, p. 457.
21. Eberhard Schütz, *Die Europäische Allianzpolitik Alexanders I. und der Griechische Unabhängigkeitskampf 1820–1830*, Wiesbaden, 1975, p. 28.
22. Ley, op. cit., pp. 261–2.

23. Judith Cohen Zacek, *The Russian Bible Society 1812–1826*, unpublished Ph.D. thesis, Columbia University, 1964, p. 154.
24. Nicolas Mikhailowitch, op. cit., II, p. 376.
25. Ibid., p. 391.
26. Schütz, op. cit., p. 96.
27. Édouard Driault and Michel L'Héritier, *Histoire diplomatique de la Grèce de 1821 à nos jours*, 5 vols, Paris, 1925, E. Driault, I, *L'Insurrection et l'indépendance* (*1821–1830*), p. 224.
28. Wendy Hinde, *George Canning*, London, 1973, p. 387.
29. Schütz, op. cit., p. 109.
30. *Some Official Correspondence of George Canning*, edited by Edward J. Stapleton, 2 vols, London, 1887, I, pp. 232, 234.
31. Harold Temperley, *The Foreign Policy of Canning 1822–1827: England, the Neo-Holy Alliance, and the New World*, 2nd edn, London, 1966, pp. 345–6.
32. N.N. Bolkhovitinov, 'Russian America and International Relations' in S. Frederick Starr, ed., *Russia's American Colony*, Durham, N. Carolina, 1987, p. 268.

Chapter 8

THE GUARDIAN AT HOME:
1815–1825

. . .

THE CONSTITUTIONAL QUESTION

Alexander's actions in the immediate aftermath of Napoleon's defeat served to raise the hopes of at least some of the Russian educated élite that changes would now take place within Russia which would complement her newly-acquired international status and bring her, internally as well as externally, up to the level of West European powers. They had seen Alexander insisting on a *charte* in France, favouring constitutional settlements in Switzerland and in the German states and even giving the Poles a constitution despite their support for Napoleon's invasion of Russia. According to Prince A.B. Kurakin (the former Russian ambassador in France), between 1813 and 1815 Alexander would 'openly express himself regarding the present organization of the internal state administration' and stated that in the near future his 'principal occupation will be this matter'.[1] In 1826 General A.D. Balashev, the minister of police, claimed that Alexander 'had the intention, from 1815, to introduce some changes in the administration of the State'.[2]

Alexander further raised hopes in his speech at the opening of the Polish *Sejm* in 1818, and in other comments shortly thereafter which suggested that he intended to extend this type of constitution to Russia. His speech expressed the hope that the Polish constitution would 'extend a beneficial influence over all the countries which Providence had committed to my care'. The text of Alexander's speech to the *Sejm* was his own and Capodistria

166

had attempted unsuccessfully to moderate it (according to Capodistria, Alexander had given him permission to make changes only to the grammar and punctuation). Alexander was delighted with his own performance and only prepared to give a little credit to higher powers for its excellence. He wrote to General P.D. Kiselev from Warsaw in March that the speech:

> . . . in the face of the whole of Europe, was not easy to draft, I appealed again with fervour to the Divine Saviour, and He understood me and allowed that which you have read to flow from my pen . . . .[3]

Others were less enthusiastic about the speech, and feared the potential effect of his words, especially on Russian youth, but its significance was generally acknowledged. A.A. Zakrevsky, at the time a member of the general staff, commented that 'the speech which the Emperor delivered to the Diet was very beautiful, but it could have terrifying consequences for Russia'.[4] N. Karamzin wrote to the poet I.I. Dmitriev in April 1818 that 'the Warsaw speeches had a powerful effect on young hearts: they dream of a constitution; they judge, they lay down the law; they start to write . . . . And it is funny and a shame . . . . Let our youth rage; we will smile'. Rostopchin, governor-general of Moscow, wrote the following year that '. . . the speech of the Emperor in Warsaw excited heads; young people demand a constitution from him'.[5] Many Russians assumed that a Russian constitution would soon follow. The writer, economist and future Decembrist Nikolai Ivanovich Turgenev later wrote that:

> In this act of the Emperor Alexander there were hopes for the Poles, for the Russians and for the whole of humanity. The world saw, perhaps for the first time, a conqueror giving to the vanquished rights instead of chains. By doing this he also pledged himself so to speak to do as much for his other subjects.[6]

'On a Constitution', an article in the journal *Syn otechestva* (Son of the Fatherland) by the academic lawyer at St Petersburg University A.P. Kunitsyn, was written in response to the Warsaw speech. It was moderate in its proposal for an assembly whose task was simply to advise the 'supreme ruler', but nevertheless assumed that constitutions were now the only form of government which were acceptable and that the details were a matter for public debate. Even those who opposed constitutional reform assumed that it was likely. When Karamzin learnt that Novosil'tsev had been commissioned to write a constitution for Russia, his concern led him to write to Alexander opposing constitutional reform and urging him to rescind the Polish constitution. He expressed the view that 'to give Russia a constitution . . . is to dress up some respected man in a dunce's cap'. In 1818 he made his point even more bluntly: 'Russia is not England . . . autocracy is its soul'.[7]

According to an account by Constantine, Alexander's younger brother, the following exchange took place between them after the Warsaw speech, which illustrated both Alexander's intentions and again his intolerant attitude towards criticism, even when it came from members of his own family:

Alexander: Soon also this great moment of joy will arrive for Russia, when I will grant a constitution to her and when, like now, I will cross Petersburg with you and my family to return to my palace surrounded by a joyous people.

Constantine: My tongue was paralysed; at last I could utter: If Your Majesty puts aside absolute power, I doubt whether this will conform to the wishes of your people.

Alexander (curtly): I do not require your advice, but I will explain my will to you as to one of my subjects.[8]

Alexander did not immediately retreat from his declared intention. A few months after his Warsaw speech, at the Congress of Aix-la-Chapelle, he made his position even plainer to Marshal Maison: 'The people must be delivered from the regime of arbitrariness; I have restored this principle in Poland, I will establish it in my other states'.[9] Yet, despite Alexander's own stated intentions, Russia did not receive a constitution, and indeed underwent no fundamental change to her government.

In May 1818, Bessarabia (which had been acquired from the Turks in 1812) was granted a 'constitution' by Alexander as he visited Kishinev on his return from

Warsaw. Bessarabia, of course, was not ethnically Russian and Alexander had demonstrated by his policies in the Baltic provinces, in Finland and in Poland, that he recognized that different forms of government were appropriate for the non-Russian parts of his Empire. The Bessarabian 'constitution' has to be seen in this light. It was not concerned with the 'rights' of the population, but rather with the establishment of a particular and separate form of administration. The whole territory was placed under the authority of a military governor-general, while the day-to-day administration was placed in the hands of a civil governor. A structure of administration was set up, headed by a Supreme Regional Council, and regulations were made concerning the languages to be used in administration and in the courts (Russian and Rumanian), the form of civil law (according to local laws and custom) and criminal law (Russian) to be used in the courts. The Rumanian social structure was somewhat simplified; Rumanian boyars were given Russian noble titles but the peasants retained their personal freedom. A similar policy had been adopted in Georgia in 1801 and shows that Alexander, at the very least, was not prepared to *introduce* serfdom into areas where the peasants were free. Despite the fact that this constituted little more than administrative restructuring it is significant that Alexander approved the Bessarabian constitution against the advice of many of his advisers. Bessarabia was a peripheral area, but separate administrations for such areas perhaps suggest that the tsar was contemplating a federal approach to the administration of the Empire. This orientation was confirmed when in early 1819 Alexander appointed Balashev as governor-general of five provinces in Russia (Tula, Orel, Voronezh, Tambov and Riazan'), leading to speculation that the country was going to be governed in far larger units than before.

Speransky was recalled from exile in 1819 and put in charge of the reorganization of Siberia, which had suffered under the arbitrary and corrupt governorship of Ivan Borisovich Pestel' (father of the future Decembrist Pavel Ivanovich Pestel'). Alexander's instructions to Speransky show that he was genuinely interested in major administrative restructuring within the Empire:

. . . you will correct everything that can be corrected, you will uncover the persons who are given to abuses, you will put on trial whomever necessary. But your most important occupation should be to determine on the spot the most useful principles for the organization and administration of this remote region. After you have put on paper a plan for such reorganization you will bring it to me, personally, to St Petersburg, so that I shall have the means of finding out orally from you the true condition of this important region, and of basing on solid foundations its well-being for future times.[10]

In 1821, Alexander established a special Siberian Committee to examine Speransky's report and recommendations, and the ensuing statutes of 1822 created a new administrative structure for Siberia as well as introducing important economic legislation.

Novosil'tsev was commissioned by Alexander to write a constitution, or rather a charter, for Russia. Unlike Alexander's very public statement at the opening of the *Sejm* in 1818, he did this in secret, and consequently the date when Novosil'tsev was entrusted with this task remains unclear. The latest research on the subject, by the Russian historian Mironenko, challenges the view that work had started immediately after Alexander's Warsaw speech. He suggests that the commissioning of this charter should not be seen as a reflection of Alexander's momentary enthusiasm at the opening of the *Sejm*, but rather as an indication that at some later, but unspecified, date in 1818 or 1819 Alexander was still serious about the possibility of granting a constitution to Russia. In May 1819 Schmidt, the Prussian consul-general in Warsaw, informed the Prussian Ministry of Foreign Affairs that work had been completed on the constitutional project, but this only referred to the first draft, which Schmidt dispatched in October 1819. This draft (entitled 'Précis de la charte constitutionnelle pour l'Empire Russe') was submitted to Alexander in October and approved by him; impatient to see the work completed, he gave Novosil'tsev a further two months to complete it. By the end of 1819 the project was no longer a secret – in November the Paris paper *Le Constitutionel* reported that it was in progress: 'The Emperor Alexander is going to lay the foundations of representative government in his vast empire, by giving a constitution to Russia'.[11]

In the early summer of 1820, Alexander was still expressing considerable interest in the work, and in discussion with the poet and administrator P.A. Viazemsky he said that 'he hoped to bring this matter without fail to the desired conclusion'. He also spoke, however, of the shortage of money needed for such a step, and that he knew 'how much such a transformation would meet with difficulties, obstacles, inconsistencies in people'. Nevertheless, Alexander clearly wanted the project to continue and even gave Viazemsky the benefit of his assistance in the difficult task of translating words from French into Russian. This is revealing about Alexander's understanding of the meaning of the word 'constitution'. He suggested that the French word *constitution* should be rendered in Russian as *gosudarstvennoe ulozhenie*, that is, 'state code'. This implies a regulation and carries no connotations about the guarantee of rights; but it would not be an inappropriate term for a set of rules for the establishment of a *Rechtsstaat*. In the final version of the charter, article 34 refers in French to the 'principes constitutifs de la charte' which was given in the Russian version as 'regulations of the charter'.

The final text of Novosil'tsev's draft proposed a federal structure for the Empire. He suggested that Russia should be divided into twelve administrative units which would be termed 'lieutenancies' (*namestnichestva*). Within each lieutenancy a duma would be set up comprising an upper and lower chamber. The members of the upper chambers were to be appointed by Alexander but the members of the lower chamber were to be elected by the nobility and by town-dwellers. It is interesting to note that Novosil'tsev envisaged that within this federal structure Poland and Finland would lose their special status, and constitutions, and would simply have become lieutenancies. At the top of the structure there would be a State Duma, with the St Petersburg or Moscow department of the Senate becoming the upper chamber and with a lower chamber being elected from members of the lieutenancy dumas.

Some historians have regarded this charter as very moderate (the Soviet historian A.V. Predtechensky, in a book published in 1957, claimed that the charter made no attempt to limit the prerogatives of autocratic power and therefore did not try to create a 'constitutional monarchy'). The content, structure and wording of the charter show the influence of the Polish constitution of 1815, but Novosil'tsev was also familiar with the constitutions of France, the United States and the southern German states. The draft *Précis* of the charter had given considerable legislative powers to the State Duma; the final version reduced these powers. Article 12 of the charter stated categorically that 'The sovereign is the only source of all authority (*pouvoirs*) in the Empire'. However, had the charter been implemented it would have imposed some restrictions on the power of the ruler. The tsar alone would have retained the right to initiate legislation but laws would have had to be examined and approved by the State Duma before they could be promulgated. Furthermore, the Duma would have had the right to reject laws and also the right of veto. The principle of *habeas corpus*, rejected by Alexander at the beginning of his reign when it was proposed by A.R. Vorontsov (see above p. 41) partly because of Novosil'tsev's opposition to it at the time, would have been established in the charter, as would equality before the laws and freedom from arbitrary arrest.

Why did Alexander fail to implement a charter which he had not only commissioned but also, having seen its first draft, had urged Novosil'tsev to complete? His comments to Viazemsky suggest that he was aware that there was opposition in certain sections of the court nobility to the introduction of any type of constitution. Alexander, however, had shown in his policy towards Poland that he felt confident enough to act against the advice of his closest advisers. He was certainly conscious of the threat which constitutional change could pose to his own authority and, both in the early years of his reign and in 1809, had been reluctant to restrict his own power in any way. But the limitations on the tsar's power which would have followed from Novosil'tsev's charter had been clear in the *Précis* and yet Alexander had not discouraged further work; on the contrary, he seemed eager that the project should be completed as soon as possible. The only unfavourable comment which Alexander made on the implications of the charter concerned the election of deputies. Perhaps already conscious of the lack of docility of the deputies in the Polish *Sejm* (the second Polish *Sejm*, which was more troublesome than the first, did not meet until late 1820), he commented that unsuitable deputies could be elected to the Russian duma, 'Panin for example'.

Alexander's retreat from constitutionalism can only be explained by the events which had taken place at home and abroad in 1820. By the end of this year, as we have seen, he was becoming disillusioned with the constitution in Poland following the turbulent meeting of the second *Sejm* in September, and had come to believe that the French constitution had not prevented the survival of revolutionary sentiments in that country. Revolts in the Italian and Iberian peninsulas further alarmed him and convinced him of the existence of a Europe-wide revolutionary conspiracy; the mutiny of the Semenovsky regiment indicated to him that Russia was not immune from the contagion of revolutionary ideas. In this atmosphere the question of introducing a constitution into Russia was shelved. In 1821 Alexander made a telling comment to the French ambassador, La Ferronays, when he claimed that he loved 'constitutional institutions' but thought that they were only suitable for sophisticated peoples and an 'enlightened nation' such as France (quoted in full above on p. 152). He never formally renounced his ideal of constitutional government but it is significant that he had not mentioned Russia to La Ferronays as an equally enlightened nation worthy to receive a constitution. The events of 1820 had convinced Alexander that Russia, and Russians, were not ready for even the moderate type of 'constitutional institutions' which he favoured. In 1823 M.S. Vorontsov altered the structure of Bessarabian administration, demonstrating that there was nothing inalienable about its 'constitution', although its autonomy was not formally abolished until 1828 under Nicholas I.

. . .

THE SERF QUESTION

The other fundamental question to which Alexander turned following the defeat of Napoleon was, once more, serfdom. The pattern of the tsar expressing his opposition to the existing situation, commissioning reports in secret and then ultimately doing nothing, parallels the fate of constitutionalism in the same period. Alexander's own personal abhorrence of serfdom has been established. In 1812 peasants (serfs and state peasants) had played a significant role in the defeat of Napoleon's army by harassing the French rearguard during their retreat and by disrupting their supply system. In September 1812 the Russian newspaper *Severnaia pochta* (Northern Mail) reported that:

. . . where the peasants, armed with peasant axes, scythes, pitchforks and spears fight with them [the French] and fall upon them, then the French are vanquished and our brave peasants beat them roundly, in the defence of faith and father-land.

There was a feeling amongst some educated Russians, and amongst some peasants, that the reward for such patriotism would be emancipation. In the immediate aftermath of Napoleon's defeat, it seemed as if Alexander was going to tackle the issue, although, as with Novosil'tsev's consti-tutional project, he did not make his convictions or his intentions public.

Peasants were emancipated in the Baltic provinces: in Estonia (1816), Courland (1817) and Livonia (1819). Alexander had shown throughout his reign that he was prepared to carry out different policies in the non-Russian parts of his Empire. He may have seen the Baltic provinces as a testing ground for emancipation throughout the Empire but in fact their social and economic conditions were so different that little could be learnt from the experience. One important difference was that in the Baltic provinces the landowners (most of whom were ethnically German or Swedish) were willing at least to contemplate ending serfdom, while very few Russian landowners were prepared to take this step. Even in the Baltic provinces, Alexander and the governor-general of Livonia and Courland, the Italian Filippo Paulucci, had to put pressure on the Livonian nobility to follow the example of Estonia and accept emancipation. The serfs were freed without land and had to negotiate contracts with the landowners to continue to work it. There is no doubt that, in general, more economic progress was made in the Baltic provinces after the emancipation than in Russia, but the peasants were normally at a disadvantage when negotiating contracts and this, coupled with the continued existence of labour dues and the loss of landlord assistance in times of hardship, meant that some of them suffered in the short term. According to the Decembrist Pavel Pestel' the Baltic peasants found themselves in a condition which was far less prosperous than that of Russian peasants, despite the 'imaginary freedom' they had been given.

Alexander restated his concern about the condition of the serfs, and his assumptions about the responsibilities which nobles had for them, following his visit to the Ukraine (Malorossiia) in the autumn of 1816:

> I found the peasants in a poor state, but noble pastures very well worked. This is the model of a foreign farm, but not of ours: in Russia the good landowner and the good proprietor should see that the peasants are rich; one's own pasture should not be the only aim of household management.[12]

Yet Alexander's position on serfdom seems to be contradicted by the response he made to sixty-five St Petersburg nobles who presented him with a proposal for emancipation. Alexander is supposed to have responded to General Illarion Vasil'erich Vassil'chikov (governor-general of St Petersburg, who presented the petition) with the words 'To whom, in his opinion, belongs the legislative power in Russia?'. On receiving the reply that the tsar alone had such power, he coldly remarked 'Then leave me to promulgate the laws which I consider the most useful for my subjects'.[13] Alexander, of course, always liked to retain the initiative for reforms, and never looked kindly upon those who took this upon themselves. The most recent study of this subject, however, by the Russian historian Mironenko, sheds doubt upon the date of this incident. It was previously thought by historians to have taken place in 1816; Mironenko thinks that it probably happened later, in 1820, by which time events at home and abroad meant that Alexander's position on reform generally had undergone a change.

Alexander continued to contemplate fundamental changes to the institution of serfdom after 1816 and seemed to be prepared to resist inevitable noble opposition. He gave a secret instruction to S.M. Kochubei, marshal of the nobility in Poltava province and future Decembrist, to prepare regulations for the emancipation of the serfs:

> In 1817 by imperial command, communicated to me in secret by the governor-general, I was entrusted to compile regulations for the free condition of the serfs. I worked on this for over a year, after which the regulations were submitted to the late monarch.

In 1817 Alexander told his aide-de-camp P.P. Lopukhin (a member of the Union of Welfare, see pp. 205–6, and son of P.V. Lopukhin, the president of the Council of State) that 'he certainly wanted to free and will free the peasants from dependence on the landowners'. He was aware of the nobility's opposition to this but threatened that 'If the nobility will oppose this, I will go withmy whole family to Warsaw and issue the decree from there'. M. Murav'ev spoke of Alexander's intention in the autumn of 1817 to issue a manifesto on the emancipation of the serfs from Warsaw. By the end of 1817 Alexander had received Kochubei's report (the date suggested that Kochubei had in fact been instructed to look at the question by Alexander in 1816 rather than 1817), but Alexander was disappointed that he had limited himself to the regulation of relations between serf and landowner rather than dealing with the whole question of serfdom, and had neglected the necessity of 'legal freedom, without which one cannot secure the lasting happiness of the peasantry'.[14]

In 1818 Alexander entrusted Arakcheev, again in secret, with the responsibility of drawing up a project for emancipation. Arakcheev had not been known as an outspoken critic of serfdom but nor had he defended it, and the choice of such a close adviser suggests that the tsar was taking the matter seriously. The task was made difficult, in fact impossible, by Alexander's unrealistic insistence at this point that the project should not offend the nobility in any way. Arakcheev therefore attempted to tackle the financial implications of the emancipation. He suggested an arrangement by which the government would buy a certain amount of land from the nobles annually, including the serfs living on the land. But as the sum Arakcheev envisaged that the government should spend on this was only five million roubles a year, it has been estimated that even if all nobles willingly participated in this scheme it would have taken two hundred years to implement fully. Despite its obvious limitations, Arakcheev's proposal did at least tackle the central issue of the financial implications of emancipation. Alexander also secretly commissioned his minister of finance, D.A. Gur'ev, to prepare a project for the emancipation of the serfs which has not survived, although some correspondence exists for 1818 and 1819 indicating that the work was proceeding at this date.

Alexander seems to have stepped back from the idea of emancipating the serfs in about 1820. He was fully aware of the opposition of most of the nobility to any tampering with serfdom, which perhaps explains why his commissioned reports were always secret. Many nobles feared that the emancipation would inevitably follow an attempt to introduce a constitution, and in this respect the fates of both constitutionalism and emancipation were linked. Rostopchin wrote to S.R. Vorontsov in 1819 that after Alexander's Warsaw speech young people demanded a constitution and that 'by constitution is understood the emancipation of the peasantry which is contrary to the wishes of the nobility . . . '.[15] Any talk of constitutional change inevitably raised the question of serfdom. Serfs were not mentioned in Novosil'tsev's constitution, as they had not been mentioned in Speransky's 1809 project, but any discussion of representative institutions or legal rights was bound to raise the problem of reconciling them with the existence of serfdom. Speransky had believed that political freedoms could and should be established before civil freedoms, which required the emancipation of the serfs ('. . . establish constitutional laws, that is *political freedom*, and then gradually you raise the question of *civil freedom*, that is the freedom of the serfs'); something which might take ten or twenty years to achieve. But others believed that the question of serfdom had to be dealt with first. N.I. Turgenev wrote 'We have a slavery of which not even a trace must be left before the Russian people receive political freedom; first everyone must be equal in civil rights.'[16] Although Alexander did not take part in these intellectual discussions, he must have been aware that rumours about the possibility of constitutional change had led to the questioning of serfdom's chances of survival within a constitutional regime.

Alexander was also conscious of the potential disorder in the countryside which could follow an over-hasty emancipation. The Russian government had been acutely aware of possible serf risings during Napoleon's invasion of 1812, arising either from a proclamation by Napoleon of the freedom of the serfs or from the general disorder and anarchy in the wake of two armies' passage through Western Russia. In the event, the invasion brought only sporadic violence but the government continued to be wary of potential peasant disturbances. In 1819 Alexander received police reports about disorders in the countryside; this seemed to confirm the warnings of his advisers that rumours about emancipation would lead to serious unrest. By the end of 1820, of course, Alexander was convinced of the existence of a revolutionary conspiracy which threatened the social and political order of Europe and from which Russia was not immune. Under these circumstances he feared any governmental policy which risked giving rise to social disorder. Symptomatic of Alexander's change of heart during 1820 was the fate of a decree on the prohibition of the sale of serfs without land. Serfs in Kursk province complained to the Senate when their noble landowner sold them without land. The Senate decided that the noble had not broken the law, but in early February 1820 Alexander instructed the Commission for the Codification of the Laws to resolve this issue 'without delay' and to submit a proposed new law on the subject to the Council of State. This was duly submitted to the Council and discussed in March and December 1820. The Council opposed the changes to the law and resolved to postpone a final decision until it had received written comments from all its members. Alexander, who had been so keen at the beginning of the year that a law should be swiftly passed, was now prepared to let the matter rest. He was aware of the opposition in the Council and, in any case, had by now lost interest in further reforms. As a result, he did nothing to speed up proceedings, and an issue about which he had expressed such concern from the very beginning of his reign was ultimately left unresolved.

.   .   .

MILITARY COLONIES

Alexander did, however, tackle the question of the peasantry (albeit mainly the state peasantry) in the setting up of the so-called military colonies. The idea was not entirely new in Russia. The Cossack communities which had traditionally defended Russia's southern frontiers performed something of the same function as the military colonies. There had also been more deliberate attempts to introduce formal military/agricultural settlements in Russia. In the reign of Aleksei Mikhailovich (1645–76) an experiment was conducted in two border areas whereby one in three adult males per household within a community was conscripted to perform both general military duties in these frontier areas while continuing to farm in peacetime. The peasants responded by mass desertions. Peter I used what he termed a 'land militia' to man the frontier on Russia's south-western borders. This militia was superseded from 1751 by six regiments of mainly Serb immigrants which perfomed similar functions until their disbandment in 1769. In the reign of Catherine II, Grigorii Potemkin settled units of light cavalry in the province of Novorossiia and military settlements were established on the newly-acquired territories between the rivers Southern Bug and the Dniester and the Bug and the Dnieper. In 1804, General Rusanov tried to encourage retired soldiers to return to agriculture by giving them land, livestock and tools. Alexander had also become familiar with the Austrian practice of creating colonies of soldiers on the southern frontier with the Ottoman Empire and was determined to establish military settlements in Russia.

There were practical reasons for Alexander to consider a different organization of Russia's standing army in peacetime. The cost of maintaining the army was enormous (over half the state budget) and the Napoleonic Wars had put a great strain on Russia's finances. Alexander was also aware of the peasants' hatred for compulsory service in the army, which he believed was partly due to homesickness and the removal of the peasant from the land. Service in the Russian army was for twenty-five years, which in most cases meant for life. The conscripts who survived the period of conscription had by this stage lost touch with their native villages and could only hope to be looked after in monasteries or in special soldiers' homes.

The first colony was set up in Mogilev province in 1810. The land chosen was crown land; the peasants living there were transported elsewhere and replaced by the transfer of 40,000 state peasants from the province of Novorossiia in early 1812. The French invasion of Russia disrupted the project, not least because the French occupied the town and part of the province of Mogilev, but Alexander returned to the idea in 1814. Alexander now chose an area near Arakcheev's estate of Gruzino for a colony. In 1816 Arakcheev was put in charge of the whole operation which was now conceived of on a far more ambitious scale than in 1810. The colonies were to comprise soldiers and peasants; the soldier and his family were supposed to assist the peasant farmer in peacetime while the peasant would support the soldiers' family when he was on campaign. The peasants were to be helped financially by being given land, a house, a horse and exemption from all taxation. The health of the colonists was to be maintained through the establishment of hospitals and provision of free medicine; an increased population guaranteed through the provision of a midwife and, at least initially, a grant of twenty-five roubles to couples on marriage; while cleanliness was to be assured through the installation of English-style latrines! Special attention was given to the education of the children of soldiers and peasants, known as 'cantonists', who would form the basis of a new army. Arakcheev was given 350,000 roubles to ensure the success of the project. It has been estimated that the colonies comprised 90 battalions of infantry in the north, 12 in Mogilev, 36 in the Ukraine (Malorossiia) and 240 squadrons of cavalry in the south; in all about 160,000 soldiers. When soldiers' wives and dependants, soldiers invalided out from the army and the 374,000 peasants involved are added, a total is reached of about three-quarters of a million people living in military colonies by the end of Alexander's reign. Original villages had been razed and replaced by specially-designed houses arranged symmetrically along a main road. Peasants and nobles whose land lay within the area designated for colonies were moved elsewhere.

The colonies did not solely comprise soldiers but also peasants (usually crown peasants) who were already living on the land selected for colonies, or who were transported to the new villages. Alexander had always shown a love for neatness and order, exemplified in his enjoyment of the details of military parades and ceremonial. He had been impressed by his visit to Arakcheev's estate at Gruzino in 1810 which was run in a regimented fashion, with immaculate peasant houses arranged symmetrically. Alexander's letter to his sister Catherine praised in particular:

> (1) the order which prevails everywhere; (2) the neatness; (3) the construction of roads and plantations; (4) a kind of symmetry and elegance which pervades the place. The village streets have *precisely this kind of neatness* for which I have been clamouring in the cities . . . .[17]

There is no evidence, however, to suggest that Arakcheev persuaded Alexander to copy his model and the idea behind the colonies seems to have been the tsar's alone. Arakcheev willingly carried out his master's instructions, although even he commented after the suppression of the revolt of the Chuguev regiment military colony in 1819 that 'I openly admit to you that I weary of all this'.

Alexander seems to have been motivated not only by the practical desire to save money on the army and the wish to create something neat and tidy in the countryside, but also by more humanitarian, idealistic, and even utopian ideas. He believed that the colonies would serve to create a new class of useful, educated subjects for the state:

> In the military colonies the soldier has his permanent place, and, on the occasion of a campaign, his property, his wife and his children buoy him up. He serves with hope and returns with joy . . . . Above all, the education of the colonists augments the number of useful people, better roads are provided, the people don't have to go ten or fifteen versts to study, and they won't have cramped living quarters.[18]

Perhaps in the euphoria of the triumph over Napoleon

Alexander felt that he had the ability to recast Russian society as well as to reshape the political map of Europe. One French observer commented that the ambitious education, for both sexes, which the military colonies were supposed to provide showed that Alexander 'wishes to advance the progress of civilization and to create for himself an intermediate class, the need of which makes itself felt in Russia more strongly with each day'.[19]

It has sometimes been suggested that Alexander had an additional ambitious aim, namely to create a class of land-owning peasantry, as the land and goods were allotted to the peasant colonists by the state. He was, of course, expressing his desire to see serfs emancipated at this time and, although this policy would not in itself have affected serfs on noble land, it could perhaps have been used to challenge the arguments put forward by some landowners about the inability of the peasantry to thrive under a different system. If the colonies had functioned as successfully as Alexander had envisaged this new class of peasants would also have been prosperous, because the amount of land and the economic concessions were generous and the equipment and livestock given to them of good quality. Arakcheev, however, made the assumption that the various committees set up to administer the colonies, of which he was head, could dispose of the land as they saw fit and had the right to deprive peasants of their holdings if it was felt that they were not using them properly. This meant that in practice the peasants were being treated in a traditional Muscovite manner: land and possessions given to them solely in return for satisfactory service. As the land and goods belonged to the state, so the state could take them away from the settler if it was felt they were no longer deserved. Alexander made no statement clarifying the property rights of the settlers but as he was aware of Arakcheev's policy there is no reason to suppose that he opposed his interpretation; as 'constitutions' could be altered or withdrawn, so could land and goods given to colonists.

The colonies were hampered from the start by the unwillingness of the peasants to have their lives forcibly improved in this way. The attraction of free medicine and good equipment could not outweigh the resentment at being transported from their homes, subjected to a military regime in their working life and facing the prospect of their sons having to become reserve soldiers and their daughters having to marry within the colony. Every aspect of the traditional peasant way of life was attacked and made subject to alien military-style regulations; peasants had to wear uniforms, perform drill and shave off their beards, and colonists in the Novgorod settlements were supposed to stand to attention whenever the commander rode by. Even the economic benefits were lessened by obligatory construction work and daily wage-rates which were far less than that outside. Visitors remarked on the orderly and prosperous appearance of the colonies; the traveller, Robert Lyall, however, recognized that this was no compensation for the imposition of military discipline and interference in every aspect of the peasants' lives:

> Upon entering the house of the peasants, what a change is to be remarked from the dirt and disorder which usually characterize the Russian cottage! Every thing bore an aspect of military regularity; the very water-pail has its assigned place, and should it happen to be found in any other, by the inspecting subaltern officer, on his morning visit, a severe reprimand, if not a stroke of the cane, is sure to follow.[20]

Matters were not helped by the lack of training given to officers in the colonies and by the prevalence of financial corruption.

By 1818 discontent was rife; in 1819 there was a revolt in the Chuguev Uhlan regiment which was brutally put down. In Zybkaia colony (Kherson province) Old Believers and Dukhobors were forcibly conscripted into the colonies and those who protested were sentenced to run the gauntlet. In 1825 the peasants in Arakcheev's model village, which had so impressed Alexander, showed their gratitude by murdering his mistress. Some settlers showed a touching but misplaced faith in Alexander's willingness to protect them from what they saw as Arakcheev's scheme and from the cruelty of punishments meted out to them. Peasants in the village of Vysokoe petitioned Alexander in 1816 to protect them from Arakcheev. Settlers unsuccessfully petitoned Alexander's brothers, Nicholas and Constantine, during their travels through Russia. In fact, Alexander had approved the punishments imposed by Arakcheev following the revolt in the Chuguev area despite their harshness; twenty-five of the fifty-two settlers who were sentenced to run the gauntlet died in the process.

Alexander was at his most stubborn in his refusal to recognize the flaws in his scheme. In a conversation with Major-General Il'en he insisted that discontent in the colonies was due only to the problems of transition, such as the grain not yet having been sown or shortages of feed for livestock. When Alexander visited a colony, of course, everything was specially prepared so that he saw smartly dressed soldiers and peasants in prosperous surroundings. Alexander made it clear that he intended the experiment to work, whatever the cost. In his words '. . . there will be military colonies at any cost, even if it is necessary to line the road from Petersburg to Chudov with bodies'. The French ambassasdor La Ferronays reported on 13 February 1820 that Alexander 'had adopted them [the colonies] with too much ardour and enthusiasm'.[21] Alexander expressed the hope that the military colonies could be extended to the whole of the army. In 1818 he told the Senate that 'When with God's help colonies achieve their existence in full and are set up according to our intentions then in peacetime it will no longer be necessary to have a recruit levy in all parts of the empire'. And in 1822 he asked Arakcheev to send him a 'general map of the proposed colonies for all the army'.[22]

Alexander maintained his support for the system of colonies despite opposition from all quarters. Lyall remarked that 'It is held in utter abhorrence by the peasantry: – it is detested by the regular army . . . and it is highly disapproved of by all classes of the nobility'.[23] Alexander's generals were opposed to them, fearing that agricultural pursuits would destroy the military spirit of the army. Some members of the nobility regarded the colonies as a sinister attempt to create a new caste which would be answerable only to the tsar and lead to a military state within a state. Although Alexander never made any move to use the colonists in this way it is true that they were intentionally segregated from the rest of Russian society and governed by their own rules. Government officials could not enter colonies without permission from the military command; colonists were judged according to their own law codes and so were outside the Russian judicial system. Members of the educated élite also disapproved of the colonies. Gavril Stepanovich Baten'kov, the future Decembrist who worked as Arakcheev's assistant in the colonies, wrote that 'Military colonies presented to us a terrible picture of injustice, oppression, outward deception, baseness, all the aspects of despotism'.[24] The writer Alexander Herzen referred to the setting up of colonies by Alexander as 'the greatest crime of his reign'.[25] Awareness of opposition possibly accounted for the gradual implementation of the scheme but did not prevent Alexander from pursuing his grandiose vision with undiminished vigour. Nor was there any retreat from the scheme in the last years of his reign, when other plans for a constitution or emancipation had been put aside. The organization of the colonies was substantially modified under Nicholas after a serious revolt in the Novgorod colonies (although the amount of land given over to colonies and the number of settlers increased markedly in his reign), and only abandoned fully after defeat in the Crimean War.

. . .

RELIGION, EDUCATION AND PHILANTHROPY

The setting up of the military colonies demonstrated that Alexander was not simply concerned in this period with the material well-being of soldiers and peasants but, more ambitiously, aimed to raise their level of education and change their whole life style. In the years following the defeat of Napoleon he showed an equal confidence in his ability to direct the spiritual life of his subjects. Alexander had, of course, undergone a spiritual experience himself in 1812 but his policies went beyond mere toleration and sympathy with those who shared his views. Instead, he actively encouraged the spread of religious ideas through his sponsorship of the Bible Society and through education reforms. As Alexander had attempted to use his new authority in Europe to mould the Quadruple Alliance in accordance with his newly-acquired religious sentiments, so at home he assumed that what had been a consolation and inspiration to himself in trying times must necessarily be of benefit to his subjects.

The British and Foreign Bible Society had been founded in London in 1804. Its main purpose was to bring the New Testament to the people of every land, providing translations where necessary. The representative of the Society in Finland in 1811 was John Paterson, who requested permission from Alexander to prepare a translation of the Bible into Finnish. Alexander gave his approval and donated 5,000 roubles for the project. Thus encouraged, Paterson and the Reverend R. Pinkerton, who was in Moscow, determined to set up a Bible Society in Russia. By good fortune, their activity coincided with Alexander's conversion, and he gave his formal approval for the setting up of the Society in early 1813. Alexander was at the height of his enthusiasm for spiritual matters. He expressed his warmest support for the work of the Society in a letter to Aleksandr Golitsyn:

> Your last letter, in which you told me of the opening of the Bible Society, interested and moved me. May the All High bestow His benediction upon this institution; I attach the greatest significance to it and am in complete agreement with your view that the Holy Scriptures will replace the prophets. In general this common tendency toward drawing nearer to Christ the Redeemer is a real pleasure for me. You may have at your disposal all monetary means necessary for the printing of the Bible.[26]

Alexander donated 25,000 roubles to the Society in February 1813 and committed himself to an annual subscription of 10,000 roubles. Modestly declaring that he did not merit the honour of being patron of the society, Alexander enrolled as an ordinary member, along with his younger brothers Constantine and Nicholas.

There is no reason to doubt the genuineness of Alexander's enthusiasm for the work of the Society. The memoirs of members of the Bible Society and of Quakers who met Alexander after 1815 testify to the strength of his religious feelings and show how easily his emotions could be roused. John Paterson reported that when Alexander met William Allen and Stephen Grellet in 1819 all three prayed together and that when they rose Alexander kissed Allen's hand, 'all three quite overcome, so that the

Emperor hastened into another room'.[27] Stephen Grellet wrote on the same occasion that Alexander was 'bathed in tears' after joining him in prayers.[28] Allen recorded a conversation three years later in which Alexander said 'when I am with you, and such as you, who love the Saviour, *I can breathe*'.[29] Alexander, of course, liked to please, but there was no particular reason for him to want to impress the uninfluential members of a foreign religious sect and the similarity of the experiences of Allen, Grellet and Paterson suggest that these were his genuine feelings. In the two years following the inauguration of the Society, Alexander continued to give it public support and considerable financial aid. Another member of the Society, E. Henderson, wrote in January 1817:

> You know what this munificent monarch has already done for the Society . . . and a few days ago, he expressed his request to our worthy president that the exertions of the Bible Society should bear no greater proportion to the spiritual necessities of the Empire. 'What is the cause?' said he; 'Do you stand in need of money? Only let me know, and you shall find me at your service.'[30]

In consequence its work flourished: by the end of 1818 the Society had published 371,000 copies of the Bible, in 79 editions and in 25 languages and dialects used in Russia.

Alexander did not limit himself to supporting the initiatives of foreign societies. In 1817 he established the Ministry of Religious Affairs and Public Instruction (known as the Dual Ministry), with Golitsyn at its head. This was an amalgamation of the Synod, the Department of Religious Affairs for Foreign Confessions and the Ministry of Public Instruction. The decree read 'Desiring that Christian piety always be the foundation of true education, we affirm the fruitfulness of uniting the affairs of the Ministry of Public Instruction with the affairs of all creeds in a single administration'. Karamzin dubbed the new Ministry the 'Ministry of the Eclipse'.[31]

Alexander's new religious orientation did not in itself favour the Orthodox Church, which lost some of its influence with the replacement of the Synod by the new Ministry. Before he had even come to the throne, Alexander had demonstrated his West European

187

sympathies to his friend Czartoryski by his scathing comments on the inability of Russians to understand his ideas and by his day-dreaming about living a blissful pastoral idyll on the banks of the Rhine or in Switzerland. In religious affairs, he showed the same pull towards foreigners, be they Quakers, Protestant sects or organizations such as the Bible Society. The Dual Ministry put all religious confessions, not only Orthodoxy, under one Ministry, in four departments: Russian Orthodoxy and Old Believers; Roman Catholics and Uniates; Protestant Churches and sects; non-Christians. This not only denied primacy to the Orthodox faith over other faiths in the Empire but, by formally associating Orthodoxy with Old Believers, seemed to challenge its position in the state as the official belief and as the only true church. The novelty of this approach, seemingly established through the initiative of Alexander, has provoked the comment by one historian that 'After it [the Dual Ministry] was abolished in 1824 such an arrangement was not attempted again until the Soviet government created the Council for Religious Affairs in 1965'.[32]

The fate of the Old Believers (that is, those who had rejected the reforms introduced into the liturgy and practice of the official Orthodox Church in the mid-seventeenth-century) was rather different, although a change of policy came about inadvertently. Old Believers had been tolerated in Russia since the reign of Catherine II. Alexander had continued this policy, but in 1816 a dispute arose within the Theodosian community (the so-called priestless Old Believers) on the question of marriage. The internal wranglings within the community involved the civil authorities and by the spring of 1820 had been brought to the attention of Alexander himself. The result was that he set up, as usual in secret, a special committee to look into Old Believer affairs. The committee received reports about what it regarded as the nefarious activities of several Old Believer communities, and two members of the committee, Mikhail Desnitsky (the metropolitan of Novgorod and St Petersburg) and Filaret Drozdov (bishop of Tver'), condemned their inactivities and pressed for a reversal of the policy of toleration. As a result of their pressure, the committee accepted their recommendation that restrictions should be placed on the participation of Old Believers in local government. The committee also became involved in regulating the affairs of Old Believer communities. The result of this was that an internal dispute within an Old Believer community had led to the re-establishment of a secret committee to deal with Old Believer affairs, something which Catherine II had deliberately abandoned when she abolished the Office of Schismatics in 1763. It was ironic that this should have taken place under Alexander who publicly declared his belief in toleration. It was unfortunate, of course, that the dispute arose in 1820, just at the time when Alexander was becoming suspicious of anyone who failed to conform and who might pose a threat to order. He wrote in July 1820 that 'to our great surprise we have found that this society, abandoning the rules of peace' included people who defended 'harmful rules, such as disobedience to the authorities and to the law, the corrupt nature of marriages and such'.[33]

Alexander also went no further in resolving the question of the economic and institutional status of the Jews in Russia. In April 1817 he established the Society of Israelite Christians, which gave financial assistance to Jews wishing to convert to Christianity. Although the policy of toleration was formally continued there was less attempt in this period to integrate the Jews into the Russian social system. After a crop failure in Belorussia in 1821 the local nobles were quick to blame the Jews for peasant impoverishment. Alexander set up a new committee to develop a new law code which would supersede his 1804 Statute on Jewry (see above pp. 51–2) but the immediate consequence was the forced resettlement of Jews in Belorussia from the land to towns, which resulted in the displacement of 20,000 people.

Although the new Dual Ministry was divided into two sections, one of which was to deal with religion and the other with education, the close association of educational matters with spiritual matters was a departure from the approach in the eighteenth century and the earlier reforms of Alexander's reign. Catherine II's legislation established secular schools and specifically laid down that teachers should not be priests (although in practice this was not always observed). Alexander had followed this tradition in the educational reforms made during the early part of his reign, and the syllabuses in schools and the new universities had been predominantly secular (see above pp. 53–4). That educational and religious matters were now regarded as complementary was shown by the fact that the head of the department for education, V.M. Popov, was also one of the secretaries of the Bible Society.

Alexander hoped that Russian education would benefit from being administered by the Dual Ministry. Kochubei argued that:

> The main goal of education is the development of morality. Experience shows that morality has no firmer foundation than religion. Therefore, religion should be the first guide for the education of youth . . . it is certain that uniting the Ministry of Education with the Directorate of Spiritual Affairs would have great benefit for education.[34]

The consequence, however, of this new administrative structure was to assert government control over staffing and syllabuses. In 1819 Mikhail Leon'tevich Magnitsky was chosen to inspect the university of Kazan', which had experienced problems over instruction and cases of student indiscipline. After conducting a mere week-long investigation he pronounced himself so shocked at the university's ungodly instruction that he recommended its closure. Alexander did not like to be pushed into anything and was not willing to accept the failure of one of his own earlier initiatives. 'Why destroy it when it can be improved?' he asked Golitsyn.[35] He was prepared, however, to instruct that the university should be reformed and appointed Magnitsky as curator. The result was a purge of non-Russian professors and the introduction of courses in religion. Less dramatic changes took place at the other universities but there were still significant changes of personnel at the top of the structure which reflected Alexander's new priorities: A.P. Obolensky, a member of the Bible Society, replaced P.I. Kutuzov at Moscow; E.V. Karneev, a supporter of the Bible Society, replaced Potocki in Khar'kov. A censor was appointed for each university, responsible to the Ministry.

At the secondary school level, 'harmful' subjects such as philosophy and practical subjects like political economy, commerce and technology were replaced by greater emphasis on the study of history, ancient languages and geography. The utilitarian, technical slant of Alexander's earlier education reforms was now reversed. At the lower, district, school level, the study of natural history and technology was discontinued and daily readings from the New Testament were introduced. At the same time uniformity in education was ensured by the banishment of the Jesuits (who had been tolerated under Catherine II mainly because of the education which they provided) first from St Petersburg in 1815 and then from the whole Empire in 1821, which meant the closure of the Jesuit academy at Polotsk. The Jesuits had not endeared themselves to Alexander by refusing to give his mistress, Mariia Naryshkina, absolution until she gave up her affair with him; but the Jesuits also opposed the Bible Society and had established their own separate system of education.

At the same time the so-called Lancastrian system of education, pioneered in Britain by Joseph Lancaster and Andrew Bell, was introduced into Russia. The charm of the system was that basic instruction could be given to a large number of pupils with a small number of trained teachers through 'mutual instruction'. The teachers instructed monitors (that is, star pupils or older pupils) who passed the information (essentially learning by rote) on to groups of pupils who also questioned each other. The appeal for Alexander and his advisers was that elementary religious instruction could be given in this way to far more children than was presently possible. The Quaker William Allen suggested that three or four young Russians should be sent to England to learn the system, pointing out to the Russian ambassador in London, Count Lieven, that although opposition to the system existed in Britain it was 'from those who are bigoted to some particular system of religion, and would prefer, that the poor should remain ignorant, unless they could, at the same time, be educated in their particular creed'. But in Russia, he continued, 'these impediments do not exist, and her present enlightened Emperor has it in his power to set the world an example, which must produce the most striking effect'.[36] In fact, Alexander had shown little desire to use the Orthodox Church, or its clergy, to provide basic instruction in Russia and seemed quite willing to adopt an educational method which was the product of a very different, and foreign, spiritual ethos.

Several Lancastrian schools were established in Russia, both on an *ad hoc* basis by various individuals (for example, by James Arthur Heard in Gomel', in Belorussia, and Sarah Kilham in St Petersburg) and, in more planned fashion, in the military colonies. In 1819 a Committee for the Establishment of Schools of Mutual Instruction was set up under the aegis of the central school administration. Allen was keen that the schools should be personally associated with Alexander and proposed that they should be set up through the Imperial Philanthropic Society (see below) with the aim 'to train up the pupils in sound religious principles; and to inspire them with sentiments of virtue, and with universal benevolence towards their fellow creatures; to develop their faculties, and to form their minds to habits of industry, order and subordination'. Such promised benefits could only appeal to Alexander, who was keen to be associated with the schools and 'expressed his desire to have a school society established like the Bible Society'.[37] He personally donated 5,000 roubles annually and paid the salaries of the two teachers at the Lancastrian school for poor foreigners in St Petersburg; and he donated 10,000 roubles, an annual sum of 7,000 roubles and the salary of Heard in Gomel'.

Both in the military colonies and in his education policies Alexander believed that Russian society could be moulded to create a new type of citizen; one who, he was convinced would be both happier and more useful to the state. This was partly a product of his own conversion and self-confidence after Napoleon's defeat but he had always shown a concern for the general well-being of his less fortunate subjects and had encouraged the establishment of philanthropic societies to assist such people. Early in his reign, Alexander had authorized the setting up of charitable societies (see above pp. 55–6). In 1816 these and other societies were consolidated into the Imperial Philanthropic Society, with Golitsyn at its head and a state subsidy of almost 150,000 roubles. In addition to taking over provision for the poor, the Society had a wide range of functions, including the establishment of poor houses and asylums, the provision of apprenticeships and tools for impoverished artisans, the distribution of literature on first aid and life-saving methods and even the provision of dowries for poor but worthy girls. The Society was not, strictly speaking, a government agency, but clearly the financial subsidy and moral support from the imperial family was of crucial importance. Following this, other private charitable associations were set up modelled on this Society, and existing ones put under its auspices. By the end of Alexander's reign there were at least twenty-one officially sanctioned charitable societies, five prison aid societies and seven mutual aid societies. Branches of the society were established in Moscow, Vil'na, Kazan', Voronezh, Ufa and Slutsk.

Alexander also showed an interest in prison reform, as had Catherine II. He allowed the Englishman Walter Venning, who was a member of the London Society for the Reformation of Prison Discipline (founded by John Howard, who had visited Russian prisons during Catherine's reign and had died in Russia), to visit Russian prisons and present a report to him. Venning submitted his report, which was highly critical of the state of Russian prisons and recommended segregation by sex and by crime (so that the truly wicked would not corrupt the others), and the introduction of vocational training. Alexander then visited the Venning brothers, John and Walter, in the spring of 1819 and discussed model prisons with considerable attention to detail ('The balconies, he observed, would not do for Russia, as they were too airy in twenty degrees of frost')![38] He expressed an interest in the establishment of a society for prisons and played a personal role in drawing up the rules and form of organization of just such a society, which was set up in 1819 as the Society for the Supervision of Prisons. Alexander became its patron and personally donated 10,000 roubles with the promise of a further 5,000 roubles annually. He even sent the necessary vestments and other liturgical items when a chapel was opened in the St Petersburg prison. His support, however, did not extend to permitting the Society to have any influence over the administration or financial organization of prisons or to have access to military prisons.

The events at home and abroad in the 1820s had as much impact on Alexander's religious and philanthropic policy as they did on his attitude towards constitutionalism and serfdom. Alexander's conviction that there was a general conspiracy of secret societies aroused his suspicion of all societies with foreign connections. Paterson recognized the relevance of foreign events for the Bible Society in a statement in 1822:

> The truth is, that the attempted revolutions in Naples, and Piedmont, and Spain, had alarmed the Emperor, and made him jealous of all societies, and all attempts to instruct the people.[39]

Masonic lodges had taken root in Russia in the middle of the eighteenth century, but had been suppressed by Catherine II towards the end of her reign. In the early nineteenth century freemasonry had revived in Russia and been tolerated by the government (Constantine became a mason, and there were rumours that Alexander himself had secretly joined a lodge), but in August 1822 all secret societies, including masonic lodges, were banned.

At the end of his reign, Alexander also became more susceptible to the warnings of conservative members of the Orthodox clergy like Archimandrite Fotii and Metropolitan Serafim against the Bible Society and Golitsyn. These eventually led him to abolish the Dual Ministry and to dismiss Golitsyn. In 1824 Fotii and Serafim attacked the German Johann Gossner, whose work had been published in Russian and for whom Golitsyn had secured 18,000 roubles from Alexander for the purchase of a building where he could preach. Gossner was portrayed to Alexander as a latent revolutionary, whose views were contrary to the laws of Christian religion and whose 'new religion' signified 'faith in the approaching anti-Christ, the on-coming revolution, the thirst for bloodshed, fulfilling the spirit of Satan'.[40] Fotii sent a series of letters to Alexander on the subject of Gossner, and on Golitsyn's collusion with him, which culminated in a letter in early May in which he warned of the revolutionary plans of secret societies in Russia. A week later the Dual Ministry was abolished, Golitsyn lost his position and resigned from the presidency of the Bible Society.

Throughout the summer of 1824 Fotii tried to scare Alexander with talk of the connection between the Bible Society and European revolutionary secret societies (which he claimed operated through the Bible Society), and with talk of links between secret societies and English Methodists who, according to him, were planning a revolution for 1836. The replacement for Golitsyn as head of the Ministry of Public Instruction, the conservative Admiral A.S. Shishkov, also denounced the Bible Society and accused it of connections with masons and English Methodists. Although Alexander never formally acted against the Bible Society, he did nothing to defend it against these attacks so that its influence waned. Paterson summed up the situation at the end of 1824 as follows:

> The good Emperor was still our protector, and did not permit our enemies to crush us, although, alas! he had given his power, as regarded all matters of State, into their hands. The fact is, he had lost all his own energy, and could not be troubled with State affairs. Everything that he should have done was left undone. His nervous system was shattered, and no wonder, considering what he had gone through since 1812.[41]

The formal suspension of the Bible Society's activities took place under Nicholas I in 1826.

Essentially Alexander lost interest in its work in the last years of his life. His philanthropic interests also declined. In 1822 Alexander had instructed that the barracks of the Litovsky regiment should be remodelled to construct a model prison. But he lost interest in the project after Golitsyn's fall and when the prison finally opened in 1826 it was as a traditional building which bore little relation to the principles of the society; indeed, there were accusations of the misappropriation of funds. The Lancastrian school movement also lost some of its charm for Alexander when it became apparent that this method could also be used by those who became sympathetic to the Decembrist cause (such as Major-General Mikhail Fedorovich Orlov and Major Vladimir Fedoseevich Raevsky) to instruct soldiers in dangerous seditious thoughts.

Alexander's record at home in the years after 1815 was not impressive: Russia proper did not receive a constitution; serfdom remained untouched; peasants and soldiers had been forced into colonies against their wish; the syllabuses in schools and universities had become more traditional. Some historians have portrayed this period as one of reaction, dominated on the one hand by the sinister figure of Arakcheev and on the other hand by reactionaries and mystics like Magnitsky and Fotii. Such a view is an oversimplification. First, Alexander was full of confidence in his own ability, at least in the period from 1815 to 1820, and ministers like Arakcheev and Magnitsky, far from dominating him, simply carried out his bidding. Even after the shock of the events of 1820 Alexander was not forced by any of his advisers to adopt policies against his will. Second, Alexander viewed both his military colonies and his religious and educational policies in a positive light. He believed that he would be bringing great material and moral benefits to his people. This was not entirely self-delusion; after all, the peasants in the colonies were materially better off and provided with educational and medical facilities, and the idea behind the Lancastrian schools was that elementary instruction should be made available to a greater number of people than presently possible. But Alexander also believed that he could mould Russian society to create new, and useful, citizens who would be not only more prosperous and better educated but also happier and more spiritually fulfilled. As Alexander was convinced that he could ensure the happiness and tranquillity of Europe though alliances and great power co-operation based on Christian principles, so he believed he could force his own subjects to be happy.

It was only in 1820 that the tide began to change against reform, and then it was essentially in response to events outside Russia rather than as a result of deepening mysticism on Alexander's part or any increased influence of his advisers. And even then, not everything was suddenly halted; Alexander continued to support the military colonies and only gradually lost interest in philanthropic institutions. Rather than portraying the period from 1815 to 1825 as one of bleak reaction it would be more appropriate to put emphasis on the period from 1815 to 1820 as one of many initiatives. The unfortunate consequence for Russia was that the schemes which were implemented – the military colonies and educational reforms – were those which most alienated the educated élite; whereas the ones which the educated élite most eagerly anticipated – essentially constitutional reform and to a lesser extent emancipation – were those which were put aside. To many educated young Russians, Alexander had failed to do for Russia what he had done for the French, the Finns and the Poles and the gap between Russia's policies and position abroad and her stagnation at home was at the root of their alienation from the regime.

· · ·

NOTES AND REFERENCES

1. S.V. Mironenko, *Samoderzhavie i reformy. Politicheskaia bor'ba v Rossii v nachale XIX v*, Moscow, 1989, p. 147.

2 Georges Vernadsky, *La Charte constitutionnelle de l'empire Russe de l'an 1820*, Paris, 1931, p. 38.

3. Grand-Duc Nicolas Mikhailowitch [Nikolai Mikhailovich], *L'Empereur Alexandre Ier: Essai d'étude historique*, 2 vols, St Petersburg, 1912, II, p. 8.

4. N.K. Shil'der, *Imperator Aleksandr pervyi: ego zhizn' i tsarstvovanie*, 4 vols, St Petersburg, 1898, IV, p. 95.

5. V.I. Semevskii, *Politicheskiia i obshchestvennyia idei Dekabristov*, St Petersburg, 1909, pp. 267, 270.

6. N. Tourgueneff [Turgenev], *La Russie et les Russes*, 3 vols, Paris, 1847, I, p. 61.

7. J.L. Black, *Nicholas Karamzin and Russian Society in the Nineteenth Century: A Study in Russian Political and Historical Thought*, Toronto, Buffalo, 1975, pp. 86, 57.

8. Recounted in A. Fatéev, 'Le Problème de l'individu et de l'homme d'état dans la personnalité historique d'Alexandre I, empereur de toutes les Russies', *Russkii svobodnyi universitet v Prage*, Prague, 1939, no. 65, pp. 26–7.

9. Léonce Pingaud, 'L'Empereur Alexandre Ier, roi de Pologne – la "Kongressovka" (1801–1825)', *Revue d'histoire diplomatique*, vol. 32, no. 4, 1918, p. 536.

10. Marc Raeff, *Siberia and the Reforms of 1822*, Seattle, 1956, p. 40.

11. Vernadsky, op. cit, p. 77.

12. Mironenko, op. cit., p. 81.

13. Ibid.

14. Ibid., pp. 79–80, 86–7, 96.

15. Semevskii, op. cit., p. 270.

16. Ibid., p. 271.

17. Richard E. Pipes, 'The Russian Military Colonies', *The Journal of Modern History*, vol. 22, no. 3, 1950, p. 206.

18. Kenneth R. Whiting, *Aleksei Andreevich Arakcheev*, unpublished Ph.D. thesis, Harvard University, 1951, pp. 145–6.

19. Pipes, op. cit., p. 214.
20. Robert Lyall, *An Account of the Organization, Administration, and Present State of the Military Colonies in Russia,* London, 1824, p. 43.
21. Nicolas Mikhailowitch, op. cit., II, p. 286.
22. V.A. Fedorov, 'Bor'ba krest'ian Rossii protiv voennykh poselenii (1810–1818)', *Voprosy istorii,* no. 11, 1952, p. 115.
23. Lyall, op. cit., pp. 40–1.
24. Semevskii, op. cit., p. 176.
25. S.B. Okun', *Ocherki istorii SSSR konets XVIII – pervaia chetvert' XIX veka,* Leningrad, 1956, p. 294.
26. Judith Cohen Zacek, *The Russian Bible Society, 1812-1826,* unpublished Ph.D. thesis, Columbia University, 1964, p. 48.
27. John Paterson, *The Book for Every Land: Reminiscences of Labour and Adventure in the Work of Bible Circulation in the North of Europe and in Russia,* London, 1858, p. 312.
28. *Memoirs of the Life and Gospel Labours of Stephen Grellet,* edited by Benjamin Seebohm, 2 vols, London, 1860, I, p. 417.
29. *Life of William Allen with Selections from his Correspondence,* 3 vols, London, 1846, II, p. 265.
30. Zacek, *The Russian Bible Society,* op. cit., p. 72.
31. Black, op. cit. p. 84.
32. Walter Sawatsky, entry on 'Alexander I' in *The Modern Encyclopedia of Religions in Russia and the Soviet Union,* edited by Paul D. Steeves, vol. 1, Gulf Breeze, Florida, 1988, p. 109.
33. Pia Pera, 'The Secret Committee on the Old Believers: Moving away from Catherine II's Policy of Religious Toleration' in Roger Bartlett and Janet M. Hartley, eds., *Russia in the Age of the Enlightenment: Essays for Isabel de Madariaga,* London, 1990, p. 226.
34. James T. Flynn, *The University Reform of Tsar Alexander I 1802–1835,* Washington D.C., 1988, p. 72.
35. Ibid., p. 97
36. Judith Cohen Zacek, 'The Lancastrian School Movement in Russia', *Slavonic and East European Review,* vol. 45, no. 105, 1967, p. 347.
37. Ibid., p. 352.
38. B. Hollingsworth, 'John Venning and Prison Reform in Russia, 1819-1830', *Slavonic and East European Review,* vol. 48, no. 113, 1970, p. 541.
39. Paterson, op. cit., p. 364.
40. Zacek, *The Russian Bible Society,* op. cit., p. 283.
41. Paterson, op. cit., p. 392.

Chapter 9

EPILOGUE: THE PARTING OF THE WAYS

. . .

DEATH OF ALEXANDER?

On 13 September 1825 Alexander left for Taganrog on the Sea of Azov and arrived on 25 September. His wife, Elizabeth, had been ill during the summer and doctors had recommended a stay in a mild climate for her health. The choice of a small provincial town surrounded by malaria-infested countryside was a strange, and fatal, one. By this date, Alexander had reluctantly accepted that hostilities would shortly break out with the Turks and Taganrog was close to Russia's military and naval bases in the south which he duly visited. He also, however, used Taganrog as a base for visits to a variety of places of interest including monasteries, mosques, synagogues, German Mennonite settlements and hospitals. After his visit to the monastery of St George on 8 November he felt unwell and was unable to eat; at first there seemed to be no cause for concern but by the time he reached Mariupol on 16 November he was running a high fever. The party returned to Taganrog, where Alexander continued to feel ill but refused to take any medication or let himself be bled, despite the protestations of Sir James Wylie, his personal physician, and Tarasov, his private surgeon. According to Wylie, as recorded by Robert Lee who was the physician of the Vorontsov family, Alexander was suffering from the 'bilious remittent fever of the Crimea'.[1] He was weakened by attacks of fever and diarrhoea, and when he finally submitted to medical treatment little could be done for him. He died in the morning of 1 December 1825, a few weeks short of his forty-eighth birthday. After a post-mortem examination the corpse was transported to St Petersburg where it finally arrived two months later. The Empress left the Crimea in April of the following year but was taken ill on the way and died during the journey.

Almost immediately it was rumoured that Alexander had not died in Taganrog and that the body in the coffin was, in fact, that of a courier named Maskov who had died during the journey south. The legend arose that Alexander, with the connivance of his doctors, his wife and his friend Prince Petr Mikhailovich Volkonsky, chief of staff, had staged his own death. Eleven years after events at Taganrog a holy man called Ivan Kuzmich turned up in Siberia who was similar in build to Alexander, well-educated and strangely familiar with the details of court life in St Petersburg and with events of Alexander's life, in particular the campaigns against Napoleon. It was rumoured that members of the imperial family had secretly visited Kuzmich and that his handwriting matched that of Alexander. Kuzmich died in 1864. Such legends about tsars were nothing new of course; if some chose to accept that the Cossack Pugachev was really Peter III then Kuzmich was a no less improbable Alexander I. There were questions, however, about the tsar's state of mind in 1825 and odd circumstances about his death which seemed to give substance to these rumours.

Alexander had frequently declared his reluctance to rule and his desire to retreat from the world. In the summer of 1819 (that is, *before* he had become disillusioned by events abroad and at home), according to the recollections of Alexandra, Nicholas I's wife, Alexander had said that:

> For myself, I have decided to rid myself of my duties and to retire from the world. Europe more than ever has need of young rulers who are at the height of their vigour; for me I am no longer what I was and I believe it is my duty to retire in time.[2]

When his comments duly provoked consternation he reassured his listeners that this would not happen immediately. Alexander reiterated his dream of retirement while he was touring in the Crimea. He was so taken with the beauty of the Crimean coastline that he talked of building a palace there for his retirement, saying 'When I give in my demission, I will return and fix myself at Orianda, and wear the costume of the Taurida'.[3] This sounds more like a man musing on a recurrent and distant dream than someone plotting to fake his own death and with the risk of facing an uncertain future. Furthermore, Alexander had always invisaged in his daydreams that his retirement from the responsibilities of office would mean a new life in pleasant surroundings; by the banks of the Rhine, in Switzerland or in a palace on the Crimean coast. He had never expressed a desire to live a harsh life of self-denial as a hermit in Siberia.

Several people close to Alexander had noted his mood of depression by 1825. In the year before his death he had experienced personal tragedy and seen his subjects suffer. In the summer of 1824 Sophia, his illegitimate daughter by his mistress Mariia Naryshkina, died of consumption at the age of eighteen. He was then deeply affected by the great flood in St Petersburg in November 1824 which resulted in thousands of deaths. On the day of his departure from St Petersburg Alexander attended mass at the monastery of St Alexander Nevsky. It was a requiem mass and it seems that Alexander was deeply moved by the service. He always, however, attended a mass before departing on a long journey and he often reacted emotionally to religious ceremonies so it is hard to portray this event as significant or unusual in any way. And Alexander's mood improved in the Crimea; it seems that relations between husband and wife were happier than they had been for a long time and that Alexander took pleasure in his many excursions and in the dramatic scenery.

Further controversy has arisen over Alexander's death because of conflicting evidence about his illness and because of unusual procedures after his death. There were discrepancies between the accounts by eye-witnesses about the course of his illness. This could be explained, however, not only by the imperfections of the memories of Alexander's companions but also by the nature of his illness. He fluctuated between appearing to recover and then undergoing further bouts of fever and nausea.

Another confusing factor was that Dr Tarasov later claimed that he had not signed the post-mortem report, which gave rise to the suggestion that he refused to be party to the conspiracy. Yet his signature did in fact appear on the report. Further suspicion arose because there was a long interval of thirty-six hours between Alexander's death and the autopsy, which would in principle have allowed time for a substitution of the body, but this could be accounted for by the confusion in the aftermath of this unexpected tragedy. The coffin was not left opened for people to view the deceased and it was never opened for public view in St Petersburg. Robert Lee, who had the account of Alexander's death from Wylie, did in fact see Alexander's body lying in state in Taganrog, but did not see his face, having been informed that it had been covered because it 'was already completely changed and had become quite black'.[4] Presumably this is why the corpse was not put on public view. It is true, however, that when the tomb was opened later in the century it was found to be empty, and there is a story that a body was secretly taken from the tomb in 1866 and buried in the Alexander Nevsky cemetery.

Despite the mystery of the empty tomb, the evidence suggests that Alexander did indeed die in Taganrog. The autopsy report is vague but there is nothing to suggest that this did not match Alexander's symptoms or that the dead body in the coffin and the autopsied corpse were not the same person. And there is no real evidence that Kuzmich was Alexander. His supposedly extraordinary knowledge about the events of 1812 only suggests that he had been present during the campaign in some capacity, or that he knew someone who had been. In fact Kuzmich apparently frequently praised Kutuzov, something which Alexander had never done for Kutuzov reminded him all too painfully of his own mistakes in the campaign of 1805–07. Kuzmich also reminisced about the entrance to Paris at the head of his troops with Metternich at his side,[5] which was simply inaccurate. It is also hard to imagine that Alexander, who had several major health problems, could really have lived until the age of eighty-six (Kuzmich died in 1864). Indeed, accounts of Kuzmich's knowledge and 'wisdom' probably serve to discount his identity as Alexander who, although he was educated to speak several languages, had given no indication of possessing any special folk wisdom or miraculous insights. The simple fact that Alexander's death took place far away from St Petersburg in rather unexpected circumstances and that the disease took hold very quickly, probably account for the rumours.

. . .

ALEXANDER AND THE DECEMBRISTS

The death of Alexander I was followed by a virtual interregnum. As Alexander had no sons, and no surviving daughters, his eldest brother Constantine was next in line to the throne. In 1819, however, he had corresponded with Alexander about renouncing his claim following his morganatic marriage to a Polish woman of non-royal blood. In 1823 Alexander had formally recognized this renunciation by preparing a manifesto which passed the succession to his younger brother Nicholas. Although Nicholas was made aware of this decision, the manifesto itself was kept a secret. Sealed copies of it, marked with the words 'Not to be opened until after my death', were deposited in the Uspensky cathedral in Moscow and with the Senate and the Council of State in St Petersburg. Uncertain of the loyalty of the guards regiments and conscious of the potential threat of Constantine's Polish forces (Constantine was governing Poland), Nicholas at first hesitated to assume the throne and took an oath of loyalty to Constantine on 9 December, as did the guards and state officials. Only after Constantine's public renunciation of the throne did Nicholas firmly resolve to take power and the troops were therefore ordered on 24 December to take a second oath of loyalty to Nicholas two days later. In this atmosphere of uncertainty the secret society based in St Petersburg known as the Northern Society decided to stage a revolt on 26 December (hence, the name 'Decembrists') in favour of Constantine (who had an ill-deserved reputation as a liberal) and demanded a constitution. Popular legend has it that when the troops cheered for a '*konstitutsiia*' they thought it was the name of Constantine's wife. About 3,000 troops were led into Senate Square by thirty officers for this purpose, but, ill-directed and confused, they posed no real threat and the majority of them remained loyal. The 'rebels' were eventually dispersed with ease when the artillery opened fire (it has been estimated that they suffered between seventy and eighty casualties). This ineffectual revolt was followed by an attempted uprising in the south, led by the Southern Society with assistance from the Society of United Slavs, but this revolt was easily quelled by loyal troops and by mid-January was at an end.

The uprisings took place almost a month after Alexander's death and therefore, strictly speaking, are relevant not to his reign but to that of his successor, Nicholas I. Certainly, the shock of the revolt had a significant effect on Nicholas and his entourage (his mother apparently kept muttering on the day of the St Petersburg rising 'God! What will Europe say?').[6] Nicholas was convinced that the revolt was part of a Europe-wide revolutionary conspiracy and that nefarious ideas had spread eastwards from Western Europe and in particular from France, traditionally seen as the hot-bed of revolution. He was confirmed in his view by the findings of the Investigating Commission which examined participants in both revolts; the Decembrist A.N. Murav'ev, for example, confessed before the Investigating Commission that he had acquired his 'insane liberal ideas during my stay in foreign countries from the spirit of the age'.[7] Nicholas took great interest in the work of the Commission and for the rest of his reign kept a copy of its reports on his desk to remind him of the threat of revolution. The Decembrist revolt, however, was not only important for the effect it had on Nicholas and on his policies but also as the outcome of the dilemmas, and the failures, of Alexander's reign. A reign which had seemed to promise far-reaching internal reforms, and during which Russia had become the dominant continental power, had ended in the alienation of a section of Russian society's educated élite.

Superficially, Alexander seemed to have much in common with the officers who led their troops into rebellion in 1825 (we know little about the motivation of the ordinary soldiers who followed their officers). Many of the leaders of the Northern and Southern Societies came from the best aristocratic families and had had a privileged, western-orientated education. They were familiar with foreign languages and the writings of the major European figures of the day; the library of Pavel Pestel', leader of the Southern Society, contained books by Rousseau, Helvétius, Holbach, Diderot, Condillac, Voltaire, de Stähl, Beccaria and Bentham. Like Alexander, many Decembrists had developed an admiration for the achievements of the French Revolution, similarly without having any direct experience of it (the Decembrists in exile in Chita apparently sang the *Marseillaise*). Many of them had fought in the campaigns against Napoleon and had entered Paris with Alexander in 1814. Many also stayed in France during the occupation (there were 30,000 Russian troops in France between 1814 and 1818 and it has been estimated that about one third of the Decembrists had been officers there) and, like the tsar, had travelled to other allied countries at this time. They too had developed an interest in the constitutional arrangements in other countries, had philanthropic concerns about welfare and had expressed their abhorrence of serfdom. Some of them also underwent religious experiences not so dissimilar to Alexander's own (for example the Decembrist Mikhail Orlov was a member of the Russian Bible Society and Mikhail Sergeevich Lunin converted to Roman Catholicism).

The shared experiences of Alexander and many of the Decembrists has sometimes been put forward as the reason why he failed to take decisive action against these secret societies despite having been informed on several occasions of their existence. Indeed, he seemed to have sympathized with the aims of the early secret society, the Union of Welfare. This grew out of an even earlier Union of Salvation (which functioned from 1816 to 1818) and was active from 1818 to 1821, when it was wound up and replaced by the Northern and Southern Societies. When Alexander was made aware of the content of the constitution of the Union of Welfare, the so-called 'Green Book', which was based on the constitutions of the German patriotic secret society, the *Tugendbund*, he remarked that the rules of the constitution were 'splendid' but warned that many secret societies started with purely philanthropic aims but then turned to plotting against the state. According to an account by Constantine after Alexander's death, Alexander often talked with him about the Union of

Welfare and in 1822 or 1823 gave him its rules to read. Behind the façade of purely philanthropic endeavours the Union of Welfare in fact aimed to establish a constitution for Russia, but Alexander was unaware of its true aims. As late as 1821 (that is, *after* the shock of the events at home and abroad in 1820), on receiving a report on the secret societies' activities from General Vassil'chikov, governor-general of St Petersburg and commander of the Imperial Guard, Alexander commented that 'you who have been in my service since the beginning of my reign, you know surely that at one time I too shared and encouraged these illusions and errors!', adding that 'it does not behove me to take action against them'.[8] This has led some historians to think that Alexander had some sympathy with the aims of the secret societies. The historian Zetlin wrote that Alexander was 'in a way, the first of the "Decembrists" – the elder brother of those who, later, were to hate him so bitterly and fight him so relentlessly' and that 'Throughout his life, even when he was floundering in the dark labyrinth of mystical searching, he had remained their spiritual companion'.[9] But Alexander was not so sympathetic as to ignore these activities and he approved Vassil'chikov's proposal to establish a small secret police force for surveillance of troops in and around St Petersburg.

The similarities between Alexander and the Decembrists were, in reality, only superficial. Alexander was forty-seven when he died and the Decembrists represented, with a few exceptions, a younger generation (the average age of the Decembrists was between twenty and thirty years old but forty per cent of them were under the age of twenty-five). Alexander was educated in the late eighteenth century and fed a diet of works of the French Enlightenment. The Decembrists, for the most part, received their education in the early nineteenth century and were influenced by the events of Napoleonic as well as revolutionary France and also by the early Romantic movement (several Decembrists were themselves significant literary figures). The type of education which many of them received – at institutions like the Tsarskoe Selo *lycée*, the Moscow School of Artillery or Moscow University (147 of the 166 Decembrists sentenced by the Supreme Criminal Court for whom information exists had some form of formal institutional education) – lent itself to debate between students and was very different from the personal instruction which Alexander had received at the hands of La Harpe. The Decembrists were not only familiar with the constitutions of revolutionary France but also with the early nineteenth-century constitutions, that is, not only the Napoleonic constitutions but also the French constitution of 1814, which was published in the journal *Syn otechestva* (Son of the Fatherland). Russian journals also published translations of, amongst others, the Spanish and Norwegian constitutions and commented on the form of government in England.

Although the events of 1812 had a profound impact on Alexander his experience was very different from that of the many Decembrists who fought in the campaign against Napoleon (some of those who participated in the 1825 rising were too young, of course, to have fought). These Decembrists, unlike Alexander, had come into direct contact not only with the enemy but also with peasants in partisan units (the Decembrist Mikhail Orlov fought in a partisan unit under General I.S. Dorokhov) in a way which was quite new to them. The experience of repelling foreign invaders from their homeland aroused shared feelings of pride and patriotism in the young officers and in other sectors of society. The future Decembrist N.A. Bestuzhev wrote that 'Vast Russia rose as one man . . . . The national fervour in Russia was great because it was a national war'.[10] 'We were the children of 1812' said the Decembrist Matvei Ivanovich Murav'ev-Apostol.[11] The combination of admiration for foreign parts mixed with a fierce pride in Russia was a common experience for young impressionable officers. A.V. Chicherin, a lieutenant in the Semenovsky regiment who died during the campaign to liberate Europe from Napoleon, commented from Bunzlau that:

> . . . the love I bear my fatherland burns like a pure flame, elevating my heart . . . . Here we continually see the achievements of civilization, for they are evident in everything – in the manner of tilling the fields, building houses, and in [popular] customs – yet never, not even for a minute, would I wish to settle under an alien sky, in a land other than that where I was born and where my forefathers were laid to rest.[12]

The experiences of the Decembrists abroad after 1815 also differed markedly from those of Alexander. Although Alexander made unofficial as well as official contacts while abroad, he did not share the camaraderie and freedom of discussion that many young Russian army officers had with foreign officers of a similar age and background at this time. The Bestuzhev brothers, all Decembrists, were deeply influenced by this contact. Mikhail Aleksandrovich Bestuzhev wrote that 'our navy, being in England in 1812, and our naval officers, annually visiting the warships of England, France and of other foreign countries, acquired an understanding of the form of government of those places'. Nikolai Bestuzhev, his brother, spent five months in Holland in 1815 which gave him his 'first understanding of the benefit of the law and of civil rights'.[13] The Decembrist Baron Andrei Rozen (a Baltic German) recorded in his memoirs the impact on the young intellectual officers of their stay in France:

> From conversation about literature, poetry and novels, they involuntarily and imperceptibly glided into discussion of Jacobins and Girondists, *Carbonari* and *Tugendbundgenossen* . . . . The extraordinary events of 1812 had also brought about a powerful feeling of the people's strength, and a sense of patriotism which no one had before had a conception . . . . Under a milder sky, in fresh surroundings, which bore the stamp of a higher civilization, under the influence of softer manners and a more humane outlook on life, many of the Russian officers acquired some new ideas about the government of their own country.[14]

Nor did Alexander have any contact with the German masonic lodges and secret societies as did some of his young officers. General I. Diebitsch (a former Prussian officer who had become a member of the general staff) reported from Meissen on the spirit of 'free thinking' amongst Russian officers who had come into contact with German societies, and warned of 'the so-called Tugendbund, the spreading of rumours, the indifference of Prussian officers towards their ruler, assimilated so well by our officers in France, the connections of these societies with Frankfurt, Berlin, Dresden, Leipzig, Bamberg, Munich, Warsaw and St Petersburg'.[15] The acquaintance of some of the Decembrists with foreign masonic lodges and secret societies was reflected in the constitutional projects of the early secret societies. The constitutions of societies like the Order of Russian Knights and the Unions of Salvation and Welfare copied some of their rules and hierarchical organization from masonic lodges. The influence of the German *Tugendbund* was particularly evident in the constitution of the Union of Welfare. Although Alexander shared some of the broad philanthropic aims of these German societies he was not directly influenced by them or, indeed, fully aware of their purposes.

The Decembrists displayed a deep sense of patriotism in their writings, which arose from their experience of the 1812 invasion as well as from the new interest in nationalism and history associated with the Romantic movement in the early nineteenth century. They were much more conscious, and prouder, than Alexander of Russian historical traditions. Although the Decembrists, no less than the tsar, looked to Western Europe for their models of a constitution for Russia, the vocabulary of their drafts reflected this new interest and pride in Russian history. In the constitution proposed by the Northern Society, drawn up by Nikita Murav'ev, the representative assembly was to be called the *narodnoe veche* (the people's assembly), recalling assemblies of this name which had met in the Russian city republics of Novgorod and Pskov from the tenth to the twelfth centuries. The title of the constitution proposed by the Southern Society, drafted by Pavel Pestel', was *Russkaia pravda* (Russian justice), which was the title of the first (twelfth-century) Russian law code. Alexander had never shown any great interest in Russia's past and traditions, and his complete orientation towards the West meant that he was also an object of criticism. The poet K.F. Ryleev, member of the Northern Society, characterized Alexander in the words 'Our Tsar is a Russian German/And he wears a Prussian uniform'.[16]

Pride in Russia made the comparison between Russia and foreign countries even more shaming, particularly as Russians felt that their country had saved Europe from the tyranny of Napoleon. The preamble of the draft constitution of the Northern Society read: 'All the European nations are attaining constitutions and freedom.

The Russian nation, more than any of them, deserves one as well as the other'.[17] The Decembrist Prince Sergei Grigor'evich Volkonsky wrote that 'in general all that we saw in passing in Europe in 1813 and 1814 engendered the feeling amongst all the young that Russia completely lagged behind in social, internal and political life'. The Decembrist Mikhail Aleksandrovich Fonvizin thought the experience of many young Russians abroad was at the root of their discontent:

> During the campaigns in Germany and France our young people became acquainted with European civilization, which made a strong impression on them so that they could compare everything that they had seen abroad with that which presented itself at every turn at home – the slavery of the vast majority of Russians who had no rights, the cruel treatment of subordinates by their superiors, all manner of the abuse of power, everywhere arbitrary rule – all this excited the discontent and outraged the patriotic feelings of educated Russians. Many of them became acquainted during the campaign with German officers, and with members of the Prussian secret society . . . . In candid discussions with them our young people imperceptibly adopted their free way of thinking and the desire for constitutional institutions, being ashamed for Russia as a deeply humiliating despotism.[18]

Another of the Bestuzhev brothers, Aleksandr Bestuzhev, summed up the feelings of patriotism and frustration felt by many with his words:

> Napoleon invaded Russia and then the Russian people for the first time sensed its power; at that time the feeling of independence awoke in all hearts, at first political and then national. This was the beginning of free thinking in Russia . . . . the military, from the generals to the soldier, having returned home only spoke of how good it was in foreign lands. By comparison the question naturally arose, why isn't it like that here?[19]

Although the mentality and experiences of the Decembrists differed in significant ways from those of Alexander, in the first few years after the defeat of Napoleon it looked as if their aspirations were the same. Alexander's speech in 1818 to the Polish *Sejm* suggested that he was seriously contemplating introducing a constitution into Russia and many Russians assumed that this would happen in the near future (see above pp. 166–7). Like the tsar, the Decembrists were aware of the two main issues which needed to be addressed in Russia – the abolition, or reform, of serfdom and the establishment of the rule of law – and believed these could only be established through a constitution. The Decembrists expressed their abhorrence of serfdom no less than Alexander. M.M. Spirodov, for example, told the Investigating Commission that his liberal ideas had arisen from witnessing the condition of the serfs:

> I saw that a fertile province pays tribute only to landowners; I saw the unceasing activity of the peasant whose fruits served to enrich the lords; I saw the latter's immeasurable wealth in grain, while at the end of the year the peasants lacked not only grain for sale but even for their own sustenance . . . I confess, my heart was gripped with pity for them.[20]

The Northern and Southern Societies both assumed that serfdom would be abolished but they did not agree on the means by which this should be done. The Northern Society proposed freeing the serfs without giving them land (as had taken place in the Baltic provinces) but did not look at the problems which would have been created by depriving the peasants of land and the nobles of free labour. The Society was no more willing than Alexander or Arakcheev to risk offending the nobles by forcing them to give up their land to the peasants. Pestel', on the contrary, urged a radical solution which was accepted by the Southern Society. He proposed that all land should be taken over by the state and divided into two categories. Land in the first category would be divided into lots sufficient to support a family of five and distributed to peasants, or anyone else, who wished to work it. This land would remain state land and could not be sold, exchanged or mortgaged. Land in the second category could be sold or rented by the state to individuals. The proposal was a radical and original attempt to tackle the issue but it was clearly not designed to be in the interests of the landowning class and would have to be imposed on it by force, something which neither Alexander nor the members of the Northern Society had been prepared to contemplate. Indeed, there were no means to coerce the nobility to accept emancipation against their wishes since the nobility provided most of the officer corps and the higher echelons of provincial officialdom. Pestel' could only attempt to tackle this problem with a proposal to establish a temporary directory which would govern the country for eight to ten years to cover the period of transition.

The insurmountable obstacle to constitutional reform under Alexander had been that it required the tsar to give up some of his own power willingly, something which had been recognized all too clearly by Speransky. The Decembrists also had to come to terms with this fundamental problem, and the issue became more acute as the possibility of Alexander embarking on constitutional reform on his own initiative faded after 1820. The draft constitution of the Northern Society envisaged a constitutional monarch, with limited powers. The tsar would have become the 'Supreme Functionary of the Russian Government', and would have retained the right of veto, control over the armed forces and the right to conduct foreign policy. Legislative power, however, would have been devolved to a national assembly comprising an upper and lower chamber. The lower house was to be elected on a restricted franchise (by literate males over the age of twenty-one with movable property of the value of at least 500 roubles). The country would be organized as a federation of nationalities, something which was influenced by Murav'ev's admiration for the constitution of the United States and which was vehemently opposed by Pestel'. The question of the means to be used to force such a constitution on the monarch was not, however, resolved. The pathetic gesture of the Decembrist revolt in St Petersburg, and the ease with which it was crushed, demonstrated clearly the mistaken assumption that the tsar would have to respond to such a threat with concessions.

The draft constitution of the Northern Society reflected the moderate views of its leaders but the majority of the Decembrists favoured a more radical solution. Many felt disillusioned with Alexander even before his retreat from reform in the early 1820s. There was talk amongst members of the Northern Society of the desirability of assassinating

Alexander (A.I. Iakubovich and P.D. Kakhovsky expressed their willingness to undertake this) but this was too extreme for most. Pestel' was one of several Decembrists who came to the belief that it was impossible to expect co-operation from a ruler to limit his powers. His constitution assumed that Russia would become a republic, and he sketched out a pyramid of representative institutions ranging from county assemblies at the bottom to a national assembly at the top. All males over the age of twenty would be eligible to vote for members of the county assemblies; thereafter the assemblies themselves would elect representatives to serve at higher levels, with the national assembly electing the five members who would make up the State Duma.

The revolts in Spain and in the Italian peninsula and the Semenovsky rebellion in 1820 halted any movement towards the fundamental alteration of the structure of government or serfdom in Russia. The early 1820s were crucial years in turning Alexander away from reform; this was also a crucial period in the development of the ideas of the Decembrists and the point at which their aspirations clearly diverged from those of Alexander. Events in Europe strengthened the radical nature of the Decembrists at the same time as they weakened Alexander's desire for reform.

The Russian periodical press kept educated Russians informed of events in the Iberian and Italian peninsulas. Nikolai Turgenev wrote of that time that 'we breathed European news'. The outbreak of revolt filled educated young Russians with the optimism that this was a Europe-wide process in which Russia would share and which would bring liberties to all European peoples including themselves. Vassil'chikov reported to Prince Petr Mikhailovich Volkonsky (the chief of the general staff) in March 1821 that 'the news about the Piedmontese Revolt has made a strong impression here. Sensible people are in despair but the greater part of the youth are in raptures over what has happened and do not hide the nature of their thoughts.'[21] Alexander's response was decisive. He instructed Arakcheev to increase his surveillance of the guards regiments and, at the beginning of 1821, established a secret police force for this purpose.

The Spanish revolt had a particular impact on the

Decembrists. They had a romantic interest in the fate of that country, partly because they felt a bond of common experience in having struggled against the French in 1812. The Decembrist A.P. Beliaev witnessed the defeat of the Spanish revolt as a naval officer aboard a Russian frigate in 1824. Even the defeat moved him to assert that the Spanish example gave him and his colleagues 'more enthusiasm for freedom'.[22] In particular, the method of revolt in Spain was of interest to many Decembrists, in that the initial success was bloodless and was achieved by a small number of soldiers. This pattern could only appeal to the Russian military, especially as there were precedents in Russia for the army spearheading *coups d'état* against tsars in the eighteenth century. The Decembrists also learnt another lesson from the behaviour of the Spanish king, Ferdinand VII, who at first accepted the constitution demanded by the rebels and then, three years later, reneged on his agreement and crushed the rebels by force with the assistance of French troops. To many Decembrists this was an illustration that rulers could not be trusted and that reform through co-operation with the ruler was out of the question. This conclusion was strengthened by Alexander's role in the Spanish revolt. In 1812, he had recognized the very constitution which the rebels demanded in 1820; but now he publicly sided with Ferdinand and ultimately approved of the French invasion. In his testimony to the Investigating Commission, Pestel' wrote that:

> The events in Naples, Spain and Portugal had at that time a great influence on me. I found in them, to my understanding, incontestable proof of the instability of monarchical constitutions and fully sufficient reasons to distrust the genuine consent of monarchs to a constitution accepted by them. These last considerations strengthened me greatly in the republican and revolutionary cast of my thoughts.[23]

Kakhovsky went one stage further: 'The breach of the constitution in France, and its complete destruction in Spain were the reasons which compelled me to agree to the extermination of the imperial family'. As for Alexander:

> He helped Ferdinand to stifle the legitimate rights of the Spanish people, and did not foresee the harm he did to all

thrones. From then on Europe cried with one voice: there is no compact with kings.[24]

Portraits of Riego and Quiroga, the leaders of the Spanish revolt, were displayed in a bookshop in St Petersburg during the abortive December uprising. In the south, the 'Orthodox catechism' of Sergei Ivanovich Murav'ev-Apostol (a series of questions and answers similar in form to a catechism but clearly aiming to use religious language and justification to challenge the authority of the ruler) was modelled on the political catechisms used in Spain to teach the rudiments of the constitution to soldiers. Murav'ev-Apostel had come across a dramatized version of a Spanish-style catechism in a French novel on the eve of the Decembrist revolt. Mikhail Pavlovich Bestuzhev-Riumin, who worked with him on the catechism, stated that 'The thought of such a production had existed for a long time in the society. It came from a catechism prepared by Spanish monks for the people in 1809'.[25]

The Greek revolt had a less significant impact but it strengthened the view that all the peoples of Europe were demanding, and achieving, change. Ypsilantis had contacts with members of the Southern Society based at Kishenev and Tul'chin, and the revolt strengthened the links between the Southern Society and the Society for United Slavs, formed by the Borisov brothers which aimed at establishing a republic in Russia, the abolition of serfdom and the liberation and then federation of all Slavic people (including the non-Slavic Hungarians).

At the same time, conditions within the Russian army deteriorated. Military colonies were as unpopular with soldiers and officers as they were with peasants. G.S. Baten'kov, a former assistant of Speransky employed by Arakcheev in the military colonies, proposed that the rising of the Northern Society should take place not in St Petersburg itself but on the Pulkovo Heights to the south of the city. This was so that assistance could then be sought from the dissatisfied colonists in Novgorod province (where a major revolt was to take place in 1831). In fact, his experience of the 'intolerably burdensome and unpleasant work in the military colonies' was an important factor in alienating him from the regime and joining the Northern

Society.[26] In peacetime, far more emphasis was placed on tedious drill and parade ground exercises. The most notable army mutiny was, of course, that of the Semenovsky regiment in 1820, although the term 'mutiny' was in fact inappropriate; in their hysterical and heavy-handed response to a peaceful protest against the excessive disciplinary measures of Colonel F.E. Schwarz, the authorities chose to interpret events as a mutiny. The regiment was dispersed and many officers were moved to the south where they became particularly receptive to the ideas of the Southern Society. In addition to this notable episode, it has been estimated that between 1820 and 1825 there were at least a further fifteen collective protests from soldiers.

Disillusionment with the prospects for gradual reform at home drove many to join the Decembrist movement shortly before the uprising. Baten'kov, for example, had believed in the possibility of gradual change and had written an 'Essay on the Theory of Governmental Institutions' in the summer of 1825 which he intended to submit to Alexander. He proposed the establishment of a Council of Deputies with limited powers to inform the tsar of his 'people's needs' without 'infringing the rights of the autocracy'. In the end, his growing disenchantment about the likelihood of reform from above, and then his dismissal from his post for indiscreet comments, resulted in Baten'kov joining the Northern Society on the eve of the St Petersburg revolt. The deep resentment against Alexander, who had promised so much and delivered so little, was at the heart of the resentment of many Decembrists. As Kakhovsky wrote of Alexander: 'He lit the spark of freedom in our hearts, and was it not he who afterwards roughly put it out?'.[27] The total disillusionment of many educated Russians by 1825 was summed up after his arrest in a letter from Aleksandr Bestuzhev to Nicholas I; he put the following words in the mouths of soldiers returning from the campaigns in Europe:

> We spilled blood but we again are obliged to sweat under forced labour. We delivered our homeland from tyranny but we are tyrannized anew by the master . . . . Why did we free Europe, was it to put chains on ourselves? Did we give a con-

stitution to France, so that we should not dare to talk about it? Did we buy with our blood primacy among nations, so that we should be oppressed at home?[28]

   . . . .

Bestuzhev's words are a damning indictment of Alexander's reign. The despair and disillusionment of many members of the Russian élite arose not only because Alexander had failed to live up to their expectations but also because Russia's position in Europe was stronger than it had ever been before. At the very time when Russia had saved Europe from Napoleon and was playing a vital part in all matters concerning European affairs, she had failed to take what many Decembrists assumed would be the natural step of adopting Western-European forms of government and social organization.

Reformers like Speransky and the Decembrists were aware of the factors which made such a development in Russia difficult, namely the existence of serfdom and the nature of Russian absolutism. Alexander, of course, equally disliked serfdom and believed that Russia should be governed by the rule of law. Ultimately, however, he was not prepared to pursue a policy on serfdom which was so clearly opposed by the bulk of the nobility, and decided that Russia was not yet ready for a constitution. Alexander, Speransky, Novosil'tsev, the Decembrists and others in the early nineteenth century faced the same dilemmas: how to free the serfs without alienating the nobility and causing social unrest; and how to introduce a modern, Western-European form of government which required the tsar to give up some of his power voluntarily. In turn, this raised the question of which of these two processes – political reform or abolition of serfdom – should come first. Early in the reign, Alexander's 'young friends' had put their trust in the absolute power of the tsar to carry out political and social reform and therefore opposed any of his power being handed over to the Senate, or to any other institution. Speransky felt the time was right in 1809 to introduce political change in Russia, while postponing emancipation, but in the event he was not able to secure Alexander's agreement to implement his constitutional project. Alexander seriously considered the possibility of changes to both the institution of serfdom and

217

constitutional reform until the early 1820s, and commissioned several proposals on both subjects; but he was always conscious of noble opposition to the emancipation of the serfs and was always wary of giving up any of his power. He then became frightened by the prospect of revolution and social unrest and grew disillusioned with the effectiveness of even 'moderate constitutions' in ensuring stability and tranquillity in European states.

Alexander had made Russia a more powerful and more influential European power than ever before, but in the process had disillusioned a group of educated Russians who expected that the transformation of Russia's international standing would be accompanied by a parallel transformation of her political and social structures. In the words of Baten'kov:

> . . . the severity of the last two years of the reign of Alexander I surpassed all that we had ever imagined about the Iron Age. The oppression was in proportion to his European glory.[29]

Pestel', and many other Decembrists, came to believe that the logic was that fundamental change was impossible under the tsar and that even a constitutional monarchy could not be trusted. By 1825 the belief amongst these Russians that reform could, and should, come from the top had died. The divorce between tsardom and at least part of the educated élite, which plagued Russia for the rest of the nineteenth and early twentieth centuries, had been firmly established by the time of Alexander's death.

. . .

NOTES AND REFERENCES

1. Robert Lee, *The Last Days of Alexander and the First Days of Nicholas (Emperors of Russia)*, London, 1854, p. 45.
2. Prince Vladimir Bariatinsky, *Le Mystère d'Alexandre Ier (1825–1925)*, Paris, 1925, pp. 17–18.
3. Lee, op.cit., p. 32.
4. Ibid., p. 40.
5. K.V. Kudriashov, *Aleksandr pervyi i taina Fedora Koz'micha*, Peterburg (sic), 1923, reprinted, Moscow, 1990, p. 29.
6. Mikhail Zetlin, *The Decembrists*, translated by George Panin, New York, 1958, p. 179

7. Marc Raeff, *The Decembrist Movement*, Englewood Cliffs, New Jersey, 1966, p. 50.

8. Zetlin, op. cit., p. 139.

9. Ibid., p. 130.

10. L.Ia. Pavlova, *Dekabristy – uchastniki voin 1805–1814 gg.*, Moscow, 1979, p. 94.

11. M.V. Nechkina, *Dekabristy*, 2nd edn., Moscow, 1982, p. 18.

12. John L.H. Keep, *Soldiers of the Tsar: Army and Society in Russia 1462-1874*, Oxford, 1985, p. 254.

13. V.I. Semevskii, *Politicheskiia i obshchestvennyia idei Dekabristov*, St Petersburg, 1909, p. 206.

14. Glyn Barratt, *The Rebel on the Bridge. A Life of the Decembrist Baron Andrey Rozen (1800–84)*, London, 1975, pp. 37, 38.

15. Semevskii, op. cit., pp. 330–1.

16. Patrick O'Meara, *K.F. Ryleev: A Political Biography of the Decembrist Poet*, Princeton, 1984, p. 204.

17. Anatole G. Mazour, *The First Russian Revolution 1825*, 2nd edn., Stanford, 1961, p. 91.

18. M.V. Dovnar-Zapol'skii, *Idealy dekabristov*, Moscow, 1907, p. 204.

19. Semevskii, op. cit., pp. 206–7.

20. Raeff, op. cit., p. 56.

21. O.V. Orlik, *Dekabristy i evropeiskoe osvoboditel'noe dvizhenie*, Moscow, 1975, pp. 73, 65.

22. O.V. Orlik, *Dekabristy i vneshniaia politika Rossii*, Moscow, 1984, p. 50.

23. Orlik, *Dekabristy i evropeiskoe*, op. cit., p. 95.

24. Isabel de Madariaga, 'Spain and the Decembrists', *European Studies Review*, vol. 3, no. 2, 1973, p. 149.

25. Ibid., p. 153.

26. John Gooding, 'Speransky and Baten'kov', *Slavonic and East European Review*, vol. 66, no. 3, 1988, p. 411.

27. Madariaga, op. cit., p. 149.

28. Dovnar-Zapol'skii, op. cit., p. 94.

29. Ibid., p. 99.

BIBLIOGRAPHICAL NOTE

The standard Russian pre-revolutionary accounts of Alexander's reign are N.K. Shil'der, *Imperator Aleksandr I: ego zhizn' i tsarstvovanie* (The Emperor Alexander I: his Life and Reign), 4 vols, St Petersburg, 1897–8, M. Bogdanovich, *Istoriia tsarstvovaniia Aleksandra I i Rossii v ego vremiia* (The History of the Reign of Alexander I and of Russia during his Times), 6 vols, St Petersburg, 1869–71, and Grand Duke Nikolai Mikhailovich [Nicolas Mikhailowitch], *Imperator Aleksandr I: Opyt istoricheskago izsledovania* (The Emperor Alexander I: An Attempt at an Historical Investigation, published in a parallel French edition as *L'Empereur Alexandre Ier: Essai d'étude historique*), 2 vols, St Petersburg, 1912. The best and most comprehensive account is by Shil'der; Nikolai Mikhailovich gives a shorter but balanced study and Bogdanovich is stronger on military campaigns than on domestic policy. All these accounts include documentary material, much of it in French (part of the first volume and the whole of the second volume of Nikolai Mikhailovich's work consist of documents, and each of the Shil'der and Bogdanovich volumes has documentary supplements). K. Waliszewski's *La Russie il y a cent ans: Le règne d'Alexandre Ier*, 3 vols, Paris, 1923–25, is a readable account, marred in places by an overt anti-Russian bias. A reliable and scholarly account in German is Theodor Schiemann, *Kaiser Alexander I und die Ergebnisse seiner Lebensarbeit*, Berlin, 1904, which is the first volume of his *Geschichte Russlands unter Kaiser Nikolai I*, 4 vols.

In English, and English translation, there are several popular accounts of Alexander's life; of particular merit is

Edith M. Almedingen, *The Emperor Alexander I*, London, 1964; other readable accounts include Maurice Paléologue, *The Enigmatic Tsar*, New York, 1937 (English edition), and Henri Troyat, *Alexander of Russia: Napoleon's Conqueror*, Sevenoaks, 1984 (English edition). There are two major and valuable scholarly biographies of Alexander in English: Alan Palmer, *Alexander I: Tsar of War and Peace*, London, 1974, which provides a good coverage of military campaigns, and Allen McConnell, *Tsar Alexander I: Paternalistic Reformer*, New York, 1970, which is well-balanced and concise, and particularly useful on domestic policy.

Some of Alexander's correspondence has been published in pre-revolutionary scholarly journals, and in particular in the journal *Russkaia starina*. Alexander corresponded mainly in French and collections of his letters to his tutor Frédéric-César de la Harpe, his sister Catherine, and Napoleon, have been published: *Correspondance de Frédéric-César de la Harpe et Alexandre Ier*, 3 vols, Neuchâtel, 1978–80; Grand-Duc Nicolas Mikhailowitch [Nikolai Mikhailovich], *Correspondance de l'Empereur Alexandre Ier avec sa soeur la Grande Duchesse Catherine, Princesse d'Oldenbourg, puis Reine de Würtemberg, 1815–1818*, St Petersburg, 1910; Serge Tatistcheff (S.S. Tatishchev), *Alexandre Ier et Napoléon d'après leur correspondance inédite 1801–1812*, Paris, 1891.

The relationship between Catherine II and Alexander is described in Isabel de Madariaga, *Russia in the Age of Catherine the Great*, London, 1981. Probably the clearest insight into the youthful Alexander can be found in the memoirs of Adam Czartoryski, although they were written many years later: *Memoirs of Prince Adam Czartoryski and his Correspondence with Alexander I*, edited by Adam Gielgud, 2 vols, London, 1888. The standard Russian work on the reign of Paul is M. Klochkov, *Ocherki pravitel'stvennoi deiatel'nosti vremeni Pavla I* (Outlines of the Work of the Government in the Time of Paul I), Petrograd, 1916, reprinted Cambridge, 1973. In English, a balanced approach can be found in Roderick E. McGrew, *Paul I of Russia 1754–1801*, Oxford, 1992. Recent articles on Paul's policies are brought together in Hugh Ragsdale, ed., *Paul I: A Reassessment of his Life and Reign*, Pittsburgh, 1979. Of particular interest is the analysis of Paul's policies by J. Keep, 'Paul I and the Militarization of Government', *Canadian-American Slavic Studies*, vol. 7, no. 1, 1973, pp. 1–15 (republished in Ragsdale's book). An account of the *coup* in 1801 against Paul, and Alexander's reaction can be found in Constantin de Grünwald, *L'Assassinat de Paul Ier tsar de Russie*, Paris, 1960. A detailed account in Russian of the events leading up to and following the *coup* is given by N.Ia. Eidel'man, *Gran' vekov. Politicheskaia bor'ba v Rossii konets XVIII – nachalo XIX stoletiia* (The Turn of the Century. Political Conflict in Russia at the End of the Eighteenth and Beginning of the Nineteenth Centuries), Moscow, 1982. A historiographical essay on the events of 1801, concluding with the official Soviet interpretation of events, can be found in S.B. Okun', 'Dvortsovyi perevorot 1801 goda v dorevoliutsionnoi literature' (The Palace Revolution of 1801 in Pre-Revolutionary Literature), *Voprosy istorii*, 1973, no. 11, pp. 34–52.

The publication of documents from the Russian Ministry of Foreign Affairs, mainly French originals with Russian translations, is now almost complete for Alexander's reign in the series: *Vneshniaia politika Rossii XIX i nachala XX veka* (The Foreign Policy of Russia in the Nineteenth and the Beginning of the Twentieth Centuries), edited by A.L. Narochnitskii *et al.*, first series 1801–15, 8 vols, Moscow, 1960–72, second series 1815–1830, 5 vols up to December 1824, Moscow 1974–82. Ambassadors' reports and other documents relating to Russian diplomacy of the period, mainly in French, can be found in the volumes of the *Sbornik Imperatorskago russkago istoricheskago obshchestvo* (Collection of the Imperial Russian Historical Society), particularly in volumes 2, 6, 11, 54, 70, 77, 82, 88, 89, 112, 119 and 127. Reports from French ambassadors at the Russian court have been published in Grand-Duc Nicolas Mikhailowitch [Nikolai Mikhailovich], ed., *Les Relations diplomatiques de la Russie et de la France d'après les rapports des ambassadeurs d'Alexandre et de Napoléon, 1808–1812*, 7 vols, St Petersburg, 1905–14; a selection can also be found in the second volume of his *L'Empereur Alexandre Ier* (see above).

The standard account in Russian of foreign policy in the reign is: S.M. Solov'ev, *Imperator Aleksandr pervyi: politika i diplomatiia* (Emperor Alexander I: Policy and Diplomacy),

St Petersburg, 1877. Although this gives a detailed account of foreign relations, it is unfortunate that the extensive quotations are always given solely in Russian, although often the originals must have been in French, and there are no footnotes or other indication of sources. The major historian of Russian foreign policy in the later nineteenth century, S.S. Tatishchev, has also written on the Alexandrine period in *Iz proshlago russkoi diplomatii: istoricheskiia izsledovaniia i polemicheskiia stat'i* (From the Past of Russian Diplomacy: Historical Studies and Polemical Articles), St Petersburg, 1890. He presents a Russian nationalist view of foreign relations and is particularly harsh on Czartoryski, whom he accuses of disloyalty by putting Polish before Russian interests. The biographies by Shil'der and Bogdanovich both give a detailed account of foreign policy; Shil'der criticizes Alexander for neglecting Russian interests. The classic French account of the French Wars is Albert Sorel, *L'Europe et la révolution française,* 8 vols, first edn Paris, 1893–1904, this is important because of its extensive use of French primary sources, although some of the judgements and assumptions about Russia are suspect. In English, A.A. Lobanov-Rostovskii, *Russia and Europe, 1789–1825,* North Carolina, 1947, has been superseded by P.K. Grimsted, *The Foreign Ministers of Alexander I: Political Attitudes and the Conduct of Russian Diplomacy,* Berkeley, 1969. Grimsted focuses on successive foreign ministers but also gives a convincing analysis of Alexander's attitude to foreign affairs in general and, more specifically, to constitutional reform outside Russia. The book includes a very full and informative bibliographical essay. A useful overview of Russian foreign policy can be found in two books by Barbara Jelavich: *A Century of Russian Foreign Policy 1814–1914,* Philadelphia, 1964, and *St Petersburg and Moscow. Tsarist and Soviet Foreign Policy, 1814–1974,* Bloomington, Indiana, 1974.

A detailed study of the early years of Alexander's policy in the Mediterranean can be found in N.E. Saul, *Russia and the Mediterranean, 1797–1807,* Chicago, 1970. Franco-Russian relations between 1807 and 1812 are examined comprehensively in Albert Vandal, *Napoléon et Alexandre Ier. L'Alliance russe sous le premier empire,* 3 vols, first edn, Paris, 1891–96. There are numerous accounts and memoirs by participants in the 1812 invasion of Russia. Amongst the most readable and informative which have been translated into English are: Philippe-Paul de Ségur, *Napoleon's Russian Campaign*, translated by J.D. Townsend, London, 1959; Mathieu Dumas, *Memoirs of His Own Time, including the Revolution, the Empire and the Restoration*, 2 vols, II, London, 1839, and *Memoirs of General de Caulaincourt, Duke of Vicenza*, edited by Jean Hanoteau, translated by H. Miles, 3 vols, I, London, 1935. The best account in Russian of the 1812 campaign is L.G. Beskrovnyi, *Otechestvennaia voina 1812 goda* (The Patriotic War of 1812), Moscow, 1962. Soviet writings on 1812 are discussed in Barry Hollingsworth, 'The Napoleonic Invasion of Russia and Recent Soviet Historical Writing', *Journal of Modern History*, vol. 38, 1966, pp. 49–51. In English see the translation of the Russian account by E.V. Tarle, *Napoleon's Invasion of Russia, 1812*, New York, 1971, originally published in Russian in 1938; Alan Palmer, *Napoleon in Russia*, London, 1967; Nigel Nicolson, *Napoleon: 1812*, London, 1985; Michael and Diana Josselson, *The Commander. A Life of Barclay de Tolly*, Oxford, 1980; Janet M. Hartley 'Napoleon in Russia: Saviour or Antichrist?', *History Today*, January 1991, pp. 28–34; Janet M. Hartley, 'Russia in 1812: Part I: The French Presence in the *Gubernii* of Smolensk and Mogilev' and 'Russia in 1812: Part II: The Russian Administration in Kaluga *Guberniya*' in *Jahrbücher für Geschichte Osteuropas*, vol. 38, 1990, pp. 178–98, 399–416; and Yitzhak Yankel Tarasulo, *The Napoleonic Invasion of 1812 and the Political and Social Crisis*, unpublished Ph.D. thesis, Yale University, 1983.

Documents relating to the period of the Congress of Vienna can be found in Charles K. Webster, ed., *British Diplomacy 1813–1815: Select Documents dealing with the Reconstruction of Europe*, London, 1921. The best accounts of the Congress in English are, from the British perspective, Charles K. Webster, *The Foreign Policy of Castlereagh 1812–1815: Britain and the Reconstruction of Europe*, London, 1963, and, from the Austrian perspective, Enno E. Kraehe, *Metternich's German Policy*, 2 vols, II, *The Congress of Vienna, 1814–1815*, Princeton, 1983. A succinct account of the Congress is provided by D. Dakin, 'The Congress of Vienna, 1814–15, and its Antecedents' in Alan Sked, ed., *Europe's Balance of Power, 1815–1848*, London, 1979. The best introduction to the subject of the Holy Alliance is E.J. Knapton, 'The Origins of the Treaty of Holy Alliance', *History*, new series, vol. 24, 1941, pp. 132–40. There are three important accounts in French on the Holy Alliance, all of which cover a wider period than the titles suggest by discussing both the evolution of Alexander's thinking and Russian foreign policy after 1815. Maurice Bourquin, *Histoire de la Sainte Alliance*, Geneva, 1954 is an account sympathetic to Alexander. A more cynical portrayal of Alexander can be found in Jacques-Henri Pirenne, *La Sainte Alliance: Organisation européenne de la paix mondiale*, 2 vols, Neuchâtel, 1946–9, in which the Holy Alliance is seen as a tool to challenge British hegemony. A recent account, which benefits from access to unpublished (family) documents, takes a balanced view: Francis Ley, *Alexandre Ier et sa Sainte-Alliance (1811–1825) avec des documents inédits*, Paris, 1975. A recent study in German favours the Pirenne interpretation: Ulrike Eich, *Russland und Europa: Studien zur russischen Deutschlandpolitik in der Zeit des Wiener Kongresses*, Cologne, Vienna, 1986. An older account in German is Hildegard Schaeder, *Die dritte Koalition und die Heilige Allianz. Nach neuen Quellen*, Königsberg/Berlin, 1934 (republished as *Autokratie und Heilige Allianz*, Darmstadt, 1963). The standard Russian work on the subject is V.K. Nadler, *Imperator Aleksandr I i ideia sviashchennago soiuza* (The Emperor Alexander I and the Idea of the Holy Alliance), 5 vols, Riga, 1886–92.

A comprehensive, succinct and balanced account of Russian policy in the Balkans is given in M.S. Anderson, *The Eastern Question*, London, 1966. Also useful is a more recent summary by Anderson: 'Russia and the Eastern Question, 1821–41' in Alan Sked, ed., *Europe's Balance of Power, 1815–1848*, London, 1979. A broad overview of Balkan developments can be found in the early chapters of Charles and Barbara Jelavich, *The Establishment of the Balkan National States, 1804–1920*, Seattle, 1977 and Barbara Jelavich, *Russia's Balkan Entanglements 1806–1914*, Cambridge, 1991. The Greek Revolt is covered well in English from the Greek perspective in Douglas Dakin, *The Greek Struggle for Independence, 1821–1833*, London, 1973, and from the perspective of Capodistria in C.M. Woodhouse, *Capodistria: Founder of Greek Independence*, Oxford, 1973. The most thorough account of Alexander's policy during the Greek revolt, which projects the view that Alexander genuinely sought a 'European' solution to the Greek question, is by Eberhard Schütz: *Die Europäische Allianzpolitik Alexanders I. und der Griechische Unabhängigkeitskampf 1820–1830*, Wiesbaden, 1975. The best account by a Soviet historian is by I.S. Dostian: *Rossiia i balkanskii vopros: iz istorii russko-balkanskikh politicheskikh sviazei v pervoi treti XIXv* (Russia and the Balkan Question: the History of Russo-Balkan Political Contacts in the First Third of the Nineteenth Century), Moscow, 1972. Some important material on the damage caused by the Greek revolt to Russia's economic interests can be found in A.V. Fadeev, *Rossiia i vostochnyi krizis 20-kh godov XIX veka* (Russia and the Eastern Crisis in the Second Decade of the Nineteenth Century), Moscow, 1958. Russian policy in Bessarabia is examined in depth in G.F. Jewsbury, *The Russian Annexation of Bessarabia, 1774–1828: A Study in Imperial Expansion*, Boulder, Colorado and Guildford, 1976.

For domestic policy the biographies by Shil'der (in Russian) and McConnell (in English) are most informative. The best general Soviet account of domestic policy, sound on factual description of reforms and constitutional projects but marred in places by crude analysis, is A.V. Predtechenskii, *Ocherki obshchestvenno-politicheskoi istorii Rossii v pervoi chetverti XIX veka* (Outlines of the Socio-Political History of Russia in the First Quarter of the Nineteenth Century), Moscow-Leningrad, 1957. A far more simplistic analysis is found in S.B. Okun', *Ocherki istorii SSSR konets XVIII – pervaia chetvert' XIX veka* (Outlines of the History of the USSR at the End of the Eighteenth and in the First Quarter of the Nineteenth Century), Leningrad, 1956. A recent work gives a well-balanced analysis of projects for constitutional reform: M.V. Minaeva, *Pravitel'stvennyi konstitutsionalizm i peredovoe obshchestvennoe mnenie Rossii v nachale XIX veka* (Government Constitutionalism and Progressive Social Opinion in Russia at the Beginning of the Nineteenth Century), Saratov, 1982. There is no study in English which is concerned with all aspects of domestic policy over the whole period but a detailed analysis is given of central and local government in John P. LeDonne, *Absolutism and Ruling Class: The Formation of the Russian Political Order, 1700–1825*, New York and Oxford, 1991, and the creation and early activity of the Ministry of Internal Affairs is examined in D.T. Orlovsky, *The Limits of Reform. The Ministry of Internal Affairs in Imperial Russia*, Cambridge, Mass., 1981. In Russian, there is a recent rather superficial account of the work of the Ministry of Justice: N. Efremova, *Ministerstvo iustitsii rossiiskoi imperii 1802–1917 gg.* (The Ministry of Justice of the Russian Empire 1802–1917), Moscow, 1983. Extracts, in English, from the constitutional projects of Alexander's reign have been published in M. Raeff, ed., *Plans for Political Reform in Imperial Russia, 1730–1905*, Englewood Cliffs, New Jersey, 1966.

Alexander's attitude towards reform in the first few months of his reign is analysed in the article by Allen McConnell, 'Alexander I's Hundred Days: The Politics of a Paternalistic Reformer', *Slavic Review*, vol. 28, 1969, pp. 378–93. Documentary records of the Unofficial Committee, in French, are published in the second of the 3-volume biography of Pavel Stroganov by Nikolai Mikhailovich: *Graf Pavel Aleksandrovich Stroganov (1774–1817). Istoricheskoe izsledovanie epokhi imperatora Aleksandra I* (Count Pavel Aleksandrovich Stroganov (1774–1817). An Historical Investigation of the Epoch of Alexander I), St Petersburg, 1903. M.M. Safonov, *Problema reform v pravitel'stvennoi politike Rossii na rubezhe XVIII i XIX vv.* (The Problem of Reform in the Politics of Government in Russia at the Turn of the Eighteenth and Nineteenth Centuries), Leningrad, 1988, is a detailed, archive-based, study of the reform proposals and administrative reforms of the first few years of Alexander's reign. The Senate reform of 1801 is analysed intelligently by O.A. Narkiewicz, 'Alexander I and the Senate Reform', *Slavonic and East European Review*, vol. 47, no. 108, 1969, pp. 115–36. This article challenges some of the assumptions made by Tel'berg in the major pre-revolutionary Russian publication on the Senate, in particular concerning the Potocki incident: G. Tel'berg, 'Senat i "pravopredstavleniia na vysochaishie ukazy" (Ocherk iz istorii konservativnykh politicheskikh idei v Rossii nachala XIX veka)' (The Senate and the "Right of Representation on Imperial Decrees" (A Study in the History of Conservative Political Ideas in Russia at the Beginning of the Nineteenth Century)), *Zhurnal Ministerstva narodnago prosveshcheniia*, new series, vol. 25, no. 1, 1910, pp. 1–56.

On Speransky the standard biography in English is M. Raeff, *Michael Speransky: Statesman of Imperial Russia 1772–1839*, The Hague, first edition 1957, second edition 1969. As well as analysing Speransky's reforms in the early part of Alexander's reign and his projects for constitutional reform, a comprehensive account is given of his later administrative reforms in Siberia. The publication by Valk of unpublished material by Speransky (M.M. Speranskii, *Proekty i zapiski* (Projects and Notes), edited by S.N. Valk, Moscow-Leningrad, 1961,) has led to some reassessment of his writings, and Raeff's biography should be read in conjunction with the important article by John Gooding, 'The Liberalism of Michael Speransky', *Slavonic and East European Review*, vol. 64, no. 3, 1986, pp. 401–24. Gooding makes a convincing case for regarding Speransky as a radical thinker who deliberately employed a degree of self-censorship when presenting his ideas to Alexander in 1809. The best account in Russian of Speransky's views, albeit written before the publication of Valk's volume, is the chapter by M.V. Dovnar-Zapol'skii on the 'Politicheskie idealy M.M. Speranskago' (The Political Ideals of M.M. Speransky) in *Iz istorii obshchestvennykh techenii v Rossii* (The History of Social Trends in Russia), Kiev, 1910, pp. 117–73. Minaeva's volume, *Government Constitutionalism and Progressive Social Opinion in Russia*, cited above, also presents a balanced view of Speransky and is generally in agreement with Gooding's analysis.

The best account in Russian concerning the domestic policies of the second half of Alexander's reign is S.V. Mironenko, *Samoderzhavie i reformy. Politicheskaia bor'ba v Rossii v nachale XIXv* (The Autocracy and Reform. Political Conflict in Russia at the Beginning of the Nineteenth Century), Moscow, 1989. This is a lucid and stimulating analysis of the reasons for Alexander's failure to introduce a constitution or emancipate the serfs. Mironenko *inter alia* discusses Novosil'tsev's constitutional charter; a textual analysis of this charter in French can be found in Georges Vernadsky, *La Charte constitutionnelle de l'empire Russe de l'an 1820*, Paris, 1931. Alexander's policy towards Poland is discussed from the perspective of Czartoryski in Marian Kukiel, *Czartoryski and European Unity (1770–1861)*, Princeton, 1955. The important and comprehensive study of Czartoryski by W.H. Zawadzki, *A Man of Honour: Adam Czartoryski as a Statesman of Russia and Poland 1795–1831*, Oxford, 1993, unfortunately came out too late to be consulted for this book. Alexander's policy towards the Congress Kingdom of Poland after 1815 is examined comprehensively, albeit unsympathetically, in Frank W. Thackeray, *Antecedents of Revolution: Alexander I and the Polish Kingdom, 1815–1825*, New York, 1980. See also Janet M. Hartley, 'The "Constitutions" of Finland and Poland in the Reign of Alexander I: Blueprints for Reform in Russia?' in the volume of conference papers on 'Poland, Finland and the Russian Empire' to be published by the School of Slavonic and East European Studies. Alexander's policy towards non-Russian parts of the Empire is examined in Jewsbury, cited above, concerning Bessarabia, and in Edward C. Thaden, *Russia's Western Borderlands 1710–1870*, Princeton, 1984.

A succinct analysis is made of the operation of the military colonies in Richard E. Pipes, 'The Russian Military Colonies', *The Journal of Modern History*, vol. 22, no. 3, 1950, pp. 205–19. A contemporary account which shows considerable insight is Robert Lyall, *An Account of the Organization, Administration, and Present State of the Military Colonies in Russia*, London, 1824. The question of military colonies is also addressed in two studies of Arakcheev: Michael Jenkins, *Arakcheev: Grand Vizir of the Russian Empire*, New York, 1969, is a popular biography; Kenneth R. Whiting, *Aleksei Andreevich Arakcheev*, unpublished Ph.D. thesis, Harvard University, 1951, is a more scholarly piece of work, which gives a convincing portrayal of Arakcheev as the subservient tool of Alexander. For general history of the army in the reign of Alexander see the appropriate chapters of, in English, John L.H. Keep, *Soldiers of the Tsar: Army and Society in Russia 1462–1874*, Oxford, 1985, and, in Russian, L.G. Beskrovnyy, *Russkaia armiia i flot v XIX veke: voenno-ekonomicheskii potentsial Rossii* (The Russian Army and Navy in the Nineteenth Century: the Military-Economic Potential of Russia), Moscow, 1973.

Alexander's policies concerning primary and secondary school education are examined in Nicholas Hans, *History of Russian Educational Policy (1701–1917)*, London, 1931. University reform is discussed in detail in James T. Flynn,

The University Reforms of Tsar Alexander I 1802–1835, Washington D.C., 1988. Philanthropic activity is examined in Judith C. Zacek, 'The Imperial Philanthropic Society in the Reign of Alexander I', *Canadian-American Slavic Studies*, vol. 9, no. 4, 1975, pp. 427–36. The best account of the Bible Society is by Judith Cohen Zacek, *The Russian Bible Society, 1812–1826*, unpublished Ph.D. thesis, Columbia University, 1964. Alexander's educational and religious policies are also examined in Walter William Sawatsky, *Prince Alexander N. Golitsyn (1773–1844): Tsarist Minister of Piety*, unpublished Ph.D. thesis, University of Minnesota, 1976. Alexander's policy towards the Jews is presented lucidly in John Doyle Klier, *Russia Gathers her Jews: The Origins of the 'Jewish Question' in Russia, 1772–1825*, Dekalb, Illinois, 1986.

A detailed account in English of economic activity in the reign can be found in William L. Blackwell, *The Beginnings of Russian Industrialization, 1800–1860*, Princeton, 1968. Useful material can also be found in the general works by M.E. Falkus, *The Industrialization of Russia, 1700–1914*, London, 1972, J. Blum, *Lord and Peasant in Russia from the Ninth to the Nineteenth Century*, Princeton, 1961, and the English translation from the Russian of M.I. Tugan-Baranovsky, *The Russian Factory in the Nineteenth Century*, Homewood, Illinois, 1970. The best study of the impact of the Continental System on the Russian economy is M.F. Zlotnikov, *Kontinental'naia blokada i Rossiia* (The Continental Blockade and Russia), Moscow-Leningrad, 1966. Alexander's attitude towards trade is examined in David S. Macmillan, 'Russo-British Trade Relations under Alexander I', *Canadian-American Slavic Studies*, vol. 9, no. 4, 1975, pp. 437–48.

The best accounts of the Decembrist movement in English are Anatole G. Mazour, *The First Russian Revolution 1825* (Berkeley, 1937; reprinted Stanford, 1961) and Marc Raeff, *The Decembrist Movement*, Englewood Cliffs, New Jersey, 1966, which is an introductory essay followed by documentary extracts. A useful introduction to the subject can also be found in chapter four of the recent general history of nineteenth-century Russia by David Saunders: *Russia in the Age of Reaction and Reform 1801–1881*, London and New York, 1992. An interesting analysis of the backgrounds of the Decembrists can be found in W.B. Lincoln, 'A Re-examination of Some Historical Stereotypes: An Analysis of the Career Patterns and Backgrounds of the Decembrists', *Jahrbücher für Geschichte Osteuropas*, vol. 24, no. 3, 1976, pp. 357–68. A brief account of the movement in Russian is given in M.V. Nechkina, *Dekabristy* (The Decembrists), 2nd edn, Moscow, 1982, who has also written a more scholarly two-volume work on the subject: *Dvizhenie dekabristov* (The Decembrist Movement), Moscow, 1955. Soviet scholarship on the Decembrists has been extensive and includes an important series of volumes of relevant documents: *Vosstanie dekabristov* (The Decembrist Uprising), edited by M.V. Nechkina, 18 vols, Moscow, 1925–84. The standard pre-revolutionary Russian works include V.I. Semevskii, *Politicheskiia i obshchestvennyia idei dekabristov* (The Political and Social Ideas of the Decembrists), St Petersburg, 1909, and M.V. Dovnar-Zapol'skii, *Idealy dekabristov* (The Ideals of the Decembrists), Moscow, 1907. Of particular interest for the study of the influence of other European countries on the Decembrists is O.V. Orlik, *Dekabristy i evropeiskoe osvoboditel'noe dvizhenie* (The Decembrists and the European Liberation Movement), Moscow, 1975. A more general history of the development of Russian intellectual thought, which *inter alia* gives some insight into Alexander's character, is A.N. Pypin, *Obshchestvennoe dvizhenie v Rossii pri Aleksandre I* (The Social Movement in Russia under Alexander I), Petrograd, 1918. N. Tourgueneff [Turgenev], *La Russie et les Russes*, 3 vols, II, Paris, 1847, is a revealing account of the growing disillusionment of young, educated Russians after 1815. Numerous biographies and memoirs of individual Decembrists have been published in Russian. Two accounts in English concerning individual Decembrists which are of particular interest are Glyn Barratt, *The Rebel on the Bridge. A Life of the Decembrist Baron Andrey Rozen (1800–84)*, London, 1975, and Patrick O'Meara, *K.F. Ryleev: A Political Biography of the Decembrist Poet*, Princeton, 1984.

There are many contemporary accounts of Alexander's reign in English. Amongst those focusing on Alexander's character and life style are J.H. Schnitzler, *Secret History of the Court and Government of Russia under the Emperors Alexander and Nicholas*, 2 vols, I, London, 1847, and

Madame la Comtesse de Choiseul-Gouffier, *Historical Memoirs of the Emperor Alexander I and the Court of Russia*, translated by Mary Berenice Patterson, London, 1904, in whom Alexander seems to have confided. Contemporary travel accounts of note include R. Lyall, *Travels in Russia, the Krimea, the Caucasus and Georgia*, 2 vols, London, 1825, R. Pinkerton, *Russia: or, Miscellaneous Observations on the Past and Present State of that Country and its Inhabitants*, London, 1833, and R. Lee, *The Last Days of the Emperor Alexander and the First Days of Emperor Nicholas I (Emperors of Russia)*, London, 1854. Life in Russia in the early part of Alexander's reign is acutely observed by the Wilmot sisters in: *The Russian Journals of Martha and Catherine Wilmot 1803–1808*, edited by the Marchioness of Londonderry and H.M. Hyde, London, 1934.

CHRONOLOGY

Dates are in New Style, that is, according to the Gregorian calendar

1777 Birth of Alexander, 24 December.

1796 Death of Catherine II and accession of Paul I, 17 November.

1801 Murder of Paul I, 23 March.
Accession of Alexander, 24 March.
Convention between Russia and Britain, 17 June.
Exile of Pahlen, 29 June.
Peace Treaty and Secret Convention with France, 8 October.

1802 Treaty of Amiens (France and Britain), 27 March.
Decree on the Senate, 20 September.
Decree establishing the Ministries, 20 September.

1803 'Preliminary Regulation for Public Education', 5 February.
Free Cultivators' Law, 4 March.
Further decree on Senate prerogatives following the Potocki incident, 2 April.
War breaks out between France and England, 17 May.

1804 'Instructions' to Novosil'tsev for an alliance with Britain, 11 September.

1805 Ratification of Treaty of Alliance between Russia and Britain, 28 July.
Battle of Austerlitz, 2 December.
Treaty of Pressburg (France and Austria), 26 December.

1806 Battle of Jena and Auerstädt, 14 October.
Turkish declaration of War on Russia, 16 December.

1807 Convention of Bartenstein (Prussia and Russia), 26 April.
Battle of Friedland, 14 June.
First meeting of Alexander and Napoleon at Tilsit, 25 June.
Treaties of Tilsit (France and Russia), 7–9 July.

1808 Alexander declares the incorporation of Finland into the Russian Empire, 9 May.
Meeting of Napoleon and Alexander at Erfurt, September to October.

1809 Speransky's proposals for a Russian constitution.
Peace of Fredrikshamn (Russia and Sweden), 27 September.
Peace of Schönbrunn (Austria and France), 14 October.

1810 First military colony set up in Mogilev province.
Decree establishing the Council of State, 13 January.
Russian withdraws from the Continental System, 31 December.

1811 Decree reorganizing the Ministries, 7 July.

1812 Dismissal of Speransky, 29 March.
Peace of Bucharest (Russia and Turkey), 28 May
Grande Armée crosses the Niemen into Russia, 23–24 June.
Grande Armée enters Smolensk, 18 August.
Battle of Borodino, 7 September.
Grande Armée enters Moscow, 14–15 September.
Grande Armée leaves Moscow, 19 October.
Battle of Maloiaroslavets, 24–25 October.

Grande Armée crosses the Berezina, 26–29 November.
Grande Armée recrosses the Niemen, 13–14 December.

1813 Treaty of Kalisch (Russia and Prussia), 28 February.
Convention of Reichenbach (Russia, Prussia, Austria), 27 June.
Battle of Leipzig, 16–19 October.

1814 Treaty of Chaumont signed (backdated to 1 March): Britain, Austria, Prussia, Russia, 9 March.
Russian troops enter Paris, 31 March.
Abdication of Napoleon, 6 April.
First Treaty of Paris, 30 May.
Alexander visits Britain, 6–27 June.

1815 Battle of Waterloo, 18 June.
'Final Act' or Treaty of Vienna, 19 June.
Holy Alliance signed by the three emperors of Russia, Austria and Prussia, 26 September.
Second Treaty of Paris, 20 November.
Proclamation of the constitution of the Congress Kingdom of Poland, 27 November.

1816 Military colonies put under the authority of Arakcheev.
Formation of the Union of Salvation, 21 February.
Decree emancipating the serfs in Estonia, 10 June.

1817 Decree emancipating the serfs in Courland, 6 September.
Decree establishing the Ministry of Religious Affairs and Public Instruction, 5 November.

1818 Formation of the Union of Welfare, early in the year.
Arakcheev submits his proposals for emancipating the serfs, February.
Alexander addresses the opening session of the first Polish *Sejm*, 27 March.
Congress of Aix-la-Chapelle, September to November.

1819 Assassination of August Kotzebue, 23 March.
Decree emancipating the serfs in Livonia, 7 April.

Alexander receives first draft of Novosil'tsev's Charter, Summer.
Revolt in Chuguev military colony, August.
Carlsbad Decrees, August.

1820 Army revolt in Cadiz, 1 January (the 1812 constitution granted in March).
Outbreak of revolt in Naples, 2 July.
Congress of Troppau, October to December.
'Mutiny' of the Semenovsky regiment, 16–17 October.
Protocol of Troppau, 19 November.

1821 Moscow conference and dissolution of the Union of Welfare, January.
Congress of Laibach, January to May.
Ypsilantis's revolt starts in the Principalities, 6 March.

1822 Congress of Verona, October to December.

1823 Surrender of the Cortes in Spain, 31 August.

1824 Dismissal of Golitsyn, 27 May.

1825 Death of Alexander, 1 December.
Decembrist uprising in St Petersburg, 26 December.

MAPS

Europe in 1815

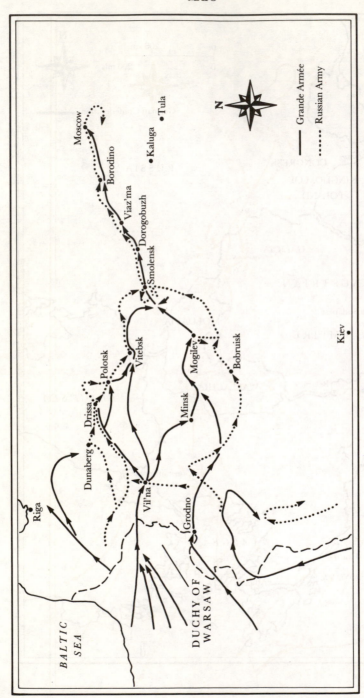

Napoleon's invasion of Russia

Napoleon's expulsion from Russia

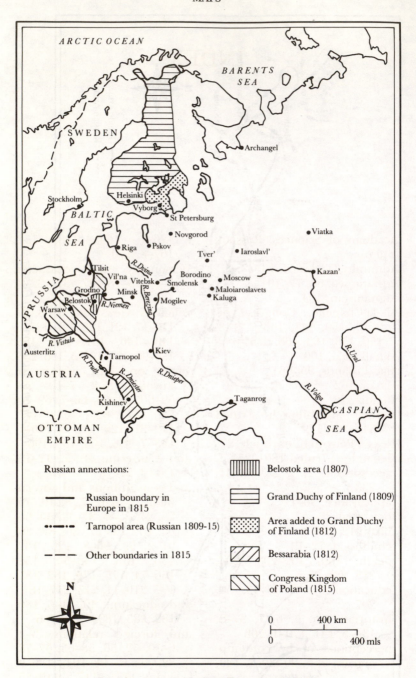

Russian expansion into Europe, 1801–25

INDEX